PENGUIN BOOKS
AN OUTSIDER IN POLITICS

Krishna Bose was a member of Parliament in the eleventh, twelfth and thirteenth Lok Sabhas. In the 1996 general elections, she was the Indian National Congress's candidate; in 1998 and 1999, she represented the Trinamool Congress and became a prominent party leader.

Professor Bose was educated at Kolkata University. She taught for many years at City College, Kolkata, where she was head of the department of English and later the principal. Her husband, Dr Sisir Kumar Bose, was a freedom fighter as well as an eminent paediatrician and the director of the Netaji Research Bureau in Kolkata. She has two sons and a daughter.

AN OUTSIDER IN POLITICS

KRISHNA BOSE

PENGUIN BOOKS

An imprint of Penguin Random House

PENGUIN BOOKS

USA | Canada | UK | Ireland | Australia
New Zealand | India | South Africa | China | Singapore

Penguin Books is part of the Penguin Random House group of companies
whose addresses can be found at global.penguinrandomhouse.com

Published by Penguin Random House India Pvt. Ltd
4th Floor, Capital Tower 1, MG Road,
Gurugram 122 002, Haryana, India

First published in Viking by Penguin Books India 2008
Published in Penguin Books 2015

Copyright © Krishna Bose 2008, 2015

All rights reserved

10 9 8 7 6 5 4 3 2

The views and opinions expressed in this book are the author's own and the
facts are as reported by her which have been verified to the extent possible, and
the publishers are not in any way liable for the same.

ISBN 9780143425427

Typeset in Sabon by Mantra Virtual Services, New Delhi
Printed at Repro India Limited

This book is sold subject to the condition that it shall not, by way of trade
or otherwise, be lent, resold, hired out, or otherwise circulated without the
publisher's prior consent in any form of binding or cover other than that in
which it is published and without a similar condition including this condition
being imposed on the subsequent purchaser.

www.penguin.co.in

This is a legitimate digitally printed version of the book and therefore might not
have certain extra finishing on the cover.

To
Sisir Kumar Bose
who is no more
and
in gratitude to
the people of Jadavpur Parliamentary constituency

Contents

Acknowledgements

Just a few words of appreciation to some who were there as I gave expression to the varied events of my life.

My older son, Sugata, was a solid support throughout. His gentle encouragement kept me going. My younger son Sumantra, however, was a severe critic. Between the indulgence of one and the strictness of the other, I found a balance.

The faces of hundreds of my devoted workers who helped in my election campaigns often passed through my mind as I wrote. They came from a wide variety of faiths and communities. Let me, in recognition of them all, mention Giasuddin Mollah of Mograhat (West), Jai Jai Ram, the Dalit organizer from the Kabitirtha area of Kolkata, and Sufal Sardar, a Christian belonging to Bishnupur (East). Ranku Ghosh, Tushar Roychowdhury and Ratan Banerjee, who managed my election office, are characters in the book.

My loyal staff in Kolkata and Delhi—Kartik Chakraborty, Anirban Bhattacharjee, K. Viswanathan, Sukhamoy Chowdhuri and Manohar Mondal—provided secretarial support and other practical assistance. My special thanks go to Ranjana Sengupta and Penguin India for seeing the book through the publication process.

SECTION ONE
AN OUTSIDER

1947: Memory and Forgetting

Even though I was born in Dhaka and grew up in Kolkata, by a twist of fate on 15 August 1947, I was in India's capital, Delhi. My memories of that day are literally covered in dust. I remember being crushed in a crowd of countless people, nearly getting trampled by horses at one point, when suddenly someone caught my hand and pulled me to safety. Was it someone in Lord Mountbatten's horse-drawn carriage, or was it the mounted police, who knows? There was dust flying everywhere, everything was blurred by the dust.

Deep into the night, we were trudging back wearily from New Delhi to the house on Nicholson Road in old Delhi. The roads were bright and silent. My companions were my cousins Dhruva and Kirti. Suddenly the silence was shattered by Kirti's resonant recitation:

Gone are you today,
O Emperor.
Your empire has vanished like a dream
Your throne lies in ruins.
Your mighty soldiers,
Under whose marching footsteps the very earth used
to tremble,
Their memories are blowing about
In the breeze in the dust of the streets of Delhi.

These were the unforgettable lines from Tagore's *Shah Jahan*. Several centuries were going through my mind in a jumbled order. The rise and decline of empires appeared trifling against the eternal journey of life and death.

The forties were turbulent times in the country's history. Someone from nearly every household was involved in the struggle for freedom—following nationalist calls for boycotts or going to jail or going underground. For the family to which I later came as a bride, the forties were a time of dangerous activities and official oppression. During the 1942 movement, my future husband was beaten up by the police for the first time on the streets of Kolkata. That rebellion triggered the first of his many spells in prisons.

We were a very small family—a 'nuclear' family, as it is termed—Father, Mother and me. We led a rather unexciting, untroubled life. I was quietly able to observe a great many things. No one noticed that I was watching.

Independence Day did not suddenly come upon us. It came towards us steadily, one step at a time. About a year before, we were sitting at the breakfast table one peaceful morning, when a bloodcurdling roar made us jump. We all ran up to the terrace. The terraces, verandahs and windows of all the houses on both sides of the street were full of people. From the direction of Ballygunj lake, a tide of raging humanity was surging down the road. In their hands they clutched lathis. A few paces in front was a terrified man running for his life. He just managed to race into the ground floor of the house opposite ours. A fierce commotion broke out in front of it. Several gentlemen of the neighbourhood had come down to the street. They were trying to calm the angry mob of Hindu gowalas, but the violent crowd was shoving them out of the way. The women of the house were standing with folded hands on the verandah—above all the din an old lady's shrill plea came to my ears: 'My sons, he has taken refuge in the house, spare his life.'

Suddenly I turned around and went towards the stairs. Father rushed forward and caught me by the hand.

'Where do you think you're going?'

'Downstairs. These people have to be persuaded. We can't let a mob of two hundred kill a man like this!'

My father looked stunned at my unbelievable foolishness. He held me tightly by the hand so I could no longer see what was happening beyond the parapet. I could only hear the noise. There was an all-mighty crash of a door being broken down. Then I heard a sound which has been forever embedded in my memory—the dull thud of batons on a human skull.

My first experience of communal riots.

I could not forgive my father for quite a while afterwards—as if the whole conflagration would have died down magically if I had been able to go downstairs. That night I came down with a raging fever and and was in delirium. In the morning our old maid and companion said, 'Your father said not to tell you, but you know, they have killed another man. The corpse is still lying on the main road.'

I rose slowly and went to the window. On the tram lines on Rashbehari Avenue lay the body of a man. Suddenly, a small car appeared from nowhere on the deserted street. It stopped and an Englishman got out. Going over to the body he covered it with a white sheet, got back into his car and drove away. In those days we were anti-British, confirmed nationalists. A bitter shame came over me. A countryman could at least have made this small gesture. In the end it was left to an Englishman. I did not know it then, but heard later that the Englishman was the editor of the *Statesman*.

The madness of the killings that gripped Kolkata for some days after Direct Action Day on 16 August 1946, known since as the Great Kolkata Killing, is a well documented historical event. We had the good fortune to live in a relatively peaceful, genteel area. Yet we, too, were singed by its flames. Close to us was the home of the linguist Suniti Kumar Chattopadhyay, a close associate of Tagore. A few yards on, was the house of the well-known poet Buddhadev Bose, 'Kabitbhavan', House of Poetry. Across the street lived the musician Sachin Dev Burman and on the street behind our house, the poet couple Narendra Dev and Radharani Devi's 'Bhalo-basa'. This translates as love but also means 'a good home' if the Bengali word is split in the middle. On the ground floor of our house stood the studio of the sculptor Pradosh Dasgupta—or did it open a little later? I do not quite remember. In other words, it was a respectable neighbourhood sprinkled with people who were involved with Bengali literature, art and culture.

I first entered the beautiful domed building of the Bengal Legislative Assembly on 12 August 1946. I remember the date—in fact I still have the card for the Speaker's gallery. That day I did not go to school because I had hurt my hand on the previous day. It was an awkward injury incurred while reading a book on the Everest expedition. This elicited much laughter and many jokes. It was a quite a feat to injure oneself, not while climbing a mountain, but while reading about it. In any case, I was sitting at home nursing my hand when Father called from work, 'Get ready quickly. The Deputy Speaker, Tofazzel Ali Sahib, has sent cards. We're going to see the Assembly in session.'

We entered the assembly hall and sat in the gallery to the left of the Speaker. The Muslim League government had declared a holiday on 16 August for their Direct Action Day. The issue was to be discussed in the house on that day. The left side of the assembly filled up with Gandhi caps. On the other side, on the Treasury benches were the members of the Muslim League—many of them wore black caps, some sported beards. After a while the debate heated up. Every time someone from one side rose to speak, the other side tried to obstruct him with shouts, yells, catcalls, desk-thumping and so on. I was completely aghast at this display of childish behaviour by grown-ups. Kamini Dutt was trying to raise an adjournment motion on behalf of the Congress. The Speaker did not give him permission, but he started to read his motion despite this. Pandemonium broke out again. Once, during an interval, I saw Bimal Chandra Sinha of the Congress and Shamsul Huda of the Muslim League, going out practically in each other's embrace. Just minutes before the two had been having a tremendous row. As they passed our gallery, I clearly heard Shamsul Huda saying to Bimal Sinha, 'So, upset because I called you a little zamindar, are you?' I thought the assembly was a very funny place. And I felt sorry for the Speaker.

From the evening of 16 August, Kolkata took on an altogether different character. Chhotokaka, my youngest uncle Benode, came with the news that widespread looting had broken out as soon as the Muslim League meeting on the maidan had ended. The next morning, as I was witnessing the communal killing in our neighbour's house, the crazed, violent crowd was saying, 'Do you know what "they" have done to us?' Our neighbour, a frail and bespectacled professor, was trying in vain to argue that whoever 'they' might have been, it wasn't this particular innocent man.

Lorry loads of people were being moved from one neighbourhood to another, in search of refuge. With them were spreading unbelievable and terrifying stories. Yet somewhere in this tide, the occasional undercurrent of a different sort of story also reached us—in some area or the other people had protected and saved those of the other community. Such stories made the world liveable again.

But these stories were like drops in an ocean. The army had been deployed to clear corpses from the streets of Kolkata. They were only able to work with gas masks on. Their job was arduous for a number of reasons. After identification, the bodies had to be separated and sent to the crematorium or the cemetery. Even death could not end the divide.

Before we could recover from the onslaught of the riots, we

heard on the radio on 24 August 1946 that an interim government had been formed. The names of the ministers were announced as well. The Muslim League had, of course, intimated that they would not join the interim government. On 2 September, the interim government took its oath of office. Were we really on the way to becoming independent? How incredible it seemed! It should have been happy news, but there was no joy; only distrust and suspicion.

In spite of all the tears, sorrow and pain, the drums of Puja sounded one day. Mihijam was a pretty little town on the Bengal-Bihar border. My father had built a house there and had named it Benubon—Bamboo Grove—after the Buddha's monastery of peace. As usual we descended on Benubon during the Puja holidays with great piles of luggage. Benubon did not have any bamboo trees, but the place was alight with kanchan flowers and fiery bougainvillaea. The custard apple tree by the well was stooping under the weight of fruit, and in the west room a neelkantha bird had built a nest in the ventilator.

Such a heavenly state of affairs was too good for our ill-starred fate. One night I dreamed that the hills around Mihijam were on fire. Kelehi mountain, Bodhma, Sundar, all the peaks were ablaze. In the morning when my mother heard about it, she said it was a very bad omen to dream of fire. In the evening, the Toofan Express brought the newspapers from Kolkata. When we got the papers we read that terrible riots had broken out in Noakhali. My cousin Jotudada said, 'So, you are dreaming national dreams these days!' Every day brought increasingly worse news. In the meantime Gandhiji arrived in Noakhali. Gandhiji had come! Everyone felt a sense of relief. We had not realized then that no one, not even Gandhiji, any longer had the power to abate the misery of the people of this land.

Our house Benubon was going to be painted. Our longstanding decorator, Ismail Mistri, did not show up despite being summoned. Finally our trusted caretaker Gokul went to find out about him and came back with the news that Ismail was very frightened and he was not going to come to work. What on earth did that mean? Why would Ismail suddenly be frightened of us? But his fear was well-founded. Riots were spreading across Bihar. Then, as now, there was a pattern to their spread. If today one community started a riot in state A, tomorrow the other community would take revenge in state B. An otherwise meek people were either in fear of their lives or crazed with hatred.

We Bengalis like to break into song when we feel threatened. If war breaks out we feel we can defeat the enemy by our singing. There was a public procession in Mihijam on the occasion of Puja. We all joined in the singing, calling on Hindus, Muslims, Sikhs, Christians, to join in the service of the motherland. On moonlit nights, the Santhal women used to sing along the lanes of Mihijam—*ltur kaney gonja dhuturari phoo-o-o*—tucked in your ear is a dhutura flower... Sometimes groups of us from Kolkata would also roam the streets singing. But there had never been such a politically conscious procession before.

But tension was mounting in the town. Section 144 of the penal code prohibiting the gathering of more than five persons, was imposed in Mihijam. Jotudada was going to Kolkata. When we went to the station to see him off we found that all the trains had been cancelled. Apparently the night before a train had passed through, and many of its compartments were strewn with dead bodies. Meanwhile, Gandhiji and Abdul Ghaffar Khan went on a tour of Bihar; at that time the message of peace started to be preached through padajatra, a long march undertaken on foot.

Soon Kali Puja was upon us—Deepavali is such a beautiful festival of lights. But no one was in the mood to put up illuminations during such a trying time for the country. Everyone was despondent. We thought we would give the lights a miss at Benubon that year. On the evening of Kali Puja darkness fell. There was no breeze. Slowly through the eucalyptus trees we saw a few lights shining in nearby houses. They were earthen lamps, with oil and coiled wicks. Gokul came forward quietly and lit the lamps in our house as well. Soon there were rows of unflickering lamps in a calm silence. But the calm was transient, merely the herald of a coming storm.

We had to postpone our journey to Kolkata two or three times, in spite of having bought the tickets. After a little peace came to Bihar, one day in early November we alighted at Howrah Station. As soon as we got off we had a novel experience. I had been through Howrah many times since childhood and never seen such a thing. There were two teams of volunteers running around. One group belonged to the Muslim League, the other to the Hindu Mahasabha. They each helped passengers from their own community. A band of them came running when they saw us. We informed them firmly that we did not require assistance.

At Christmas, friends and feasting would create a festive atmosphere in our house. This had grown into a longstanding tradition. One reason was that my American aunt Anna and I both had our birthdays around that time. Aunt Anna was the wife of my maternal uncle Kiran Roy who had met her while a student at the Massachusetts Institute of Technology (MIT). Christmas and our birthdays used to be celebrated together. That year Aunt Anna was not with us—she had left India for good, and returned to Boston, her hometown. Still, there was no less festivity. The room was decorated with colourful paper chains and Chinese lanterns. Father asked what I wanted as a birthday present. The previous year I had asked for a charkha, a spinning wheel, and my Gandhian whim had caused my mother much irritation. This year I asked for books.

I bought the books of my choice at Oxford Book Shop—the short stories of Munshi Premchand, Louis Fischer's *The Great Challenge*, Cecil Beaton's photo albums, *Happy and Glorious* by Lawrence Houseman. There was singing, sitar playing.

Whatever the turmoil and suffering in the outside world, for me, personally, the year 1946 ended in happiness and glory.

I wonder if, at the beginning of 1947, we had any inkling of how the year would unfold for us. I do not think so. On 23 January, which was Netaji Subhas Chandra Bose's birthday, the tricolour flew over every house. In the morning we awoke to the songs of the prabhat-pheri— the dawn rounds. At a quarter past twelve in the afternoon, conch-shells were blown in every household to celebrate the moment of his birth. In the evening many homes were lit with lamps as well, just like at Diwali. People held Subhas Chandra Bose in extremely high esteem, though compared to the previous year perhaps the romanticism had waned somewhat.

There had certainly been more fanfare on Subhas Chandra's birthday a year ago. A huge procession had traversed the distance from Deshapriya Park to Deshabandhu Park. Jotudada had gone to join the procession. I was not given permission to go and so felt a tinge of envy. However, I was very excited when I was allowed to go to a huge public meeting the next day in Deshapriya Park. Shah Nawaz Khan of the Azad Hind Fauj was speaking at that meeting. Along with Dhillon and Sahgal, Shah Nawaz was the hero of the entire country. The three officers of the Red Fort trials of Delhi! The slogan of the time was 'Lal Qila se ayee awaz! Sahgal, Dhillon, Shah Nawaz!'

As a young girl I was an admirer of Jawaharlal Nehru. One reason was that I had been charmed by Nehru's autobiography, which I had read in my father's library. On a later occasion I received Discovery of India as a prize for standing first in school. I first saw Jawaharlal Nehru, face to face, in December 1945. Jawaharlal Nehru came to speak at the convocation of the Jadavpur Engineering College. On the day of the convocation I dressed in a khadi sari and arrived at the huge pandal at the college. My Mejomama—literally, second-eldest maternal uncle— Surendra Kumar Roy, was one of the founders and a guiding spirit of Jadavpur College. As he himself had studied at Harvard University, he introduced several customs in its mould at Jadavpur College. At the start of the convocation, all the students of the college from 1911 to 1945 marched past with a band in attendance, while holding up their class flags—'Class of 1912' for instance—and took their seats. Minutes later the boys came and handed out flowers to those of us seated along the aisles. , We were to greet Jawaharlal with a pushpa-brishti, a rain of flowers, when he entered with the ceremonial procession. I gazed in impatient anticipation towards the academic procession of multi-coloured gowns coming forward, somewhat hampered by my short stature. I spotted some Gandhi caps and threw the flowers in my hands in the direction of Nehru's cap. The flowers landed with a plop on a Gandhi cap. I saw that it was not Jawaharlal Nehru, but Sarat Chandra Bose. Nehru was walking next to him. I think I was a little disappointed that day. Today I wonder if destiny had a hand in it. A decade later, I married his son Sisir.

In February, the naval revolt started in Bombay. Its ripples reached our city as well. Student demonstrators and the police engaged in pitched battles on the streets of Kolkata. One thing was becoming clearer by the day to all concerned—it would no longer be possible for the British to rule the country relying on the British Indian Army and the British Indian police. In May we heard the Cabinet Mission proposals on the radio. It seemed that perhaps a way to resolve the communal problem had been found and that independence was within reach. But after oscillating between hope and despair, the Cabinet Mission proposals failed as well.

In January 1947 we were once again celebrating Subhas Chandra's birthday with pomp and in our eyes the soldiers of the Azad Hind Fauj were still heroes. This time I went to two relatively small public meetings. At one of them the principal speakers were the Indian National Army's Colonel Thimayya and Colonel Shaukat Malik, and at the other, Colonel Stracey, an Anglo-Indian officer of the INA was the main speaker. The INA was still a historic example of Hindu-Muslim-Sikh-Christian unity, though that was no longer reflected in actual politics.

In those days when we spoke of Independence Day we meant 26 January, which today is celebrated as Republic Day. On 26 January 1930, in Lahore, the Indian National Congress had passed the resolution for complete independence and between then and 1947 it was celebrated as India's Independence Day. That year on 26 January, Father took me to Kalika Theatre to see *Balsena*, a play based on the boy soldiers of the Azad Hind Fauj. The audience included Ananda Mohan Sahay, one of Netaji's comrades-in-arms, the INA officer Habibur Rahman, the composer Dilip Kumar Roy, who was also Netaji's class friend, and Sarat Chandra Bose. In April we used to observe a national week in memory of the Jallianwala Bagh massacre. That April we felt we must be commemorating the last 'national week'— independence was near; now, new 'days' and 'weeks' worthy of observance were surely on the way.

My matriculation examinations were due to start on 17 April. Owing to the uncertainty in the country, the exams were postponed. The postponement of examinations means nothing to young people today, but that was not the case in our times. In a way, we were the pioneers of the postponement of exams. After several further postponements a date was fixed in June. On 20 June it was decided that Bengal was to be partitioned. That evening, sitting by the radio in the living room, Father, Mother, Chhotokaka and I were engaged in a 'news analysis', as newspapers would put it, of the state of affairs in the country. Listening to the radio announcements proclaiming that the partition of Bengal was inevitable, our mental state was peculiar. We had sought our country's independence, had we not? Independence was on its way. But had we wanted quite such an independence? Bengal had made sacrifices again and again, from the time of the Swadeshi movement to the Quit India movement of 1942 and the Azad Hind movement, in the hope that India would be free one day. Was it really inevitable that this hope could be fulfilled only through the partition of India and the vivisection of Bengal? Chhotokaka got up and started to pace the room, reciting:

> The death that follows in the wake of victory,
> The noble sadness of fulfilled hopes,
> Bequeath to the life of eternal humanity
> A wistful peace.

We sat there, in the wistful sadness of our fulfilled hopes. The beautiful lines of Tagore gave expression to the anguish in our hearts.

After the matriculation exams I was sitting around at home with nothing to do. A letter arrived from my Mejokaka—my father's younger brother— Nirad Chandra Chaudhuri, in Delhi. I was to be sent forthwith to Delhi. Mother would also go with me. We arrived in Delhi on 31 July 1947.

The date 15 August was creeping up steadily. Preparations were afoot all over the country. I was a little concerned. If I had been in Kolkata I could have gone to a prabhat-pheri or a public meeting, but there was no way of joining in any festivity in Delhi. Uncle Nirad would not be in favour of it—in fact he rather disapproved of the entire event. Unlike the rest of the family, he was an admirer of the British Empire. He was writing his autobiography. Sometimes in the evening he would read long excerpts from his manuscript to me. He told me he was going to name it *The Autobiography of an Unknown Indian*. About a couple of days before Independence Day, Uncle Nirad called me. He said, 'So, you think you can't join in all the *hoojug* (an untranslatable Bengali term meaning collective fad) if you stay here? That's why Binu (Chhotokaka) is sending all the newspapers from Kolkata. If you want to join in any of this Mafeking you can do so, I have no objection.' My memory of Delhi that day is like the work of an impressionist painter—dust flying everywhere, a tide of humanity vaguely visible. Somewhere in this, there was a state drive and the hoisting of the flag.

The fanfare of the Independence Day celebrations had hardly ended, the lamps from the illuminations of the festive night barely been extinguished, when trouble broke out in various parts of the country. Punjab was in the grip of terrible turmoil. Killings and lootings were going on unabated in the city of Delhi as well. One day, Uncle Nirad returned from the office in a rather disconcerted state. On the way back he had seen many perfectly respectable people happily carrying away things looted from the shops.

However, we had not quite fathomed how bad things really were in the city. It was 5 September. Our long-serving manservant, Dhanu, had not returned home the previous night after his duty at the Akashvani-All India Radio office. Early in the morning Dhruva, Kirti and I got on our bicycles and headed for the Akashvani office to enquire. The roads were empty anyway that early, but they seemed particularly deserted that day. I was cycling fast, my sari billowing up in the wind. After a while Kirti said to me from the next cycle, 'Your sari is blowing in the wind, fix it—everyone is looking at you.'

I had not still acquired full control over the cycle. Clutching the handle with one hand and trying to control the sari with the other, I looked around. The road was empty, not a soul to be seen. Who could be looking at me? Looking up, I was amazed. On each side of the street, on the balconies of every house, on the roofs, the windows, there were crowds of people looking down at the three of us. There was great astonishment in their expression. Was my sari responsible for quite such a reaction, I wondered.

All of a sudden, someone blew a whistle very loudly. At the

crossing in front of us stood some army personnel—they were blowing the whistle and it was meant for us. The three of us got off our bikes and padded up to face the army. 'Where are you going?' they demanded to know. They looked astonished as well. We said we wanted to go to All India Radio. Stunned, they replied, 'Are you mad? Don't you know what carnage is raging all over the city! Curfew is in force. This spot, where we are standing, was the scene of a terrible riot just a little while ago—there was shooting.'

At last the mystery of why all the people were staring at us in amazement was solved. The soldiers said to us three children, 'Leave this area as quickly as possible.' I had never cycled so hard in my life. I do not remember for how long. At some point we reached Connaught Circus and I collapsed by the side of the road. I was not going to be able to cycle any more, whatever the risk. Dhruva managed by some means to get a tongawalla to agree to come along. The three cycles were put on the tonga and we got on as well. We must have roamed the whole of Delhi trying to find a way back home that day.

After that, Delhi became engulfed in violence. There was non-stop curfew. If we stood on the terrace we could see fires and smoke all around. A few days before, Zubeida, the daughter of a Muslim friend of Uncle Nirad's, had been staying in our house. We used to call her Zubeida-baji. She had left just before all the trouble started. Our downstairs neighbour was a Sikh gentleman. One day he was stabbed—he had got on a tonga and the tongawalla had knifed him and run off. He took off his pagri and tied it around the wound on his stomach and drove the tonga home himself. A few days later, he died.

All the shops and markets were closed because of the continuous curfew. We had a large tin of egg powder in the house. For a few days Mother and Kakima used it to feed us various kinds of egg dishes. We were trying especially hard to keep our daily life normal. As part of this attempt, Uncle Nirad decreed that we would not be allowed in conversation to use, in either English or Bengali, various words such as murder, loot, rape, and so on. Suddenly it was announced one day that curfew would be lifted for half an hour. Dhruva and Kirti were immediately despatched to the market and on other 'must-do' errands. A little while later Dhruva returned from the post office carrying a pile of mail. Among the dozen or so letters was a letter with news of my matriculation results. Father had written asking me to return to Kolkata as I had to be admitted to college.

It was decided that Dilipkaka, Mother and I would attempt to return to Kolkata even though it entailed some risk. Corpses lay strewn on the roads, in the courtyard of the station, by the railway tracks. By the time the train reached the Yamuna bridge, I could not bear to look out on either side. Whichever way I turned, there were dead bodies. Apart from us there was a Punjabi family in the compartment—just evicted from Lahore. A girl of about my age was sitting next to me. Suddenly the girl cried, '*Dekho, dekho, keysa khun girta*!' (Oh, look, look, how the blood is running.) Startled, I looked out to see a child's body, blood still trickling from it. My heart froze. Not only at the death of this unknown child, but more than that at the glee of the young girl on seeing that death.

The girl had started to talk about how all the members of her family had been lined up and shot. Orphaned, she was travelling to Kolkata that day with her neighbour's family in search of shelter. I understood everything she said, but felt an unbearable pain. How merciless could human beings become!

Then there was a new scene. Some things were being thrown out of the windows of various compartments. Naively I asked Mother, 'I wonder what those pillow-like things they are throwing out are?' Human beings were being thrown out. It was like a game. Some villainous-looking people were pulling the chain and stopping the train at frequent intervals; they would then select people from different compartments and throw them off the train; whether the victims were dead, half-dead or alive, I could not tell.

A little while later they appeared in our compartment as well. A tremendous argument started between them and our Punjabi fellow-travellers in their own language. At first we had no idea what was going on. Then we realized that we were the subject of their discussion. Mother, Dilipkaka and I were on their hit list. They were preparing to throw us out through the windows as well. Their argument was very simple. Bengal and Punjab were the two provinces in which Pakistan had been created. As we were Bengalis, we must be from Pakistan, hence the death sentence. The young Punjabi girl challenged them and engaged in a heated exchange. I watched in some surprise. Just a little while ago I had seen her satisfaction at murder. She was telling them we were respectable people. 'This is a professor,' she said, pointing at Dilipkaka. I do not know whether it was because of her fiery defence, but the executioners departed, saying they would be back.

As evening wore on into night, the train entered Kanpur station. The platform was lined with white soldiers, or 'tommies', as they used to be called. They surrounded the train, searched every compartment and took several people into custody. The men who had made trouble in our compartment were among them. We all heaved a sigh of relief. But my nationalist pride took a terrible knock. I could never forget that—post-independence—I had been relieved to see the face of a British soldier.

There was no more trouble after leaving Kanpur. The train sped along in the darkness of the night. I could not sleep. I felt I was racing towards an unknown future. Whether in personal life or in the life of the country, an uncertain path lay ahead. I started to build castles of sand as I lay on the bunk—I built them and tore them down endlessly. The train ran across northern India towards the newly partitioned Bengal.

One Woodburn Park

When I entered One Woodburn Park as a bride, the sun had already set on the house. Its days of glory were over. The men who had made history in that house and the historic figures who had frequented the place were no more. In that darkness after sundown the marriage of Sisir and myself, was the first glimmer of light, a harbinger of auspicious days. On hearing that I was going to be married into the Bose family, a very near and dear aunt had commented, 'Krishna, remember it is darkest under the lamp. Compared to the luminaries who had come before, the next generation is bound to look rather dim.'

As a newly married couple, when we entered the house together for the first time, I could hear the celebratory music of the shehnai. As our car entered the portals, a number of beautiful women in red Benarasi saris received us. One came forward with a pitcher of water and poured it on the wheels of the car as an act of ablution. An elderly lady, with a tiny silver bowl full of honey, stepped into the car. She dipped her finger in the honey and touched my lips and ears. This was symbolic—whatever they say to you will be as sweet as honey. However, in spite of that symbolic gesture, it would not be quite correct to say that whatever was uttered by the in-laws was invariably sweet. I was rather quiet by nature and did not say much to anyone, honeyed or otherwise.

As we stepped out of the car, we were made to stand at the foot of the marble staircase. There was a makeshift oven there with a huge pan of milk on it. The bride was supposed to enter the house only after she saw the milk boiling over. This ritual was meant to herald a world of prosperity for the newly-weds. I stood there and shivered in the December chill—my feet bare on the cold marble floor. It took quite some time for the milk to boil over—a sure sign that prosperity would be delayed for the couple.

Next I was taken to the kitchen where Satyabadi, the long-time cook of the household, stood at the door. A white sheet covered a number of pots and pans on the floor; these were full of various kinds of cooked food. Satyabadi lifted the cover and said, 'Baudidi have a look.' I looked. This ritual was to ensure that the bride would always have abundance in her kitchen and pantry. There were more rituals to go through. I stood on a flat black marble bowl full of milk and red paint and held a slippery fish in my hand. If you held it right, you would negotiate the slippery path of the householder's life with ease...

That first evening at Woodburn Park I was very sad. Indian women traditionally felt sad when they left their father's house. It was usual in those days for girls to be married off when they were even younger than I was. I had passed my university exams and had just joined as a lecturer in a Kolkata college. Still, I was the only child of my parents. My leaving the parental home would create a void in their life. I felt saddened by that thought. But what surprised me even then, was the overarching atmosphere of gloom in Woodburn Park. I did not understand why at that time. As a matter of fact, this was the first joyous event in the family after the rather untimely death of Sisir's parents. All the brothers and sisters felt their absence keenly. Two garlanded photographs of Sarat and Bivabati, Sisir's parents, were placed on one side where I bowed and did pranam. I heard sobbing around me. In this atmosphere of grief and sorrow, I became a part of Woodburn Park.

For a few days Woodburn Park was a typical marriage house.

It was crowded with friends and relatives from far and near. There was an all encompassing busy atmosphere. The day after the arrival of the bride is known as Phulshajya. Flowers, sweets, jewellery, and dresses, all arranged on decorated trays, come from the bride's father's house. In the evening there is a reception at the bridegroom's house. I heard instructions being given right from the morning: 'Tell the shehnaiwalla to play the shehnai when the *tatta,* the gifts from the bride's house, arrive. Keep the verandah ready for the trays...' In the meantime my cousins, Dhruva and Kirti, arrived with most of my gifts packed in trunks loaded on a truck. I could see that the tradition of receiving and giving of gifts was taken very seriously here. But for our family, which was originally from East Bengal, gift-giving was not such an elaborate affair. On the day of the wedding it was the turn of the bridegroom's family to send gifts, which they did very tastefully. I somehow managed to whisper to Dhruva and Kirti that my family should not send things in trunks. They obviously conveyed the message because in the evening the trays bearing the gifts arrived decorated in a proper manner.

Soon relatives and friends started to leave and the house became quite empty. The crowd of relatives and friends and the perpetual activities that are part of an Indian marriage have an advantage. In a western marriage the couple go off for their honeymoon immediately after the ceremony. They are supposed to get to know each other better away from family. But in an Indian wedding, it is not just the two persons who get to know each other—it is the two families who come closer. In the process, the young couple also get to know each other. Now which custom is better remains debatable.

I had now to start a conscious process of adjustment to the new environment that I found myself in. It was not very easy. The background from which I came and the context in which I found myself were totally different. I was brought up in a nuclear family—my parents and myself. Since I grew up as an only child,

I never acquired the diplomatic skills to deal with worldly matters. I had to learn the hard way through experience. I had one advantage. I found that my husband was totally indifferent to worldly intrigue. So very soon we got on well with each other. And thus began a life where both of us sailed happily through all the deceptions, the betrayals and broken promises.

I had a lonely life as a child but the atmosphere in my parental home was warm, friendly and scholarly. There was music, there was appreciation of painting, art criticism, photography and a general engagement in academic activities. These were part of my life. I was learning classical music from the maestro Tarapada Chakravarti. I was also learning to play the sitar. I used to go for photographic expeditions to the alleys and by-lanes of Kolkata. The noted painter Gopal Ghosh and the sculptor Pradosh Dasgupta would frequent our home. Sometimes, we would go to visit the great portrait painter Atul Bose or the famous *pata* painter Jamini Roy. They were close family friends.

On Sunday mornings, there would be family reunions when the uncles gathered at our place. Over cups of tea and snacks, intellectual debates would go on. Topics would vary from the novels of Thomas Mann to George Orwell's newly published *Nineteen Eighty Four*. If we got tired of debates, one of the younger uncles, Manmatha, would play the organ and we would all sing Tagore songs. I can still hear strains of *Paush toder dak diyechhe, aye re chole ay* (the winter month of Paush calls, come along and join). My father, Charu Chandra Chaudhuri was the eldest of six brothers. His interests ranged from law to literature, mathematics to music. The second brother, Nirad, a writer, and the third one, Kshirode, a physician, were already well known in their own fields.

One danger of being an only child is that parents wish you to be adept at everything. The right words would be used for every occasion. My father was determined that his daughter must be accomplished. Not just any ordinary accomplishment necessary to pass muster in the marriage market; he meant accomplishment in the real sense of the word. All the days of my week were filled with learning different skills. Once a week, vocal music and instrumental music on the sitar; twice a week the tabla or percussion player would come for music practice while weekends were reserved for the Bengali Music College. I was preparing for the Sangeet-Visharad exam at the Bhatkhande Music School. On top of this I was studying for an honours degree in English literature. The pressure was too much. What was inevitable under such pressure happened.

Tarapada Babu, my music teacher, was a renowned vocalist. He felt sure, that were I to devote a couple of hours more to my practice, I could soon become an accomplished singer. He complained I was not putting in that effort. The only way to distract his mind from that was to get into an argument about the Paul Klee painting of two upside down birds that hung on our sitting room wall. Tarapada Babu declared, 'However you may try, I am not going to recognize that one as a great painting.' My teacher disliked abstract art. He was quick to anger but at the same time, he was very affectionate. Though an exponent of classical Indian music, he wrote and composed modern Bengali songs. When his first book of songs was published, he gave me a copy. On my asking him to write something in the book he wrote a beautiful poem. The first line ran something like this— 'the garland of songs that I brought for you was not to your liking I know . . .' So it was not possible to put in that extra bit of diligence which would have enabled me to score ten out of ten. But I did become quite skilled in different branches of art.

So this was the atmosphere in our home. There were two opposites at work. Although I was rather solitary and introspective by nature, the environment around me was full of warmth and life. The atmosphere in which I now found myself was definitely cold. When all the relatives left after the wedding ceremony, an uncanny silence descended. The house was huge, but the rooms were desolate. The silent marble staircase went up to the third floor. The mood everywhere was stony. This was a strange quirk of destiny. This desolate, abandoned look did not at all become the house which once upon a time had been full of life and had witnessed history being made within its four walls. This house at one time was looked upon as the political nerve centre of Bengal. Sisir's father Sarat Chandra Bose and his illustrious uncle Netaji Subhas Chandra Bose were key players in the political struggle for India's freedom. Mahatma Gandhi and Jawaharlal Nehru stayed in the Woodburn Park house when in Kolkata. Gandhiji would hold prayer meetings on the terrace of the house with crowds on the street outside the gate shouting 'Gandhi Maharaj-ki jai' It was my misfortune that I saw Woodburn Park as a hopeless and uninspiring edifice.

I thought about this later and came to the conclusion that I arrived at Woodburn Park when it was going through a period of transition. The old world had ended, but the new world had yet to gain stability. Lively and joyful days returned again. But that change was rung in by the next generation. Father, mother and children made up their individual units. The old world was completely lost. Every transition brings with it a sense of loss and pain and I went through that experience. I used to feel suffocated. I seemed to live in a make-believe world detached from reality.

I look back and see the dining room in my mind. It was actually a dining hall—the room was huge. There was a big mahogany dining table, surrounded by beautiful chairs. A lovely chandelier hung from the ceiling with crystal lamps on four sides. On two sides, high up on the walls, were large oil paintings of Sisir's forefathers. One had to strain one's neck to look at them. We all sat round the table for dinner. My sister-in-law sat at the head of the table. She was absolutely silent and did not utter a word, from soup to pudding. On the right sat her husband, my elder brother-in-law. He talked incessantly. Now and then he looked at his wife and said, 'So you understand.' She did not reply. Instead the younger sister, who sat to his right, made one or two comments. Across the table my husband and I sat side by side. At the bottom of the table facing my sister-in-law was my younger brother-in-law. My husband and my younger brother-in-law continued to eat in silence and with solemn faces. I wondered why they did not discuss anything. Why were there no arguments? No jokes?

My elder brother-in-law went on talking to himself. He was a bit of a hypochondriac. My husband was a doctor so he would look at his doctor brother and say, 'In the morning I had a mild headache.' The doctor ate his dinner in silence. 'My limbs are aching. Maybe I am going to have fever.' The person to whom this was addressed was always silent. I felt uncomfortable—why could he not say something? My brother-in-law said at last—'Why do I feel like this?' It was a direct question which had to be answered. The doctor brother raised his head, looked in an absent-minded way, thought deeply for a little while and then said—'Who knows why?' My brother-in-law retorted angrily, 'If you do not know, why have you become a doctor?' A very relevant question. I started to enjoy the conversation. The atmosphere became somewhat normal. My brother-in-law's eyes fell on me. The bearer had just served chicken. He looked at my plate and remarked, 'What, only that much? Take some more chicken.' I felt embarrassed. I usually took the food, played with it but did not eat anything. I had not been feeling well because I was pregnant but the family did not know. Somehow I felt grateful that he had noticed I was not eating much. In my in-law's household there was a general attitude of indifference. No one showed much curiosity about anyone else's affairs. That seemed to be the rule. I came from a home where much depended on whether I smiled or wept. The indifference appeared to me to be downright negligence. That I was nearly starving had first been noticed by our old cook Satyabadi. He had asked my youngest sister-in-law, 'Has the new Baudidi taken any religious vow?' Surprised, my sister-in-law had responded, 'What do you mean?' Satyabadi said, 'She has not touched fish for quite some time.'

Whenever I think of Satyabadi and the dining room a strange experience comes to my mind. I was going to have my first child. My mother wished to arrange a *sadha* ceremony for me at her place. The *sadha* ceremony was the Indian version of the western custom of a baby shower. The mother-to-be was offered a ceremonial lunch and gifts were given to her on the occasion. We were told it was the custom to first have the ceremony at the in-laws' place, only then could it be held at the parental home. Usually elderly ladies of the house organized such ceremonies. There was no one at our Woodburn Park house to take charge of this event. My youngest sister-in-law offered to help. She said even if it was for the sake of keeping up the tradition, she would arrange a formal meal. An auspicious day was fixed. Satyabadi cooked all the traditional dishes from fish-head curry to the dessert of rice pudding. I was spending a few days with my mother, but I was ordered to come back before lunch. The auspicious time for the *sadha* meal would last till ten minutes past two o'clock. Having arranged everything, my sister-in-law, who was a lecturer in a college, left because she had a class to take. I decided to wait till my husband returned from his hospital duties so that we could have lunch together, even though the *sadha* was an exclusively women's affair and he was supposed to have no role in it. The grandfather clock on the landing of the marble staircase struck two. Still there was no sign of my husband. Satyabadi said, 'Baudidi, the auspicious time will be over soon. Let me serve your meal.' We usually had our lunch on the southern verandah where there was an oval marble dining-table. Dinner was, however, served in the formal dining room where the table was formally laid with crockery and cutlery. Dinner was prepared by the Muslim chef.

It was a rather warm day. Satyabadi chose to serve the meal in the dining room. He shut the three large glass doors that opened on to the verandah. He also closed the wooden shutters. The dining room became cool and dark. Satyabadi spread a Bengali newspaper on one side of the mahogany dining table. He put on a dim light. He put a large bell-metal plate on the table. There was a neat, round mound of rice on the plate and numerous small bell-metal bowls with different kinds of food were placed around the plate. A heavy bell-metal glass of water was on one side. 'Only five minutes left, Baudidi, you had better start,' said Satyabadi and left. My unique *sadha* ceremony started. There was the huge, silent dining hall, dimly lit where I sat on a single chair. All the other chairs were empty. In front of me were the rows of bowls, the plate, the glass of water. A heavy, stony silence descended on me and the huge, dark room engulfed me. It was an uncanny feeling. I looked to my right. There, high up from the ceiling, hung the two oil paintings of Dadabhai and Ma-Janani, Sisir's grandfather and grandmother. Their names were Janakinath and Prabhabati and they looked down upon me with sympathy and affection in their eyes, as if they wished to say 'Do not fear, here we are with you.' I looked to my left. There on the wall hung pictures of Dadamoni and Didimoni—Akshay Kumar De and Subala De—Sisir's maternal grandfather and grandmother. They also looked at me very fondly. I looked once to my right and then to my left. By the touch of some magic wand, the portraits came alive and an ethereal affection poured from the eyes of the forebears for their unborn descendant. Then I came back to reality from my world of dreams. There were footsteps on the stairs. My husband lifted the curtain, saw me sitting there and asked, surprised, 'What is the matter?' I said, 'Nothing. Come and have lunch.' So we sat down, chatted and shared the fish-head curry and rice pudding. I do not think anyone ever had a *sadha* ceremony like the one I had.

Apart from One Woodburn Park, another address became

part of my life. That was Netaji Bhawan on 38/2 Elgin Road. No one lived in that house any more. It was a museum with two carefully preserved rooms—a bedroom and a sitting room. Netaji had used these rooms when he was Congress President. But a great historic event had also happened in this house. While under strict police surveillance he escaped from this house, went abroad and formed the Indian National Army. Sisir drove him from Kolkata to Gomoh on the first leg of the great escape. Now though it was a museum, I found that some sort of social work was still done in the house. Sisir ran a charitable child health clinic there.

Ever since my engagement to Sisir, I had heard a great deal about Netaji Bhawan but I was not aware of its actual activities. Some time before our marriage, I showed an art book with Kalighat *pata* paintings to my future husband. He liked the painting of a mother and child very much. He borrowed the book from me and said he would like to use the picture for a child health exhibition that he had planned at Netaji Bhawan. About this time my future in-laws invited me to a programme at Netaji Bhawan. It was my father-in-law Sarat Chandra Bose's birthday. But I felt shy and did not go. My uncle Dr K.C. Chaudhuri, aunt Amala and my cousin Kirti went and everyone asked Kirti why I had not come. Kirti in his usual enigmatic manner said, 'Well, you see, she just did not come.'

I have to confess that on the first night after marriage—which we call *phulshajya*—our conversation centred around Netaji Bhawan. I asked what Netaji Bhawan was. My husband replied, 'It is my temple.' From then on Netaji Bhawan became an intrinsic part of my life. In the early days after our marriage, sometimes Sisir would just disappear. I would look for him and his younger brother and sister would say, 'Oh, if you can't find Laldada (as they called Sisir), he must have gone to Netaji Bhawan. That's his place. He is always there.'

In my bedroom, just beside my bed was a small writing table

with my Olivetti typewriter on it. Both were wedding presents from my father. I had taken up freelance journalism apart from my teaching and was the art-critic of a little known evening daily. I needed a typewriter to write my art reviews, so the first wedding present that Father bought for me was an Olivetti typewriter. The second purchase was a Rollichord camera. This made my mother very anxious. When would the saris and jewellery be bought, she wondered. As it happened, my husband used the typewriter more than I did. Late into the night he would be typing on the machine. The archives of the Netaji Research Bureau were being prepared and Netaji's letters and speeches were being collected. Historical documents were being copied and preserved. Sisir carried on a correspondence with innumerable people all over the world. Every night I fell asleep listening to the tak, tak, tak, tak sound of the typewriter. In the meantime I continued my attempts to adjust to strange surroundings but it did not seem as though I was making much progress. The only ray of hope, in the otherwise unreal and cold atmosphere, was the sincere and intimate relationship that Sisir and I shared. It was not very demonstrative but it was a deep bond of partnership. My husband was never interested in worldly affairs. He could not take part in tittle-tattle. He always talked about and dreamt about big things. It could be about Netaji Bhawan or how the Netaji Research Bureau could be made into a world class institution which would preserve the history of Netaji and India's freedom struggle. It could be about the Institute of Child Health—how the life and health of the children of India could be improved. The Institute of Child Health had been founded by my paediatrician uncle, Dr K.C. Chaudhuri. He had with him a fine band of young doctors dedicated to the well-being of the children of our country. The Institute of Child Health developed as a unique institution within a few years of independence.

I used to love to read books, to visit art exhibitions, to sing, to play the sitar. I soon found that Sisir also enjoyed going to art exhibitions. We regularly went to the No. 1 Chowringhee Terrace Art Gallery or the Art in Industry, then situated on Park Street. I still had the job of an art critic in the obscure evening newspaper. We often went to the studio of the well-known portrait painter Atul Bose or to the studio of the famous painter Jamini Roy. They were friends of my father and looked upon me with affection. They accepted Sisir also into their close circle. Atul Bose gave me a painting by Jamini Roy as a wedding present. He said Jaminida had painted it at his request. The landscape painter Gopal Ghosh had given me a wedding present of his painting of the Chilka Lake in Orissa. He had also painted designs on the two wooden seats where the bride and bridegroom would sit during the wedding ceremony. One day an interesting incident took place at Jamini Roy's studio. Sisir and I had just said goodbye to the painter and were about to leave when Sisir pointed to a particular painting and casually remarked, 'Isn't that mother and child painting slightly different from your usual ones?' This excited Jamini Babu and he called out to Patol, his son, who used to be with him in the studio. But even before Patol could come, the painter himself wrapped the painting in a newspaper, put it in Sisir's hands and said, 'Baba, my dear son, keep it in the room where you work.' Since then the painting has always hung in Sisir's chamber.

My music practice, however, suffered a setback. The days when all the seven evenings of my week were full of music were no more. Besides, as Tagore had said, '*Ekaki gayaker noheto gan*' (music is not just for the performer). The presence of a listener was essential. In my father's house the family would all sit down for a musical evening, but that salon-like atmosphere was missing at my in-laws' place. The musical atmosphere came back to Woodburn Park as my children grew up. We would burst into song at the slightest provocation. No formal occasion was necessary. As we sat round the marble dining table we would thump the table and sing in chorus a family favourite, Tagore's

Prangane more shirish shakaya Fagun mashe ki ucchashe (in the spring month of Fagun how the shirish tree blossoms into flowers).

My writing continued, though somewhat fitfully. The PEN in Kolkata was quite lively at that time and many well-known contemporary authors and novelists used to attend the meetings. The poet couple, Narendra Deb and Radharani Debi, had made me a member of PEN. Narendra Deb was the secretary of PEN, while famous Bengali authors Premendra Mitra, 'Banaphul', Annada Shankar Roy were members, as were a number of lesser known persons. Niharranjan Ray, the reputed art historian, used to say the 'N' in PEN stood for non-entities.

It was about this time that Netaji entered into my writing. It was to draw the attention of the public to the work that went on at Netaji Bhawan that I started to write on related topics. Most of these reports were not in my name but as a special representative or art critic. On 23 January 1956 which was Netaji's birthday, Sisir organized an exhibition on Netaji's life. Sisir, helped by the devoted Naga Sundaram, worked hard day and night to set it up. There was no permanent museum at that time. It drew a large number of visitors. I wrote a review of the exhibition for the magazine *Desh* as their art critic. Someone mentioned the review to my brother-in-law, Amiya, so one morning at the breakfast table he read the review carefully. He had no idea I had written it. He looked up from the magazine and announced to the family, 'The fellow writes quite well.'

In those early days at Woodburn Park, two little children became a perpetual source of joy for me. They were the son and daughter of my brother-in-law, Amiya. His three-year-old daughter was fond of me. Her ayah, Kshiroda, used to bring her to me and announce, 'It is Khuku's meal time.' I would feed her. Her six-year-old brother was particularly attached to me. In a newly-wed bride's room everything looked fresh and interesting to him. He spent hours with me and helped put away the silk saris and jewellery in my wardrobe. Sometimes he crawled under my writing table, pulled out papers and hunted out colourful advertisements. If I happened to be in the bathroom, he would urgently knock on the door and call, 'Kakima, Kakima.' Something very serious seemed to have happened one day when he knocked impatiently. 'What is it?' 'Do you know only three days are left before my birthday!' I replied, 'Is that so? What wonderful news.' Indeed, children are a source of eternal happiness. The poet Wordsworth realized this when he wrote, 'Heaven lies about us in our infancy.' He also realized the transitory nature of this feeling, how with passage of time it evaporates '...into the light of common day'. Very soon there was another child in the family. It was our baby son. He came trailing '...clouds of glory'. He brought the message of happiness— ananda —from paradise: *Nandaner ananda sambad*, as Tagore put it. Our life started to revolve round him.

Our Woodburn Park house had a small annexe attached to it. After the birth of our son we moved to the annexe, which was like a doll's house. The three tiny rooms were made into a sitting room, a bedroom and a child's room. The mezzanine was Sisir's chamber. Since there was no space for a patients' waiting room, a curtain was put up under the staircase where there was place for only one person. If there was more than one person, then they had no alternative but to loiter in the courtyard outside under the Kalojam tree. We had made a vain attempt to shift to the annexe earlier, but my two huge wardrobes could not be taken up the narrow staircase. In the process the beautiful wardrobes were damaged, much to the chagrin of our Chinese carpenter, Tham, who had made them as wedding gifts from my father. This time a couple of steps were taken off the staircase for the movement of the furniture. Tham made a tiny square table for us, which served as a dining table for two, and in the absence of any dining space, was put at the head of the staircase. A window opened on to the view of the tennis courts of South Club.

Movement was restricted and there was lack of space. So what! Sisir and I spent some of our happiest days in that small cottage. We were still part of a loose joint family structure and the family continued to gather formally around the dinner table in the evenings. But on the whole there was more freedom in the new set-up. There was a small kitchenette behind the garage where our nanny-cum-cook, Jamini, started to work. We still used to drive about in the historic Wanderer car which later became part of the Netaji Museum. This was the car in which Sisir had driven his uncle Subhas when he escaped from the Elgin Road house in 1941. Sisir had repaired the old car but it still broke down frequently in the middle of a journey—Sisir and I, with the baby in my arms, pushing the car, were a familiar sight on the streets of Kolkata. However, in spite of occasional non-cooperation, the Wanderer kept our life on the move. I was a working mother. In the mid-fifties this was not very common in Bengali society. Sisir drove me to my workplace and on our way we dropped the baby and the nanny at my mother's residence. On his way back from hospital duty, Sisir collected us and we came home. That was our normal routine. Our doll's house became very hot in summer. To escape from the heat, we drove to the Ballygunj lake in the evenings. The south breeze cooled us, as Sisir and I sat on the grass and the baby played dangerously near the water. For a change, we sometimes went to Park Street, again in the Wanderer. We parked the car and strolled on the street looking into shop windows. However, the season changed and dark rain clouds appeared on the horizon. Our hearts leapt up at the sight. The monsoons were upon us. On the first day of the rains Sisir and I rushed up to the terrace of our doll's house and got drenched. Tagore's monsoon songs call people to come out to the Neepa forest and bathe in the first showers of the monsoon. We had no Neepa forest, but our little terrace was transformed into a monsoon landscape. Sometimes when it rained for long, Woodburn Park got waterlogged and our little house looked like an island. We made paper boats and the boats happily bobbed around in the water to the glee of our baby son.

One night in 'Chhoto bari' as we used to call the annexe, my mother-in-law visited me in a dream. I was in a somewhat depressed mood. My attempts at adjustment with the joint family had nearly collapsed. I was confused and did not know how to keep everyone happy. Our scriptures say it is impossible to please human beings, so you try to please the One whose pleasure is the pleasure of all—*Yasmin tushte jagat tushta*. I was too young for such a philosophical approach. Was anything wrong with me? What was the reason of my failure, I wondered. In my dream I saw my mother-in-law come down the steps from the terrace. She sat down on the narrow bed in the baby's room. She told me, 'Must you waste your time on insignificant brooding? Who says you have failed in your duties? You have not. Here I am. What happened to your music? It looks like you have given it up. Instead of frittering away your time in idle thoughts, why don't you sit down with your music?' I woke up and for a few seconds, was unsure whether I was still in my dream or back to reality. That evening I sat down with my harmonium after a long time and sang for hours. Father had said he would send Jagadish to accompany me on the tabla at least twice a week so I could keep up my music practice. Like many other mistakes in my life, it was a mistake not to listen to Father's advice. But I was so preoccupied in trying to strike a balance between my professional life and the duties of a mother that I thought that it would be futile to try to keep up my music. It would have been impossible even to continue my job of teaching in college if Mother had not been such a wonderful babysitter. There came a time when I could not drag the children to her place. Then she came over for the day. In Bengali society a mother spending a lot of time in the married daughter's house was frowned upon, but my mother did not care about social censure.

One evening Sisir was about to go out on his rounds to see

his patients. He suddenly asked me, 'I am going to see a child in Thakuma's house, would you like to come along?' 'Thakuma? Who is that?' I asked perplexed. Sisir said, 'Come along, let me take you to her.' Thakuma or grandmother happened to be Basanti Devi, wife of Deshbandhu C.R. Das, the political guru of Subhas Chandra Bose. According to Woodburn Park traditions the new bride was to be presented to Thakuma soon after the wedding. But in those times of indifference in Woodburn Park nobody had bothered to take me to her. That evening I met her for the first time and for both of us it was love at first sight. When she entered the room she ignored me, turned to Sisir and burst out: 'So at last you brought your wife to me. Don't you know your mother would have brought her over on the morning after *phulshajya*. Who do you think you are!' She went on for quite some time and Sisir kept on smiling with a guilty expression. Then she turned towards me. I developed great admiration and love for the courageous lady and she in turn poured all her affection on me. From then on we made frequent evening visits to the south verandah of her Nafar Kundu Lane house. She used to relate anecdotes of bygone days—days that she passed with her husband Deshbandhu and with Sarat and Subhas. She said, 'Believe me, there is not a day or night that I pass when I do not think of Sarat and Subhas. How much they suffered for our country. The long imprisonments broke their health.' Tears came to my eyes. But she sat erect with her eyes dry and told me, 'My tears have long dried up.' There was a ring of sadness in her voice. She was still there but those whom she loved so much were no more. One evening as we were leaving after our visit Thakuma gave us a bundle of letters. Letters that Subhas had written to her. She also gave us a marble Buddha that had been brought from Burma (Myanmar) by Subhas in 1927. Basanti Devi said there was a belief that it was inauspicious to keep a Buddha in a home because one could be inspired to renounce the world and become a monk. So Basanti Devi had taken it away from him. These gifts formed the nucleus of the Netaji Research Bureau (NRB), an Institute of History, Politics and Current Affairs, which Sisir established in 1957. Sisir added his own gift, the Wanderer, to the archives of NRB. The car was no longer our private property. It belonged to the nation from 1957. Large numbers of people came to see the car which was placed on a dais at Netaji Bhawan.

About this time Sisir was offered a Rockefeller Fellowship to Harvard Medical School for advanced training in paediatric radiology at the Children's Hospital in Boston. I was delighted with the news. Here was a chance to escape from the pettiness of daily drudgery and a welcome escape from my attempts to adjust in the extended family. Sisir's colleagues had advised him not to accept the fellowship. Their argument was that it took a couple of years to establish one's medical practice. If he left just after setting it up, he would have to begin again from scratch. However, both of us had made up our minds to go.

Our travel plans got delayed. The reason for the delay was strange. My new passport arrived on time but there was no news of Sisir's passport. On enquiry it was found that Sisir's name was on the blacklist of colonial subjects, turned citizens, who had taken part in the freedom movement. He would need special clearance from the central government—after more than ten years of independence, a freedom fighter's passport could not be released! The Institute of Child Health authorities wrote indignant letters to the Delhi passport office. We waited for the passport. In the meantime a wedding took place in the family. Sisir's youngest sister's marriage was fixed. She and I were more or less contemporaries and both of us taught in Kolkata colleges. My mother had asked me to give up my teaching soon after Sisir and I got engaged, but when I came to know my youngest sister-in-law also taught in a college, I decided not to give up my profession. I had been selected for the job after a tough interview. There were many candidates. The interviewers sat around a horse-shoe-shaped table and grilled me for quite some time. An elderly gentleman sat apart in an armchair and got into a discussion with me on Christopher Marlowe. I told my friends that I did not expect to get the job but they said that I would most probably be selected. That is why they grilled me. Well, I did receive the appointment letter soon after. I would teach in this college as Professor of English Literature for forty long years and serve for eight years as its Principal.

If my mother had her way, I would have been married off when I was sixteen, soon after my school-leaving exams. But my father put his foot down and declared there was no question of marriage before graduation. I then went in for post-graduate studies and did my Masters in English Literature from Presidency College. I had the good fortune to have as my teachers the legendary Professor Taraknath Sen along with Subodh Chandra Sengupta and Amal Bhattacharjee. Among my classmates were Dhritikanta Lahiri Chowdhuri, Benode Kishore Roy Chowdhuri and Arun Kumar Dasgupta. In a traditional Bengali wedding ceremony the bride is carried on a wooden seat around the bridegroom seven times. This onerous duty fell on Dhriti and Benode along with my cousin Kirti when I got married. When I started to look for a job, strangely my father opposed the idea and my mother encouraged me.

We had been looking for a suitable boy for my sister-in-law. My sister-in-law was very tall. Sisir met the boy and came back to report that he was as tall as a palmyra tree. There is usually a formal engagement ceremony before the actual wedding which in Bengali is called *Paka Dekha*. When my father had asked Sisir's family when we could have the auspicious ceremony of *Paka Dekha*, Sisir's elder brother told him that *Paka Dekha* was banned in the Bose family. There were bans on various rituals or customs in the family imposed by Ma-Janani Prabhabati, Sisir's grandmother. For example, no children in the family had birthday parties. I observed the ban on my son's first birthday. But when he had his second birthday in London and the third in Boston, I happily broke the rule. Since then, other children's birthdays have also been celebrated. Ma-Janani had decreed that there should be no matrimonial relations with families bearing the surname Dutta. I never understood the reason for this particular rule since she herself came from the Dutta family of Hatkhola and had a happy married life. So what was wrong with the Duttas? The ban on the final, formal engagement ceremony was imposed by Dadabhai (Janakinath). The marriage of his second son Sarat with Bivabati, the daughter of the Dey family had been fixed for some time. But the search for a suitable bride for Satish, the first son, was still on. Ma-Janani had a weakness for fair complexions. At the same time she was particular that the girl must come from a high caste, kulin family. Hence the delay. Bivabati's father Akshay Chandra asked Janakinath if the final engagement or *Paka Dekha* ceremony could take place, since the marriage was going to be delayed. Janakinath said in reply, 'My word is paka, final.' From that day there were no *Paka Dekha*s for Bose family boys. However, the girls were exempt from the ban. So my sister-in-law did have a nice engagement ceremony. On the day of the ceremony I happened to help the eldest aunt, the wife of Satish, in the kitchen. She was the only dark-complexioned daughter-in-law of Ma-Janani, albeit from a kulin family. She was a simple and nice person who lived just opposite our Woodburn Park house.

I did not meet many members of the extended Bose family till much later. I cannot really explain the reason. Maybe there was no one to take the new bride to visit all the branches of the family. Most of the Bose men of the generation of Sarat and Subhas were no more. The eldest brother, Satish Chandra, had passed away. The second brother, Sarat Chandra, my father-in-law, had died in February 1950. The third brother Suresh Chandra was still alive. He lived with his family in a house on Moira Street, not far from Woodburn Park. I came to know this branch of the family much later. The fourth brother, Sudhir Chandra, was no more, while the fifth brother, Sunil Chandra, had also passed away recently. Their wives were present at the time of my marriage. And in nearby Bakulbagan lived Subhas Chandra's youngest sister, Kanaklata, who had welcomed me as a new bride with a silver bowl full of honey. Apart from Thakuma, Basanti Devi, I became close to Auntie Emilie, wife of Netaji Subhas Chandra Bose, whom I met for the first time in Vienna in December 1959, on our way back from the United States. When Sisir and I got married she had written to us from Vienna, 'May you be as happy a couple as your parents Sarat and Biva were.'

The youngest uncle Sailesh and his wife, our aunt Bhakti, were away in Europe at the time of our marriage and they came to visit us in Kolkata more than a year later. I was presented to them, and when I did pranam, Kakababu, that is uncle Sailesh, hugged me affectionately. He appeared to me like the last of the Forsytes, a representative of a bygone generation. Bhakti, our Chhoto kakima, was a cheerful and friendly sort. She took upon herself the duty of taking me to visit all the near and distant branches of the Bose family. I visited many of the Bose clan for the first time and was overwhelmed by the affectionate welcome I had from everyone. The only relatives I knew from the beginning were Sisir's maternal uncle Ajit Dey and aunt Surama. They were wonderful people and a solid support to Sarat Chandra's family, particularly during the freedom struggle when Sarat and later, Sisir went to prison and my mother-in-law was left helpless with the younger children. With the marriage of Sisir's youngest sister, a chapter was closed in the saga of Woodburn Park—the chapter I have described as a period of transition and a new phase began.

We were about to leave for Boston. But just when we were ready to leave two incidents happened which nearly jeopardized our travel plans. Nothing has been smooth sailing in my life, but what could I do? It was my destiny. So I reminded myself that a storm made the tree stronger provided it could stand firm in the face of it. I came down with typhoid fever and the date of our departure had to be postponed. For three weeks I was critically ill. My mother came to stay in our doll's house and took charge of the baby. When I was recuperating my father brought his music system and his records to cheer me up. Nobody could be quite as caring as one's parents. You never had to ask—they would always be there with their silent support. I was still very weak when I started to pack our suitcases. There was a short wooden gate at the top of the stairs in our tiny doll's house so that the baby would not fall down. But one day someone forgot to put the latch on. The baby pushed the door and rolled down the stairs. We rushed him to the children's hospital, anxious about the deep cut on the forehead. The doctors attended to him. My paediatrician uncle consoled me, 'Don't worry, everything will be all right.' And aunt Amala, herself a pediatrician, kept on saying, 'The baby is all right, the mother needs attention.' It felt like ages until my husband put him on my lap with his head bandaged. We decided not to postpone our journey and took him in the aeroplane with the bandage on. The stitches were taken off at the Boston Children's Hospital.

In the late fifties, with the Bose brothers gone from the scene, politics in West Bengal was dominated by Dr Bidhan Chandra Roy. Of course, in Delhi it was the Nehru era. Prime Minister Nehru inaugurated the Children's Hospital of Kolkata where my husband was part of a team of young doctors. I remember Nehru looked particularly bored during lengthy speeches. But he was genuinely pleased to see my husband and his sisters. He had seen them as children when he used to come and stay at Woodburn Park. In the second general election after independence, in 1957, I cast my first vote. I was a voter in Ballygunj, my parents' locality. But it was in Bhowanipur, where I stayed with my in-laws, that the election was more interesting. Siddhartha Ray won from that seat as the Congress candidate. My father was one of the secretaries of the West Bengal Legislative Assembly and in my younger days, I had spent a lot of time in the corridors of the beautiful assembly building. I also sat in the Speaker's gallery and watched the proceedings day in and day out. I saw Ishwardas Jalan and Saila Mukherjee as Speakers too. As a constitutional expert, my father wrote most of the Speaker's rulings. I was interested in electoral politics. I became friendly with everyone in the Assembly. The chaprasis moving around in red and gold uniforms, would greet me with a salaam and say, 'Here comes didi'. Somebody joked, 'You seem to be the princess of the place.'

After my marriage, Sisir and I often went to watch the sessions. On one of our first such visits Siddhartha Ray spotted us in the gallery. When the session had adjourned temporarily, a chaprasi came and informed us that the Speaker Sankardas Bannerji had asked us to tea. I came to know later that Manuda (Siddhartha Ray) had sent a note to the Speaker saying, 'Sarat Chandra Bose's family has come, the Speaker should take note.' I was touched by his gesture. After a year, Siddhartha Ray resigned from the Congress and created a political sensation. He then contested as a candidate of the leftists. When he came to campaign in my little cottage at Woodburn Park in 1958, I was down with typhoid. Manuda pleaded, 'Just somehow get into the car and come and vote for me.' His wife Maya baudi protested and said, 'Getting well is much more important.' Anyway, even without my vote, Manuda managed to win as a Congress rebel.

Woodburn Park was devoid of any political activity at that time. My husband had to work hard for his livelihood and the rest of the time he devoted to history. He meticulously collected all the material relating to his uncle Subhas Chandra Bose, his father Sarat Chandra Bose and the freedom movement. People's memories are proverbially short, so Sisir devoted all his energy to preserving the historical and political legacy of his uncle Subhas and his father Sarat so that the next generation may learn something from their lives.

It was nearly ten years after independence. Still our days of Camelot were not over. We did not know how long we would have to pay the price of partition and other misdirected policies. In the international arena, newly independent India was looked upon with respect. Woodburn Park and the men of history who resided there had played a pivotal role in the struggle for freedom, but at the beginning of the fifties, Woodburn Park lost its glory with the sudden death of Sarat Chandra Bose. He had been elected in June 1949 to the West Bengal Legislative Assembly in spite of stiff opposition from the Congress high command of those days. His sudden death on 20 February 1950 created a void in national politics and a leader of that stature never emerged from Bengal in the years to come.

It is common to read about the decline and fall of empires. Sometimes we experience a decline and fall in the life of a nation or even in the saga of a family. Small and mediocre men come to power, ideals and idealism lose their sheen but we somehow continue to exist. In this darkness a little lamp flickered in Netaji Bhawan in the hope that some day the generations to come would seek inspiration from the Bose saga.

In September 1958 Sisir and I left Woodburn Park for the New World, to America, which was an unknown continent for us in those days.

Between Family and Profession

When in 1958 I arrived at what was then known as the Idlewild airport in New York, America was a strange place for us. We Indians were objects of curiosity to Americans. There were not many women in saris on the streets of New York or Boston. An American woman wanted to know if my husband rode an elephant when he came to marry me. On being told, he came in a motorcar she was disappointed, 'What, you mean in an auto?' was her response.

Sisir and I were the first members of the Bose family to arrive in America. But my personal bond with America, particularly New England, was deep-rooted. One of my maternal uncles had graduated from Harvard and another from the Massachusetts Institute of Technology. In those days Indians went to study either at Oxford or Cambridge. But my maternal grandfather was a freedom-fighter and sending his sons to the US was his form of protest against British rule. In my childhood I had an American aunt from Boston who taught me to say, 'You are welcome', in reply to 'thank you' and not the formal English response, 'Don't mention it'.

During the drive from the Idlewild airport to New York city, I passed a cemetery with tall slabs of stone. New York at first sight did not match my idea of Manhattan skyscrapers painted by John Marine. It was more like an enlarged version of the cemetery I had just passed. The tall imposing buildings suffocated me and I was happy to leave soon for Boston. However, I learnt to enjoy New York much later. We took a train to Boston and got down at the small Back Bay station. In the soft sunlight of an autumn afternoon Boston looked pleasant and friendly. The cab driver chatted with us and said he had passed through Kolkata when he had served in the Korean War. I have always chanced upon interesting cab drivers. One discussed Tagore's *Gitanjali* with me and another talked about the cave paintings of Ajanta. He had been to Ajanta when he was a soldier in the Second World War and camped in Mumbai. The most interesting remark, however, was from a New York cab driver who said, 'A good guy like Gandhi had to be assassinated! What a shame for the world!'

We settled down in an apartment on Huntington Avenue. It was near Harvard Medical School and the Boston Children's Hospital. Huntington Avenue was a broad road with streetcar lines in the middle—very much like Rashbehari Avenue in Kolkata where I grew up. I had to cross the street carefully because I was not used to cars being driven on the wrong side of the road. Sisir even managed to have an accident. He was hit and knocked down by a Volkswagen. Sisir got up and apologized to the gentleman who was driving the car. The gentleman was surprised, saying, 'People here sue the driver, they don't apologize to him.'

I learnt to do all my household chores myself. This was a new experience for me because back in Kolkata we still had reasonable domestic help. I got up early to prepare breakfast because Sisir had to reach the Children's Medical Centre by eight o'clock in the morning. I would put my son in a stroller and go to the supermarket, which at that time was a novelty for me. On my way to the supermarket I said 'Hi' to my neighbours. 'How are you this morning?' everyone asked. Our neighbour, Mr Shruhen, often brought cookies from his kitchen for my son while the elderly couple next door offered roses from their garden. The barber at the small Barber's Salon at the corner of the road regaled me with all the gossip of the locality whenever I took my son

Sugata for a hair cut. Soon we became part of Boston life. Sisir's professor also told him that the honeymoon was over and that he must take up all sorts of responsibilities at the Boston Children's Hospital as part of his training.

Boston and Kolkata seemed to have something in common. It was not an outward similarity but a similarity of spirit. If you go sightseeing in Washington, you get an idea of the city. The affluence and prosperity of New York, as also its downside, would be obvious to a visitor. But you have to live in Boston to grasp its spirit. The Bostonians say Boston grows on you. In comparing Delhi and Mumbai to Kolkata we Kolkatans also say the city grows on you. Today's Boston is not the same as that of the late-fifties. It has changed, but whenever I go back to that area I feel the character of the city has not changed much. And it has been my destiny to go back to Boston and to Cambridge on the other side of the River Charles, again and again.

We were told that Bostonians by nature were rather full of themselves, another trait we Kolkatans shared with them. Outsiders were not considered at par with them. On proposing a toast to Boston, John Collins Bossidy wrote:

And here is to good old Boston
The home of the bean and the cod
Where the Lowells speak only to Cabots
And the Cabots speak only to God.

There was a joke about Abbott Lawrence Lowell who was the President of Harvard University in the early twentieth century, and President Taft of the USA. A visitor had come to Harvard and enquired about Lowell. He was told, 'The President is in Washington seeing Mr Taft.'

We had arrived in Boston in autumn when the fall colours were at their brightest. The leaves of trees took on various shades of yellow, brown and gold. People drove to the countryside to

enjoy the riot of colour and to see the turning of the leaves. Then
came winter. Nature looked grim. The trees shed their leaves and
the bare branches looked empty and sad. But one early morning—
it was 9 December, our wedding anniversary, to be precise—I
woke up and found Boston transformed into a fairytale city.
The night before there had been a silent snowfall in the city and
all the bare trees, the houses, the road with the streetcar lines, the
rows of cars parked on both sides were covered with a blanket of
snow. I was reminded of Robert Bridges' poem *London Snow*,
'When men were all asleep the snow came flying.' I marvelled at
the dazzling whiteness all around.

If winter came, spring could not be not far behind. In April
we were in Washington to see the cherry blossoms in bloom. But
that year's cherry blossom festival was totally ruined by an
untimely snowfall. However we were pleased with that first visit
to Washington. Sisir and I visited all the historic sites. Whenever
he visited historical museums like Mount Vernon with all the
memorabilia of George Washington or the Lincoln Museum
where the assassin's route was marked by footsteps, Sisir collected
ideas for the future Netaji Museum in Kolkata. He was also
charmed by the historic sites in and around Boston. If you
followed the freedom trail, you reached the Old South Meeting
House where the conspiracy of the Boston Tea Party was hatched.
There was the house of Paul Revere. He rode on horseback from
this house to alert the American soldiers about the movement of
the British Army.

Listen my children and you shall hear
Of the midnight ride of Paul Revere.

There was the Old North Church. Lamps were flashed from
the tower of that church to inform American freedom-fighters
about the route taken by the British. 'One if by land, two if by
sea' was the signal. We came from a country which had colonial

rule till only a decade ago, so we felt a kind of affinity with the American War of Independence.

We became very friendly with the Welz family. Mrs Laura Welz took us to the countryside to experience the springtime beauty of nature, to Sudbury to see the Wayside Inn made famous by H.W. Longfellow:

A hurry of hoof in the village street
A shape in the moonlight, a bulk in the dark
That was all, And yet through the gloom and the light
The fate of a nation was riding that night.

In winter our favourite haunts were indoors—the Boston Museum of Fine Arts, the Institute of Contemporary Art, the Isabella Gardner Museum. With the advent of summer we would frequent the open air Esplanade Concert by the River Charles or the Art Festival on Boston Common. We would sometimes drive down to Salem or Revere beach.

The well-known Bengali poet Amiya Chakravarty and his European wife, Haimanti, were good friends of ours. Professor Chakravarty was teaching at Boston University. I remember going with him to a literary meet where T.S. Eliot read his own poems. I still have my copy of *Murder in the Cathedral*. On the first page is written: 'Inscribed for Dr and Mrs S. Bose—T.S. Eliot.'

Sisir was undergoing rigorous training in paediatric radiology. He had night duty and weekend duty at the Children's Medical Centre. Sometimes my son Sugata and I joined him for lunch in the hospital dining room. Paediatric radiology was unknown in India at that time and Professor Neuhauser would declare to his students that Sisir would be known as the 'Father of Paediatric Radiology' in India. Neuhauser had a body of international students training under him. Frank Bensing, an artist from New York, painted a group of students from all over the world, surrounding Professor Neuhauser. On my later visits to the

Children's Medical Centre of Boston, I found the painting still hanging on the wall in the Radiology Department. Neuhauser later gave me a portrait of Sisir done by the same painter as a farewell gift at our farewell party. I was given a big envelope meant for X-ray plates and Neuhauser said, 'Before a student leaves me, I usually ask him to interpret a difficult X-ray and this time I want you to pass that test. See if you can interpret the very complex case I have given you.' Somewhat confused, I opened the huge envelope and there was Sisir's portrait. A difficult case indeed!

On the weekend of 4 July in 1959, Americans were getting ready to celebrate their Independence Day. On 3 July, I was brought to the Boston-Lying-in Hospital. The nurses and the doctors said, 'Please, hold on till tomorrow, it is going to be a very auspicious day.' But I could not comply with their request. On the eve of American Independence Day, on 3 July, our daughter was born. There was my doctor Dr Brian Little who held my hand and said, 'Mrs Bose, think of the beautiful Himalayas' as the baby was born. There was also some excitement. It was not very common for an Indian baby to be born in Boston in those days. Before I fully succumbed to the anaesthesia I heard the nurse say, 'Can you hear me? It is a daughter. A sister for your son to play with.'

We had arrived in New England as a family of three. We left the shores of America a family of four. We decided to cross the Atlantic by sea. There was a heated discussion about the British ship, the *Queen Elizabeth*. Dr Neuhauser's choice was the French ship, the *Liberte*. He assured us they would serve good wine. But I chose the American liner, the *United States*. At the port of New York we walked towards the ship, a camera bulb flashed somewhere. On board, I saw the photograph of the four of us. We looked like a refugee family uprooted from home and going towards an unknown destination.

As a matter of fact we were going back to India. That winter we travelled all over Europe. We landed at the port of Southampton. After a brief stay in London we went to Paris and from Paris to Munich, Munich to Vienna, Vienna to Rome. Long ago I had seen a film about a hotel which changed hands several times during the war. It was occupied by the British, French and Germans, and the director brought out the characteristics of the different nationalities. I went through the same experience during this European tour. There were the cold and formal English people—since then I have seen that the English have changed a lot and are not that cold any more. But in those days they appeared to be extremely reserved, especially since I came from a child-friendly American environment. In London, eyebrows were raised if the children made any noise. The French were different altogether. Their motto seemed to be:

Unborn tomorrow, dead yesterday
Why fret about them
If today be sweet?

We travelled in Europe by train. At the French-German border station Kehl, German officers came up in disciplined formation to check our passports but I found them very warm and friendly towards children. We felt the strongest affinity with the Italians who loved their afternoon siesta and were as lazy and noisy as us. We spent a very happy white Christmas in Vienna with Auntie Emilie, Anita, and her grandmother whom we all called O'Mama. Emilie was our aunt and very dear to us. She was the wife of Netaji Subhas Chandra Bose and Anita was their only daughter, who was about to finish high school at that time. Auntie Emilie and I celebrated our common birthday on 26 December with a family lunch at a Viennese restaurant. We also met other friends of Netaji in Vienna, including Mrs Fullop-Miller, Mrs Naomi Vetter and Director Richter.

In January 1960 we were back in Kolkata. When our car

entered the portico of One Woodburn Park we could see a green ribbed glass dome that hung above the portico which was—just as we had left it—swaying gently in the breeze.

Our family life went on more or less in the usual mode. Sisir worked all morning at the Institute of Child Health, the children's hospital in Kolkata. In the evening he saw patients in his own chamber. This time he had a larger chamber since we had moved into the ground floor of our Woodburn Park house. It was a life of struggle for a doctor trying to establish himself. Things were not made any easier by his near total absorption in building up a historical institute at Netaji Bhawan. For a long time he was quietly collecting material, documents, photographs and so on relating to his uncle Subhas Chandra Bose. It was a difficult task since many of the significant events of uncle's life had taken place in different parts of the globe. It was Sisir's mission in life to preserve the memory of the great patriot for generations to come—he established the Netaji Research Bureau, an institute of history, politics and current affairs at Netaji Bhawan, in 1957. Netaji Bhawan was the ancestral home of the Boses built by Netaji's father Janakinath Bose in 1909. Netaji went to Presidency College from this house and this is where he worked as the President of the Indian National Congress in 1938 and 1939. And most importantly, his great escape from India took place from this house on 16–17 January 1941. Sisir, then a young medical student, drove Netaji from the house in his Wanderer car and took his Rangakakababu—as Sisir called Netaji—up to Gomoh railway junction. In commemoration of these events, Sisir's father and Netaji's elder brother Sarat Chandra Bose, had declared the house a historical site as early as 1946. On his return from the US the first thing Sisir did was to establish a Netaji Museum on the second floor of Netaji Bhawan in 1961. On the first floor, Netaji's bed room and sitting room were already open to the public. Prime Minister Jawaharlal Nehru was the first important visitor to the new Netaji Museum. Ignoring the hints of his officers to hurry up, he spent a lot of time in front of each photograph and document. He commented that to build up any such institute one must have a man who would dedicate himself to the work. 'Have you found the man?' he had asked. He was speaking to the man himself.

I was back at work in my college. I was a professor of English literature and also the head of the department of English in a Kolkata college. A working mother's life with two young children was bound to be difficult. My mother lent all-out support to me. My father was not a regular visitor but he took a great interest in the education of the children. So far as I was concerned, my main aim in life was to bring up my children and to give them a good education. Sugata was doing very well in his primary school. Soon Sarmila started school and she also excelled in her studies. In 1968 my younger son Sumantra was born. He was much younger than his siblings but he also had to suffer his mother's hankering for academic excellence in her children. By God's grace none of them disappointed me.

Sisir went to Tokyo in November 1965 to attend an international paediatric conference. But as usual, Subhas Chandra Bose dominated his trip. He used to write home every day to me and to our son and daughter telling us how he had met many people in Japan who knew his uncle, Netaji. He visited the Renkoji Temple where Netaji's remains were kept and when the priest Mochizuki (senior) asked him if he wanted the urn to be opened, Sisir assented. Special prayers were held throughout the day and offerings of fruits and flowers were made. The urn was then opened. Mochizuki said, 'You are the second person for whom I have opened the urn.' Sisir asked who the first person was. The reply was, 'Prime Minister Jawaharlal Nehru.' Sisir was very moved by the experience, but it was also an emotional strain for him. From Tokyo he flew into Taipei—the place where Netaji Subhas Chandra Bose's aircraft met with an accident on 18 August 1945. Netaji died at Taipei's Nanmon hospital later that night. Sisir visited the airport and the city crematorium. He walked into the Taiwan foreign office one day and asked to meet any officer with whom he could communicate in English. As Sisir entered the room, the Chinese officer looked up and stared at him in a peculiar manner. Sisir introduced himself by saying, 'I am the son of Sarat Chandra Bose and . . .' the man smiled and said, 'As you entered and walked towards me, you looked strangely familiar. Now I know why.' It turned out he was at one time the Chinese Consul at Kolkata and had met both Sisir's father and uncle Subhas. When Sisir explained his mission in Taipei, the Chinese officer said it was the first time he had heard about the tragedy. The present regime had come to power in the island after the communist uprising in mainland China in October 1949. In August 1945 the island had been under Japanese occupation. He expressed surprise why no one from India had enquired about this earlier. Sisir said that the Enquiry Committee set up in 1956 did not come to Taipei and the reason given was that India did not have diplomatic relations with the island. The officer said, 'So what, diplomatic relations or no diplomatic relations—in a matter like this we would have cooperated!' The evening Sisir returned from his trip we talked almost the whole night through about his experiences in Japan and Taiwan.

The Japan visit led to Netaji's sword being brought to India. General Fujiwara and other officers of the Japanese army had spotted Netaji's sword in an antique shop in Tokyo. General Fujiwara had been one of Netaji's comrades-in-arms and had played a significant role in the formation of the Indian National Army. The sword had been presented to Netaji by the Japanese revolutionary, Mitsuyo Toyama, when Netaji visited Tokyo in 1943. Fujiwara brought the sword to Kolkata and presented it to the Netaji Research Bureau in an impressive ceremony held at Netaji Bhawan. In the presence of the governor of West Bengal, Padmaja Naidu, Fujiwara handed over the sword to Sisir. The sword was later taken by a special train to Delhi where it was received by the President of India and Prime Minister Indira Gandhi at the Red Fort. People thronged to have a view of the sword. The inscription on the sword read: 'Destroy the evil and protect the good'.

The palatial Woodburn Park house was one of the most beautiful residential houses in Kolkata. But, as often happens in a joint family, it is not possible to share the family house equally. In our case the eldest and the youngest brothers wanted to sell the house. Sisir could not care less where he lived so long he could carry on uncle Subhas's work. But One Woodburn Park was no ordinary address. Once it had been Bengal's political hub and a focal point for the activities of Sarat and Subhas Bose. Mahatma Gandhi came and lived in this house as Sarat Bose's guest and held prayer meetings on its terrace. So did Jawaharlal Nehru. In fact, the room in which Sugata and Sarmila grew up was known as Nehru's room. Fortunately for the family, a way out was found. The Indian government offered to acquire the house as a historical monument. We got ready to move out of the house in 1968. There is an interesting anecdote here. An aunt of mine whom I called Charu mashima, was a rather spiritual person. Often what she said came true or what she dreamt, materialized. In the course of an ordinary conversation I happened to mention to her that I had hoped my son would finish school while we were still at Woodburn Park. She said, 'I do not think you will have to move before he finishes school.' I was taken aback. Already one of the brothers had bought an apartment and moved his law chamber there. Finishing school meant five years more! But as it turned out, the government delayed the process and we moved six years later in 1974.

In March 1971, Sisir and I were invited to dinner by the deputy high commissioner of Pakistan—he was a good friend of ours, as were some other Pakistani officials. They used to attend Netaji Bhawan functions and often came for dinner to our home and we often went for dinner to their place. I remember Mr and Mrs Kibria at a dinner in our Woodburn Park home. After dinner our children sang patriotic songs. When they started singing *Dhana dhanya pushpa bhara, amader ei Basundhara*, they joined in the singing and their eyes became moist. We sang in chorus— *Sakal desher rani se je amar janmabhumi*—the queen of all countries is our motherland. Our dinner at the Pakistan High Commission in Kolkata was on 26 March. The newspapers had brought the news of a severe military crackdown on Mujib-ur-Rahman's movement for an autonomous East Pakistan. Sisir asked me at the breakfast table, 'Do you think the dinner will be cancelled?' There was no cancellation. It was one of the most unusual dinners I have ever been to. It was a small gathering. Our Pakistani diplomatic friends, the deputy high commissioner Hossain Ali, Anwarul Karim and others were extremely disturbed. There was no news of their relatives in Dhaka, Bogura and other places. They poured their hearts out to us. They detested the West Pakistan authorities. Soon after, one morning Sisir and myself with some others stood in the premises of the Pakistan High Commission in Kolkata as the Pakistan flag was lowered and the Bangladesh flag went up. Someone put a bouquet of flowers in my hand and I offered it to our friend who had just become the high commissioner of the incipient nation of Bangladesh.

Netaji Bhawan became one of the active centres for the Mukti Juddha or liberation war of Bangladesh. Streams of people from the other side of the border kept coming. I, along with a group of women, worked day and night under the guidance of Bina Bhowmik (Das). Bina-di was a revolutionary from pre-independence days. She had attempted to assassinate the governor of Bengal, Stanley Jackson, during her convocation at the Kolkata University and had spent years in jail. When the Bangladesh war broke out in December 1971, Kolkata was under black-out orders. In dim light, we worked at Netaji Bhawan. Suddenly there would be news, for example, that Jessore had fallen to the

Indian army and the Mukti Bahini. There would be celebration, a round of sandesh—the Bengali sweetmeat. The next moment we would be told the information was premature—fierce fighting was still going on and we would be bitterly disappointed.

From March to December 1971 Sisir and some of his doctor friends set up a hospital at the Bongaon border. It was called the Netaji Field Hospital. I visited the hospital several times with Sisir. One doctor I remember was Dr Satyen Basu Ray, a noted surgeon, who rendered yeoman service. He used to take me around and introduce me to the young wounded Bangladeshi soldiers. One soldier I met had lost contact with his wife who had been abducted by the Pakistani army. When word came that she had been found, the young man was so happy. He told me he would welcome her home with honour and love. Sisir looked after the sick children in the refugee camps near the border.

In September that year, Sisir and I visited Europe. We went to Vienna, Prague, East and West Berlin, Wiesbaden, Bonn, Hamburg and Zurich in search of history. We met people who knew Subhas Chandra Bose We gathered photographs, documents, and a whole range of archival materials on him. We spent time with Auntie Emilie in Vienna where I prepared a paper on *Important Women in Netaji's Life*. There were four such women—his own mother Prabhabati, his adopted mother Basanti Devi, wife of C.R. Das, his sister-in-law Bivabati—Sarat's wife and, of course, Emilie. We met Miloslav Krasa in Czechoslovakia, Alexender Werth and Lothar Frank in Germany, and A.C.N. Nambiar in Switzerland. There were two conferences on Subhas Chandra Bose—one at the Oriental Institute in Prague and the other at Dresden hotel in Bonn. On my return to Kolkata Sagarmay Ghosh, the renowned editor of the Bengali literary magazine *Desh*, asked me to write about my experiences. I wrote an account that blended travel and history, which was serialized in *Desh*. It was later published as a book *Itihaser Sandhane*—In Search of History.

The Bangladesh war ended in a victory for India and the Liberation Army of Bangladesh. Sisir had a memorable meeting with Mujib-ur-Rahman in January 1972, within days of his return to Dhaka from a Pakistani prison. Sisir drove an ambulance with medical supplies across the border and reached Dhaka. Mujib was very emotional. He remembered Sarat Chandra Bose and Subhas Chandra Bose. He embraced Sisir and wept. He told Sisir he came into politics for the first time in 1940 under the leadership of Subhas Chandra Bose during the Holwell Monument agitation in Kolkata. I had the opportunity to meet Mujib when he came to Kolkata and Mrs Indira Gandhi held a dinner for him at the Kolkata Raj Bhawan. After the victory, Mrs Indira Gandhi was our heroine and I was thrilled to meet her and Mujib. After dinner Suchitra Mitra presented Tagore's *Chitrangada* for Mujib and the guests. Mujib's two sons were also present. It was heart-rending three years later when we learnt of the massacre of Mujib and his family. At that historic dinner the guest who sat beside me was Sambhu Mitra, the well-known theatre personality. We discussed whether it would be humanly possible for Mujib to hold on to the immense popularity that he enjoyed at that moment.

The Netaji Research Bureau had taken on an international character ever since the sword ceremony and the visit of Japanese friends in 1967. On 23 January 1972, Mujib's recorded message was played to the birthday assembly at Netaji Bhawan. He said, 'Netaji Subhas Chandra Bose would be an eternal inspiration through the ages to all people who fought for freedom from oppression.' January 1973 saw the first International Conference on Netaji at Netaji Bhawan organized by the Netaji Research Bureau. It brought together people who had participated in history with those who were writing history. From then on there was international participation almost every year at the annual Netaji birthday assembly and every three years we had a full-fledged international conference.

At last, it was time for us to move house. Charu mashima's prophecy had come true. Sugata had finished school and had started to go to Presidency College. It was very hard to find a place which would also fit our budget. Sisir had no time to go house hunting since General Fujiwara and a Japanese delegation had come to Kolkata. Sisir and our NRB member Atul Sen took them to Imphal where they offered homage to the souls of Japanese soldiers who gave their lives in the Second World War. Even the Emperor of Japan had sent cigars to be offered at the battlefield of Imphal. It fell on me to look for a house. The day was fast approaching when we must leave our Woodburn Park home and we were yet to find a new place. I could only pray to God. Sugata asked me jokingly, 'What have you said in your prayers? Have you placed your order for an ideal house?' I said, 'I would like the address to be Sarat Bose Road. I would like a south-facing house and some morning sunshine from the eastern side. A tiny garden to tread on. And lastly, a marble staircase as we have in Woodburn Park.' Of the five wishes, four were fulfilled. The marble staircase was missing. I named the house, Basundhara.

We were all very sad when we left Woodburn Park. It was a kind of trauma. I told Sisir and the children that in this house my father-in-law's good deeds—punya as I called it—threw an invisible ring of protection around us and we were leaving that charmed circle. That first night away from Woodburn Park, Sisir and I spent at Kenilworth hotel. The new house was not yet quite ready. The children were sent to my parents house. I could not sleep. I had injured my little finger while packing and my finger bled as did my heart. I got up, picked up my pen and wrote a poem in Bengali *Farewell to Woodburn Park* which was later published in *Desh*. This calmed me down.

Farewell to Woodburn Park
When visitors from the future crowd into this house
They will say, look how

History is engraved on its every brick.
Wandering from room to room
They will hear murmurs in the breeze,
The cold white marble will find its voice.
Extraordinary men had dreamt dreams here
Their dreams had made them homeless, freedom-mad,
Defiant of the boundary between life and death.
Those who charted the course of revolution,
Where are they today?
But, visitors from the future,
You will not know the others who were here
The quotidian joys and sorrows, the pain of their simple lives.
The oboe has played plaintive melodies here in *bhairavi* and
behag
To a daughter's departure and the arrival of a new bride at its
door,
Its yards enthralled by a child's sweet clamour.
These little affective bonds, myriad small accounts of grief,
love and tears,
Will none of this meet your eyes?
Perhaps not the stuff of History,
Will it not inspire a poet to compose a grand Epic of Life?

Soon Basundhara became the centre of all our various
activities. One of the last literary meetings that I had at Woodburn
Park was a meeting of the PEN of which I was a member. Many
of the well-known littérateurs of the time came. The poet and
novelist 'Banaphul' presided. Each one, including myself, read a
poem on Subhas Chandra Bose. An anthology of the poems was
published later. One of the first significant PEN meetings held at
Basundhara was to celebrate the release from prison of the well-
known novelist and writer, Gourkishore Ghosh. He had been
imprisoned for opposing Mrs Indira Gandhi's emergency.

At Woodburn Park I always had a stream of guests, mostly
close associates of Netaji and those related to the INA movement.

S.A. Ayer, the publicity minister in Netaji's Azad Hind government, stayed with us more than once. He sat with me on the south verandah and related many anecdotes about Netaji. The same happened with Abid Hasan—he almost became a member of the family. He and the others would invariably become deeply emotional while reminiscing about their great leader. The tradition of guests coming to stay continued in Basundhara. On the eve of Netaji's birthday we usually had a big dinner in the rear garden and musical soirees were held in the first floor drawing room. Apart from literary and musical meets, there was an annual doctors' gathering of Sisir's class of Kolkata Medical College. There was happiness and joy all around and we did not mind the usual struggle in our private life and at Netaji Bhawan. My small world of family and the wider space of activities at Netaji Bhawan had no defined boundaries.

In 1969, we were happy when Indira Gandhi threw out the old deadwood of the Congress party. She visited Netaji Bhawan at Sisir's invitation as her father had done. We also came to admire her leadership during the Bangladesh crisis of 1971. But we were deeply disturbed by the methods used by the government to crush the Naxalite movement of the late sixties and early seventies. The familes of many of our close friends suffered. Their sons were involved in the movement and some were arrested and some shot dead in so-called encounters. Then Indira Gandhi clamped the Emergency in response to Jaiprakash Narain's movement which made her very unpopular. The climax was the general election of 1977 when the people of India threw her out of power. The election results poured in throughout the night. Sisir took the small radio to bed. I dozed off, only to be woken up by Sisir telling me that Indira Gandhi had lost to Raj Narain whom everyone looked upon as a buffoon. She did, of course, storm back to power in 1980.

On the home front, an exodus took place in the late seventies. Our elder son and daughter left home for studies abroad. My daughter was the first to leave. She had done very well in her school-leaving exams and joined Bryn Mawr College in Pennsylvania for undergraduate studies. Next year Sugata, left for Cambridge University, to do his Ph.D. He had graduated from Presidency College and had come first in the university exams. Sisir was a very reserved person and I never knew how he felt when the children left home. I was sad and missed them very much. I was particularly concerned for my daughter who was very young and had only just left school. I was not sure if I did the right thing by exposing her to an alien culture at that tender age. She had led a very protected life in Kolkata. I could not sleep well for one year till she came home for her summer holidays. During her vacations we arranged public concerts for her since she sang very well. I was never that worried about my son Sugata. My younger son Sumantra, in the meantime, grew up as an only child. We had a new member in the family though—that was Basco, our long-haired, honey-coloured miniature dachshund.

My life for the next decade-and-a-half revolved round the correspondence with my children. We remained an unusually close-knit family—father, mother and three children. The two other very close members of the charmed circle were my parents. My mother by then was sick and crippled and could not visit me. But I went every day to see my parents and look after their needs. My father came regularly to our home and was always a friend, philosopher and guide to the grandchildren.

Sisir and I went to Japan in 1979. For Sisir it was a second visit. I had the good fortune to meet some of the Japanese generals and others who knew Netaji well. I met General Katakura and General Arisue for the first time. I had known General Fujiwara and General Isoda before. General Fujiwara remained our constant companion throughout the trip. We met Mrs Tojo, wife of Japan's wartime Prime Minister Tojo. She and her daughter remembered Netaji's visit to their home. I also met Mrs Kimura, wife of General Kimura. The most poignant moment for me was the visit to the Renkoji Temple where the remains of Netaji Subhas Chandra Bose have been preserved since September 1945. Sisir and I were accompanied by Generals Katakura, Arisue and Fujiwara. Mochizuki junior, the son of the old priest, showed us round. Rashbehari Bose's daughter came to meet us at the Nakamuraya restaurant in Tokyo which once belonged to her parents. Many other friends of India like Mrs Matsushima (daughter of Mrs Emori who looked after Netaji's young Tokyo cadets), the Tagore scholar, Kazuo Azuma, and the family of General Shidei, who had been killed in the August 1945 air crash, came to meet us. I was asked to speak at the Tokyo PEN on Tagore and Bose. On the way back from Japan we visited Taiwan, Singapore, Malaysia and Thailand. The visit to Taiwan was very poignant for me. I saw the airport, the old hospital and other places associated with Netaji Subhas Chandra Bose. At Kuala Lumpur I met Janaki Athinahappan, the second in command of the Rani of Jhansi Regiment—the women's wing of the Indian National Army. We were also supposed to go to Burma. But I fell ill and had to return to Kolkata from Bangkok. At Bangkok I again met several associates of Netaji among whom were Iswar Singh Nirula, Darshan Singh Bajaj and a German resident, Walter Meyer. The trip to Japan and southeast Asia resulted in my second published book. A sort of sequel to *Itihaser Sandhane*, I called it *Charanarekha Taba*—Your Footprints. The editor of *Desh*, Sagarmay Ghosh, had extracted a promise from me that as soon as I returned, my historical and travel experiences would be serialized in his literary magazine. It later came out as a book from Ananda Publishers.

Sisir and I had met Indira Gandhi several times during the late sixties and seventies. Most of these meetings were on occasions related to Netaji Research Bureau. She released various books published by the Bureau in ceremonies held in the prime minister's residence. Sisir admired Indira for having dealt a blow to the old guard of the Congress which his uncle Subhas could not, or rather did not, choose to do. He had gracefully resigned from the then Congress while Indira Gandhi had wrested power from the Congress high command. However, Sisir never went overboard: he did not praise her sky high, nor did he desert her as many did when she was thrown out of power. On one occasion when Sisir had met her she told him, 'You have again brought out a volume on Netaji? You had another International Seminar at Netaji Bhawan. Will you go on only with this work? What about doing something else?' On another occasion at the Kolkata Raj Bhawan, she confided in Sisir her utter despair about the infighting in the West Bengal Congress. She told him how disgusted she was with the factionalism in the West Bengal Congress. She told Sisir, 'Every time I come to Kolkata I never know who is fighting whom at what point.'

In the 1982 assembly elections, Indira asked Sisir to contest from the Chowringhee constituency which had traditionally been the Congress chief minister's seat. He was a bit taken aback and was hesitant. But it was not a request. It was almost an instruction from her and that also at the last moment when there was no time to consider. So the newspapers had the headline, 'Bhadralok goes to politics.' Sisir was at the height of his professional career. There were innumerable homes in Kolkata where he had treated children, from middle class Bengali households to families of big industrialists to the city's diplomatic corps. His professional career was hampered by his entry into politics. People were somewhat confused by his three incarnations—Sisir Bose, the Netajiwallah who devoted himself to the Netaji Research Bureau; Sisir Bose, the well-known paediatrician and head of the Institute of Child Health, and now Sisir Bose, the political leader. Sisir won the elections and became a Congress legislator for the next five years. Indira Gandhi had perhaps wanted him to play a significant role in West Bengal politics, but the factions within the local Congress were apprehensive of a Bose coming up in politics. After Indira Gandhi's assassination, he lost the only connection he had to the highest echelons of power in New Delhi and also someone who belonged to his own generation and understood his political values. He soon became disenchanted with the Congress leadership and after a few false steps more or less withdrew from politics. He belonged to a different era and could not adjust to the pettiness of contemporary political life.

In the eighties, Sisir, our younger son, Sumantra, and I made several trips to Europe and the US. We had spent our early householder days in Boston and destiny brought us back to the New England area as Sumantra joined Amherst College in 1988. Our nest was empty at Basundhara. Sarmila was at the Kennedy School and Sugata, after finishing his Ph.D. and a three-year research fellowship at Cambridge, started teaching at Tufts University and the Fletcher School. We continued to visit our children. We also went regularly to see our Auntie Emilie in Vienna and later in Germany, once she moved in with her daughter Anita.

On my return from one of the trips abroad in the early eighties, I was informed that I had been appointed the Principal of my college. I rushed to the director, Arun Sen, who was the head of the consortium of City Colleges. I pleaded with him to release me from the Principal's job because education had become extremely politicized. I wished to remain in the academic arena and not get into university administration. Besides I was busy with my writing. I was a regular broadcaster on All India Radio, I participated in TV programmes and wrote scripts for documentary films. I knew all this would get disrupted. But the rector insisted that I accept the responsibility.

It was admissions time. The students' unions pressurized the authorities to take in undeserving students. Their aim was to see that their political protégés got admitted. The Principal and professors would be *gheraoed* or imprisoned till they agreed to absurd demands. The students' organizations were the wings of their respective political parties. When I took charge two unions were in a fierce fight: one affiliated to the Congress and the other to the Communist Party of India (Marxist). Soon the Congress was thrown out by force. I hoped it might be easier to tackle one union. But a fight for power broke out between the CPI(M) and their own ally, a small left party called the Revolutionary Socialist Party (RSP). After some time, the smaller party was squeezed out. I heaved a sign of relief and thought now at least peace will reign. But it was not to be because two factions within the CPI(M) started to fight each other.

One of Tagore's songs says *Jibaner dhan kichhui jabe na phela*—no experience in life will be wasted. All this experience did help me when much later I went into parliamentary politics. When I look back, however, I wonder how I coped at that time. After being gheraoed for hours I had somtimes called the union leader and proposed, 'Are not you also hungry?' It was my good fortune to have the trust of my students. They felt that whatever political colour they might have, if they came to me with a just demand it would be considered.

Sisir was kept busy with Netaji Bhawan and the Institute of Child Health. He trained a fine batch of medical students who later took charge of the hospital. He had his share of trouble with employees' unions. At that time even hospitals were politicized by our communist rulers. The year 1989 was the birth centenary year of Sisir's father, Sarat Bose. He was a very distinguished political leader in pre-independence India who, some say was overshadowed by his famous younger brother, Subhas Bose. But it is also believed that Subhas Chandra Bose would not have become Netaji without the solid political and financial support he had from his elder brother Sarat. We celebrated Sarat Chandra Bose's centenary at Netaji Bhawan with due pomp and dignity. Tony Benn, the British MP, came to give the Sarat Bose Centenary Oration. A message of greetings arrived from the MacSweeny family of Ireland. Terence MacSweeny had died after a hunger strike during the Irish freedom struggle. The ambassador of Ireland recalled the bond between Ireland and India in their struggle against British imperialism. The Sarat Bose Centenary ended with a musical concert in his memory. We had booked the big auditorium Kala Mandir and were looking for a good vocalist or instrumentalist to perform when Sarmila arrived from the US. She sang Tagore, Atul Prasad, D.L. Roy, and Rajanikanta songs in memory of her grandfather.

Sisir, by now, had some able help for his historical work from Sugata. He had made a documentary film *Rebels against the Raj* which had won critical acclaim in Delhi. The then President of India Zail Singh had seen it and said it should be shown on TV so that the youth of India could be inspired. But Sisir was not in the good books of the government of the day. Ajit Panja, the information and broadcasting minister in Rajiv Gandhi's government, refused to comply with Zail Singh's suggestion.

The first half of the nineties was a mixed bag. There were moments of great joy alternating with moments of great anxiety. In June 1992, Sumantra graduated from Amherst College and Sisir and I went to the commencement. We stayed with Sugata and Sarmila came from London to join us. I was very proud of Sumantra. He had done extremely well. I have said earlier that Sumantra grew up almost like an only child since his elder siblings had gone abroad for studies when he was quite young. The education system in West Bengal had been going down fast for some time. When Sumantra reached middle and high school, the system had collapsed. The teaching standard was very poor, the examination system corrupt and inefficient. A student who had real merit could not be sure if he would get the result he deserved. I could see that a talented person like Sumantra would be very frustrated. Amherst saved him from that predicament. Commencement day began as a very hot summer day. I remember I arrived in a white cotton sari and as the ceremony progressed, the temperature continued to fall dramatically and soon we were shivering in the cold.

Sisir was not very well and the exposure to cold did not help. After we came back from Boston to London, Sisir suffered a congestive heart failure. He was hospitalized for quite some time. Sugata and I spent days with him at St. Charles hospital. During visiting hours Sarmila, Sumantra and Alan, my son-in-law, came. From then on Sisir suffered sudden fluctuations in the state of his health so I was always on tenterhooks. Sisir happened to feel unwell at the most extraordinary places. We were in the temple city of Ujjain for a celebration of the anniversary of 21 October, the day the Provisional Government of Free India was formed in Singapore in 1943. Sisir addressed a big meeting. There was a huge procession on the streets of Ujjain with Sisir and me on a flower-decked carriage, while a chhatradhar held a decorative umbrella over our heads. All this exhausted him. And in the afternoon on the steps of a fourteenth-century temple in a deserted area, he collapsed. A car was sent to fetch a doctor as we sat down and waited on the steps. There were many other such dramatic moments of concern for me.

Our daughter Sarmila's marriage in the winter of 1990 was a most joyous event in our family. Alan and Sarmila got married in a church in London. As Sisir walked down the aisle with Sarmila in her white bridal gown, I sat with Sugata and Sumantra with tears in my eyes and thanked God from my heart. An Indian wedding followed in Kolkata, conducted by the ninety-year-old Sanskrit scholar Gaurinath Sastri. He was the priest who had conducted our marriage ceremony and when Sarmila was a baby he had promised me, 'I married you and Sisir. If I am still alive, I will preside over your daughter's wedding also.' He kept his promise, but he died soon after.

The most poignantly happy moment of our life was the birth of our first grandson, Tipu, two-and-a-half years later, on 2 June 1993. Sisir, Sugata, Sumantra and I had all gathered in London for the event. But Tipu refused to be born on the date the doctors had predicted. He was late by two weeks. So Sugata had to leave for Talloires in France where his university ran a summer programme in an eleventh-century Benedictine monastery. Sisir and I joined Sugata at Talloires two weeks after Tipu's birth. He had a beautiful place on the shore of the Lake Annecy. That summer, Sugata drove us from France through Switzerland to Germany. It was a memorable drive. We reached Augsburg where Anita and Auntie Emilie received us. Auntie gave Sisir permission to publish the letters that Subhas Chandra Bose had written to her in the thirties and forties.

As we left Talloires on our way to Germany, Sugata took a photograph of Sisir and myself on a bridge in Annecy. Both of us look radiantly happy. That photograph captures a most happy chapter of my life. Tipu's birth had given us a new fulfilment. All our children seemed to be settled in their respective fields. Sugata had made a name as a historian; Sumantra was doing well as a Ph.D. student at Columbia University and after a successful academic life Sarmila had settled down. But the most precious member of our family was Tipu. That photograph of Sisir and myself reflects my mood. I could say in Shakespeare's words, 'If it were now to die, 'twere now to be most happy'.

SECTION TWO
IN POLITICS

The First Campaign

It was the first nor'wester of the season. It had been a very sultry summer day. In the afternoon I started for Sangrampur, a remote village, about an hour and a half's journey from Kolkata. Lalan was driving the closed and covered jeep. I sat in the front beside the driver while Ratan, a young party cadre, my security guard and Sumantra sat at the back. We left the congested city and entered Bishnupur which was always green and leafy with banana trees and bamboo groves lining the road. But as we entered Mograhat the landscape changed. Here there were wide open paddy fields on both sides of the roads. Now and then there were stretches of road lined with tall, slender green trees which looked so graceful. Dark clouds had already gathered in the sky, making the green paddy fields take on a darker shade of green.

A couple of days earlier, the chief minister of West Bengal, Jyoti Basu, had addressed an election rally in Sangrampur in support of the candidate of his party – the Communist Party of India (Marxist) or CPI(M). His meeting drew a sizable crowd. The newspapers, however, reported that the villagers came just out of curiosity to see the chief minister, who had completed nineteen years in this august office. Once he got up to speak, many started to leave the meeting. A darshan of the long-serving chief minister had been enough.

In that sweltering summer of 1996 I was a newcomer in politics. It was my first Parliamentary election and I had been nominated for the contest by the Indian National Congress. I had an uphill task as the seat—Jadavpur—was known to be a stronghold of the other side, the redoubtable CPI(M). My supporters in Sangrampur demanded an election meeting in their village. Being a newcomer to politics I could not expect a bigwig from my party to come to counter Jyoti Basu's rally, so it fell on me to take on the challenge.

On my way to Sangrampur, I addressed a few roadside meetings. As I approached Sangrampur our workers informed me that a huge crowd had gathered at the meeting site. They seemed to be surprised by the turnout. They had organized the meeting at a crossing by the railway track. They lamented that if they had any inkling about the popular response, the nearby school ground where the chief minister had addressed the meeting would have been chosen as the venue. Now the crossing was overflowing with people and the crowd had spilled over on to the railway track. My supporters said they would not underestimate my role as a crowd puller in future.

I took my seat on the dais. The dais, of course, was a simple, four-legged wooden platform called taktaposh in Bengali. There were three tin chairs placed on it. Sangrampur was a predominantly Muslim area. Two venerable-looking bearded Muslim gentlemen with white caps occupied the other two tin chairs. The ritual of garlanding took some time. I have always felt somewhat amused by the ritual. But young cadres of all political parties take the ritual very seriously. The guests on the dais are garlanded one by one. The ceremony proceeds in slow motion. Different people are called upon the stage and are asked to garland different guests. It is a time-consuming affair but cannot be dispensed with or even abbreviated. This is often followed by a tilak being put on the forehead or by the pinning of badges.

That evening the crowd was indeed large for a small village like Sangrampur . No wonder the organizers were thrilled. My Parliamentary constituency was well-known as being a strong communist bastion. Since independence and partition in 1947, practically no non-communist had won the seat, except once, and that too just after the assassination of Mrs Indira Gandhi in 1984 when there was a sympathy wave for the Indian National Congress. The winning candidate was Mamata Banerjee, an unknown young Congress worker at that time who defeated the veteran communist leader Somnath Chatterjee. But in the next election in 1989 Mamata was defeated and the seat went back to the communists. The CPI (M) easily retained the seat in the Parliamentary election of 1991, defeating the Congress candidate, a former vice-chancellor of Kolkata University.

The sky looked menacing when I got up to speak. In the meantime, the two venerable-looking Muslim gentlemen had made their speeches. The elder one introduced me and told the audience how happy they were to have me as a candidate. In my speech I told the villagers that I could not promise them anything because I was sure that—like me—they were tired of promises. I told them I was an outsider in politics. I said, 'I can only assure you that being an outsider perhaps I understand your problems and if I reach Delhi, I shall certainly try to give voice to your needs and aspirations.'

The nor'wester lashed us at this point. The sudden gust of wind snapped the microphone wire. I stood silently as someone repaired the line. Big drops of rain started to fall but no one in the crowd moved; they waited patiently for me to resume my speech.

If that stormy evening election meeting has left an indelible mark in my memory, the other memorable incident was the visit to a village, late one morning, in the same Mograhat segment of my constituency. The village was a little away from the main road. It could not be reached even by a three-wheeler, let alone a car. A van was brought for me. A van in local parlance meant a flat wooden platform on wheels pulled by a cyclist. Women and half-naked children came out of the huts and surrounded my

van. Somebody placed a green coconut in my hand. There was
no straw, so I tried to sip the cool coconut water directly from
the coconut. I seemed to be stuck in the frame of a Satyajit Ray
film. The women surged towards me. One of them spoke almost
in a whisper, '*Ma, tumi jitle amader ektu jal diyo*—Mother, if
you win the election, please give us some drinking water?' I was
taken aback and deeply moved. These simple village women
wanted drinking water from me! After fifty years of independence
we were unable to supply potable water to the villages. I made a
note of the village and when the opportunity came, I provided
drinking water for them. Some of the women took me inside
their houses. By the time I said 'khuda hafiz' to them I had come
to know many of their pressing problems and priorities. There
were no proper roads, no schools, no electricity, not even safe
drinking water. That summer, I learnt at close quarters, something
of the basic problems of rural Bengal, problems that persisted
even after nearly twenty years of uninterrupted, much-trumpeted
communist rule.

My constituency, however, was in part one of the Kolkata
constituencies. Seven constituencies of the state legislative
assembly made up my Parliamentary constituency. Of these four
were urban segments in the heart of Kolkata, namely Behala
West, Behala East, Kabitirtha, and Jadavpur, which was the name
of my Parliamentary constituency. Adjoining these were three
rural assembly segments, namely, Mograhat West, Bishnupur East
and Baruipur—all an hour or a couple of hours drive from
Kolkata. The two experiences I have just related took place in
Mograhat. I had been warned by all and sundry that Mograhat
was a notorious criminal-infested area. Some criminals, not so
long ago, had played football with a severed head in a place
called Netra in the area. But I found the villagers, the majority
of whom were Muslims, to be friendly and hospitable. However,
there were local mafias, dacoits and others, euphemistically called
'anti-social elements', operating in the area who were affiliated

to various political parties. They often changed their political loyalties too. This made Mograhat pretty dangerous. That summer we were having the Parliamentary and state assembly elections at the same time. The Congress candidate for the state assembly from Mograhat belonged to the area, but was known to be associated with groups whose reputation was supposed to be suspect. Despite being a local leader, he was unable to visit the area and had to stay in a neighbouring town since his life was under threat from rival groups. I felt puzzled sometimes by the intricacies of such politics. In fact, this man, Abul Bashar, with several criminal cases against him, could only enter his constituency by attaching himself to my entourage. Now and then, we had to campaign together. He would enter his own locality along with me—a complete newcomer and outsider. We sat on either side of the van and went to villages in the interior. I could not help wondering at times what I was doing there because he and I were poles apart. I was told by my party that he was a fit candidate for the place. A tough person was needed in that area. A mild-mannered woman and an academic might be all right for the Parliamentary constituency as a whole, but was absolutely unsuited for an assembly segment where muscle power was the key necessity.

I would get a comfortable lead from Mograhat that year. My colleague would also scrape through to win a seat in the state assembly by less than a hundred votes—even though he ended up spending more time in jail than in the legislature. The natural beauty of Mograhat did not match its mafia reputation. Every time I entered Mograhat I was enchanted by the tree-lined lanes and the expansive green paddy fields. I invariably sang Tagore's popular song *Dhaner khete raudra-chhayay lukuchuri khela re bhai lukuchuri khela* whenever I saw the play of sun and shade on Mograhat's amazing spectrum of green. I enjoyed sitting on the grass with veteran Muslim leaders of the villages. I was usually the only woman at these gatherings, which were organized by a young man called Ghiasuddin Molla, who was in charge of my campaign in Mograhat. I interacted with the women separately in their homes.

I began my election campaign that summer of 1996 on a most inauspicious note. The campaign was launched from a spot near the Karunamoyee bridge in Behala East—a very congested Kolkata area. The assembly candidate of that segment was a robust, young woman called Sonali Guha, a loyal follower of Mamata Banerjee. She was with me on that day. There was some argument among the workers about the place from where the procession should start off. The choice was either the front of the temple of goddess Karunamoyee on one side of the bridge or the small bust of Gandhiji on the other side of the bridge. I expressed my preference for Gandhiji's blessings for a political event.

So on a hot summer morning we started our walk, which in political parlance, is called padajatra. I was asked to fold my hands and do namashkar to the people on both sides of the road. Sometimes there were urgent whispers from the workers— 'Didi, look up at the balconies' or 'Baudi, look up at the first-floor windows', which I dutifully did. Men and women peered from the windows, the less inhibited came out on to the balconies. As a new entrant into the political fray, I was an object of some added curiosity. According to tradition, I had to keep the ghomta, the edge of the sari that worked as a veil of sorts, on my head.

Behala's narrow lanes and by-lanes were notorious for their potholes, which looked more like craters of various sizes and shapes. The inevitable happened. I tripped and fell flat. I tried to protect my face with my right arm where I felt a twinge of excruciating pain. It was a congested lane in a very poor area of Behala. Someone rushed out of a nearby dilapidated one-storey house with a steel tumbler of water for me. I smiled and got up, reassuring everybody that nothing serious had happened. Anyway, this was going to be news since there were a couple of journalists covering our padajatra. We moved to the next stop, Joka, where we had a workers meeting. Then the workers of another part of the constituency took charge of me. We drove down to Jadavpur where there was a big gathering of workers in a large hall. There was a lot of slogan shouting in the name of Somen Mitra who was the president of the West Bengal Congress at the time. He arrived amidst flowers and slogans. There was a lot of activity. I shared the dais with him and put on a smiling face though I could hardly bear the pain in my right arm.

On returning home I found my whole right arm had turned dark blue. Gomma, my long-time attendant and house-keeper, rushed in with some ice cubes. The more she applied these on the arm, the more ghastly blue it turned. My husband, Sisir, appeared on the scene. He was shocked. Apart from his other incarnations, professionally my husband was a physician, a paediatrician of considerable repute. He at once summoned the orthopaedic surgeon and good friend Dr Ashok Sengupta. Ashok put my arm in a sling and said there had been profuse internal bleeding which would take at least six weeks to heal. I had a five-week long campaign ahead of me. It was an ordeal!

On the other side of Behala—in the segment known as Behala West—the state assembly candidate from our party was Kumud Bhattacharya. I had never met him before, but had heard about him. There was a funny thing I remembered about him from the mid-seventies when he was a student leader. For some reason there was a conflict between two factions of students in front of Presidency College. The anti-Kumud faction took out a procession and shouted a peculiar slogan—'Kumud Bhatchaj wak-thu'. I had never heard such a slogan before, so I remembered it. It was not the usual murdabad or death to you. Translated in a rather inadequate fashion, it would be—'I spit on you—Kumud Bhatchaj'.

Anyway, here he was to be my campaign comrade. To begin with, he was not very pleased with me. I was unable to do namashkar to voters while I campaigned, as my right arm was in a sling. I raised my left hand, waved, sometimes I showed, the symbol of the Congress party, which was the hand or rather the palm. Kumud was annoyed and told me that raising the left hand would send a wrong signal. Voters would consider me a leftist. Our fight was with the CPI(M), a left party, and the ruling coalition was called the Left Front—so I must not raise the left hand. He advised me to rest till my arm healed. I chose to disregard this unsolicited advice.

Anyway, after one or two padajatras, or rather truck jatras, he changed his opinion. As I have said before, being a newcomer in politics I was an object of curiosity. So as we passed in a procession and our boys cried themselves hoarse—here comes so and so our Parliamentary candidate, an academic and writer by profession, wife of Sisir Kumar Bose, daughter-in-law of Sarat Chandra Bose etc. etc.—curious faces appeared, chinks in windows opened up. Women smiled, even waved. Later I discovered many were my students. I had taught for forty years at the City College for Women in south Kolkata and had at least two generations of former students by that time. Seeing the popular response to my candidacy, Kumud became rather keen on joint campaign appearances, even though he considered me to be a candidate of the Mamata faction of the Congress. He was a loyalist of Somen Mitra.

The campaign gathered momentum. I became gradually aware of the factionalism within the Congress. In 1996 there were two warring groups in the West Bengal Congress. One was led by Somen Mitra, the West Bengal Congress president. The other was led by the Youth Congress president, Mamata Banerjee. Congress leaders in Delhi, like Pranab Mukherjee who had no popular following in Bengal, tended to take Mitra's side in party squabbles. The adherents of the two camps had a deep revulsion for each other. Everyone knew about it, but I was not quite aware of the extent of the hostility.

In December 1995, upon reaching the age of sixty-five, I had retired from the City College for Women, named Shivnath Shastri College. At the end of March 1996, Mamata came to see me at home, one evening, and asked if I would agree to contest the Jadavpur Lok Sabha seat. Sisir was also present, but he kept quiet and did not comment at all. Jadavpur, everybody knew, was a tough seat—it was known as a red fortress. 'But that is a lost seat,' I told Mamata. She emphatically replied, 'No, no, you'll win it' 'Do you really think so?' I asked unconvinced. After a cup of tea, Mamata left. I was not very sure whether I had said yes or no. Things were left somewhat vague. But Sisir smiled and said, 'So you accepted her proposal. Did not even ask my opinion, what I thought about it.' 'Have I said yes?' I wondered.

Bengali newspapers next morning had a big front page headline: 'Mamata's surprise candidate—Krishna Bose'. Congress nominations are usually decided by a central committee in Delhi. Later I was told that Pranab Mukherjee, the head of that committee, had apparently asked Mamata—'Do you really want Krishna Bose? I mean, after all she does not belong to our lot.' Mamata had firmly and in her usual aggressive manner asserted, 'That is final. I have already told her,' to which Pranab babu softly said, 'All right, if you so wish.' This conversation was reported to me, later, by others. The not so subtle rivalry in the West Bengal Pradesh Congress resulted in some candidates being chosen from Somen Mitra's list and some being chosen from Mamata's list. So far as I was concerned ordinary Congress workers were generally happy with me. But among the gruppenfuhrers—group leaders—I was looked upon as Mamata's choice. The Bengal Congress has a history of being faction ridden. The Somen-Mamata feud was nothing new. Sometimes it could be a clash of ego on the part of faction leaders. The central Congress leadership also often played one against the other.

Of the seven assembly segments that comprised my

Parliamentary constituency, three candidates were from Mamata's list and four from Somen's list. The next five or six weeks I had to be in many joint campaigns with candidates for the state legislature. One of Somen's candidates, Ram Pyare Ram, was the most difficult one to manage. After some attempts I gave up trying to work with him and carried on in the Kabitirtha assembly segment by myself. Ram Pyare Ram was a short, stocky man, perpetually chewing paan. One side of his cheek was always swollen because there would be a paan tucked inside, which led some to believe he had a tumour in his left cheek. When I found he was not only not cooperating but even trying to sabotage my election, I had to speak to Somen Mitra. I was assured by Somen that Ram Pyare was a wonderful man: 'Do you know he is always to be found in the Kantapukur morgue?' This was the place where dead bodies of persons killed in political clashes or accidents were brought. How his perpetual presence in the morgue made him a wonderful man I could not quite fathom.

Kabitirtha is a Muslim-majority area near the port—an Urdu-speaking non-Bengali Muslim area unlike Mograhat which was inhabited by Bengali Muslims. I addressed a number of big meetings in Kabitirtha and also visited the homes of well-known Muslim citizens. In the port area there was one pocket of Hindi-speaking Bihari Hindus, mostly from the Yadav community. And at least one ward had educated middle class Bengalis as well. The response of the various castes and communities to my candidacy was quite enthusiastic. As I addressed a meeting or moved in an open jeep, the people roared in unison: 'Jitega, jitega Krishna Bose jitega', Krishna Bose will win! The scene is etched in my memory. I passed through a market where huge quantities of shemai, vermicelli in cream, were heaped in front of the wayside stores. People buying sweets, the blinking coloured bulbs that decorate some of the shops and the sudden renting of the air by shouts of 'Jitega, jitega'. I did win—and with a huge margin from this segment.

Baruipur, another assembly segment south of Kolkata, on the other hand, was always relaxed. Sisir sometimes joined me on my campaign visits to Baruipur. He walked with me and the assembly candidate, Sobhandeb Chattopadhyay, along the roads of the town of Baruipur. I addressed my first ever big rally at Baruipur in a huge open field known as 'Rasher Math' where about twenty thousand people had gathered. As I stood on the high podium to speak I saw only heads of people all around. I do not remember what I said, but people said I spoke very well. A tape of that speech was played in Baruipur by Sobhandeb throughout our campaign. Sobhandeb and I had no problem working together.

In the Bishnupur assembly segment, the assembly candidate Mahadeb Nashkar was Somen's man, but did not pose any problem for me, unlike the paan-chewing Ram Pyare Ram of Kabitirtha. He only wanted a little more money than the others when disbursements were made to the different assembly segments. He confessed that he had paid a certain sum to someone in the party to get the ticket to be a candidate. This was a shocking revelation for me, an innocent in politics.

The CPI(M), of course, had geared up to give me a tough fight, especially in the Jadavpur assembly segment. I found Jadavpur the most interesting segment of the seven that made up the Parliamentary constituency bearing that name. Jadavpur, in the past, had been totally hostile to any non-communist candidate. My predecessors had trailed by the largest margins in this segment. I always used to have an argument with my election agent Ranku Ghosh, whom everyone called Rankuda—I wanted to go to Jadavpur more often but he said: 'Jadavpur is a lost cause. What is the use of wasting your time there? You concentrate on the other segments which will give you leads.' But I felt that if I could address myself to the electorate of Jadavpur I might even be able to influence them. I admired the people of Jadavpur. Their forefathers had come from erstwhile East Bengal as refugees at the time of partition. They had suffered and struggled and today their children and grandchildren have established themselves in life. If they believed in a leftist ideology, I saw no harm in that. Leftism was not the monopoly of the Bengali communists. The first leftist leaders in India were Jawaharlal Nehru and Subhas Chandra Bose and both belonged to the Congress. And there were some really idealistic left leaders among the communists whom I admired. But having been in power for twenty years, the idealism of the most of the communists had evaporated. My fight was not against leftism as such, but against the ruling Left Front in West Bengal headed by the CPI(M). Having started reasonably well in the area of land reforms, the CPI(M) had failed miserably in the fields of education and health. I believed I could get the swing vote in Jadavpur from those who usually voted for the communists.

In a way Rankuda was right. Most of the segments other than Jadavpur gave me leads. At the last stage of the counting my destiny depended on the number of votes by which I would trail in the Jadavpur segment. I succeeded in reducing the margin considerably, in comparison with the Congress's past performances, and thus won the Parliamentary seat that year. In the two elections that followed in 1998 and 1999, my efforts at communicating with the Jadavpur electorate worked and I won even in the Jadavpur segment with a big majority. After the split in the Congress party in Bengal in 1998, I chose to be with the Trinamool—Grassroots—Congress. I won the Parliamentary seat in 1998 by nearly 80,000 thousand votes of which the Jadavpur assembly segment supplied a lead of nearly 16,000 votes. When I entered the counting centre for the Jadavpur assembly segment in 1998, I found our boys with tears in their eyes—tears of joy. They said, 'Didi, we are winning here!' It was unbelievable. The boys said, 'We will hold our heads high in Jadavpur after a long time.'

The transition in the opinion of the voters was silent and

subtle. In 1996 after many heated arguments with my election agent, Rankuda, I managed to go to Jadavpur to campaign. I began by addressing small wayside meetings. When I rose to speak I could see small clusters of people gather at a distance on the opposite side of the pavement. They seemed to be afraid to come any closer. People shopping at wayside stalls stopped and listened. The balconies and windows also showed one or two faces. And, then occasionally, one or two people from the opposite pavement —women more often than men—would cross over to me and say in a lowered voice, 'We liked what you said.'

It was customary for speakers on the campaign trail to scream, shout, rave and rant until the strain on their throats made their veins reach bursting point. I was an exception in this regard. I spoke clearly and with authority, but there was no question of raising my voice. I was not going to shriek. At a huge gathering at Behala chowrasta, as I came down from the podium after making an election speech, an elderly gentleman approached me and said: 'That election speeches can be made without screaming and shouting I learnt today listening to you.'

The character of the Jadavpur campaign meetings changed dramatically as people became less frightened. They came to the meetings in larger numbers. By 1998, as a Trinamool Congress candidate, I found that the voters of Jadavpur had undergone a transformation. As I stood on a jeep and passed through the streets of Jadavpur, hundreds of men and women thronged the streets and cheered. Women were particularly sympathetic. But late in the campaign even in 1996, as I stood on the jeep under a scorching sun, women pleaded—'Can we bring you a glass of water?' Some said, 'Let us give you an umbrella, the heat is unbearable.'

I was told by veteran politicians that the use of an umbrella would not go down well with the voters. I had never agreed with that view. Now when the women offered me umbrellas, I could see how stupid that notion was. Next day I brought out my Burmese umbrella, bought in the Indo-Burmese border town of Tamu. I had walked over to Tamu from More in Manipur and bought it. The lovely, grey umbrella was small and round, and just covered the head. It allowed people to see my face clearly. In 1999 I was asked on a TV programme if there was any particular reason why I used that beautiful umbrella. I answered, 'It is my lucky mascot.'

I had no idea of the physical strain involved in a Parliamentary election and that too with one arm in a sling. There were nearly 1.5 million voters in my constituency. As I have stated earlier, it comprised seven assembly constituencies—four urban and three rural. There were some Muslim-majority areas; others like Bishnupur had a considerable Christian population. There were a large number of people who were, indeed, very poor and lived in temporary wayside hutments. There were also the middle class Bengalis and a few prosperous and rich people. Within a period of five to six weeks I had to address this medley of people.

My day began early in the morning. I usually set out in a closed jeep driven by Lalan. I was given an armed security guard by the government because many of the places I had to go to, like Mograhat, could be very dangerous. A young worker of the party called Ratan was asked to accompany me. I found out he was very good at finding places in the huge constituency. He seemed to have a map of the whole area in his head. So I went from place to place, driving many miles in a day. Sometimes I managed to come back for a quick lunch and left again immediately. I finally returned around midnight. Soon I became sun-tanned, lost weight and looked like a *petni*—that is a woman-ghost—straight out of a story by Rajshekhar Bose alias Parasuram whose *petni*s are immortal characters in Bengali literature. At midnight I ate a little, holding the fork with my left hand. Sisir was worried about me and persuaded me to take a vitamin B-complex tablet before going to sleep.

Downstairs, my election office was basically run by two men.

One was my election agent, Rankuda, and the other was Tushar who helped him. The two had known each other for a long time, but now and then they fell out. Rankuda was rather short-tempered and shouted at Tushar at the least provocation. Tushar generally did not mind but sometimes even his patience ran out. So very often a drama would be enacted when one or the other would stage a walk-out from the office, only to make up a couple of hours later. Taking Ratan into account, I would say I had only two and a half workers to carry the burden of running my election machinery. Looking back, the fact that I won three times in a row from this tough constituency with this meagre staff, seems nothing short of a miracle.

The other thing I learnt, the hard way, was how important money power is in an election. After a day's gruelling campaign I would come home to find everyone clamouring for money. The cadres who worked in the different neighbourhoods demanded money. The first need was for paint and brushes to paint election slogans on the walls. Property owners disliked this form of electioneering but they were helpless. Then, of course, there would be demands for cloth banners and paper posters proclaiming the virtues of the candidate. The major expenses were on the day of the election when one had to have agents at each election booth—in my constituency there were nearly 1300 booths. Hundreds of party workers had to be put into action and fed breakfast, lunch, and sometimes dinner as well. A continuous supply of tea, coffee, and cigarettes had to be kept up too.

The other big day was the counting day. Counting agents had to sit through at least three days and two nights through the painstaking process of counting the paper ballots. Another flow of food and beverages had to be maintained. It was a constant headache for me to organize the funds for these expenses. The continuous pressure for money from different quarters was enough to make one go mad. I spent most of my pension funds and Sisir contributed his income and savings to make the campaign possible. I also noticed from the way the Congress party disbursed its funds, how corrupt the politicians and the political system had become. Without state funding of elections, this malady will be hard to cure.

At the very outset of the election campaign I had attended a small meeting of municipal councillors of our party. This was at the house of one of our Behala councillors, Bhola-babu. On my arrival at the meeting the very first question Bhola-babu asked me in Bengali was '*Apnare abar ai ghora-roge dhorlo kan?*'— How is it that you have been infected by this horse disease? I myself wondered, sometimes, what had made me jump into this unknown arena, akin to gambling and horse-racing, where many like Bhola Babu thought I was an utter misfit.

However, in spite of the physical exertion, the financial worry, and the scorching heat of the summer of 1996, I did enjoy the campaign. I liked meeting diverse people. I also had a close glimpse of the abject poverty and sub-human condition of the people of rural Bengal, and that too only at a stone's throw from Kolkata. The primary schools were mostly in ruins with no roofs, no toilets, no doors or windows, no boundary walls. Cattle grazed happily, while children sat in filth and squalor. There was no electricity and no safe drinking water in most of the villages, after fifty years of independence and twenty years of communist rule in the state of West Bengal.

I got used to addressing huge gatherings in Kolkata and its outskirts. I uttered not a word against my incumbent rival, Malini Bhattacharjee, from the CPI(M). She was an academic like me, albeit a rather doctrinaire communist who I was told was called 'Stalini' in certain circles. Both of us had read and taught the same subject—English literature. A journalist who interviewed me had asked who my favourite poet was. I had answered, 'Browning.' His philosophy 'God is in heaven and all is right with the world' gave me confidence. To the same question my rival had answered 'Shelley'. His *Prometheus Unbound* was her inspiration. After being elected, when I entered Parliament, many greeted me saying—so Browning won over Shelley!

As the election campaign was nearing its end, I was told that Jyoti Basu, the chief minister, had severely attacked me in some of his speeches. I did not know I was even worthy of his attention. At a big meeting in Behala's Sarsuna Park, there was a demand from the audience that I answer some of his criticism. I would have preferred to ignore it, but since there was persistent demand I had to say something. I remember I arrived at the meeting at the end of a string of meetings in Mograhat and Bishnupur. On arrival I found my husband Sisir and my elder son Sugata already there. In those last days of the campaign I was joined by my whole family. The three children were a great help. It was impossible for me to cope with the demand for personal appearances at public meetings because it was just not physically possible to be present at so many different spots. Various family members fanned out in different directions. Sisir went to a few selected meetings. Sometimes we suddenly met each other at a meeting. Sisir was speaking at that Behala rally when I arrived. He reminded the audience that Netaji Subhas Chandra Bose always said his family was coterminous with his country. All his countrymen were his family and none of us could claim any special credit for being a family member.

This was in reply to Jyoti Basu who had said it was improper for me—as a member of the Bose family—to be a Congress candidate. I said Subhas Chandra Bose had resigned from the Indian Civil Service(ICS) to join the Congress under Gandhiji and Deshbandhu Chitaranjan Das. He was Congress president for two terms. Even when his army was proceeding towards the Indian border during the Second World War, the soldiers carried the Congress flag with the charkha amidst the tricolour. If Subhas Chandra Bose could commit so many acts of 'impropriety', I could be forgiven for one—that is, being a candidate of the

Congress party. Jyoti Basu had made another bizarre statement—that I did not belong to the Bose family at all. I did not quite understand his logic, but I suppose he meant that I had merely married into the Bose family. I told the audience, 'You have just heard my husband say that Netaji considered his family to be coterminous with his country. So as one of his countrymen, along with all of you I belong to the family from which Jyoti-babu can not push me out.' The audience responded with thunderous applause.

Polling day arrived at long last. I cannot express the sense of relief I felt the moment campaigning stopped—a day before the election. I came home from the last meeting, lay down in my bed and fell fast asleep. The activity had shifted downstairs to the election office. Rankuda was in command. Tushar had occasional arguments with him, but was kept busy since he was in charge of food to be distributed at different election centres. The office was full of young workers who had come to pick up important papers and get last minute instructions. Sugata was in charge of the finances. Both Sisir and I had gone bankrupt by then, having spent even the savings meant for our old age. Since in India we have no social security, the future looked bleak. But I was too exhausted to worry and slept on peacefully.

On the day of the election, however, I had to get up early and visit election centres to stiffen the morale of our boys. Sumantra came with me. Sugata and Sarmila were left in charge of the office. Only I and my election agent Rankuda would be allowed to go inside election booths. So Rankuda took a different route from mine. I chose the most difficult segment—Jadavpur. It is in a way impossible to fully convey the flavour of election day in Bengal. We had to be prepared for large-scale vote rigging. In 1996 the CPI(M) had been in power in West Bengal for nearly two decades. A few very small parties were their adjuncts and formed what they called the Left Front coalition. However, the CPI(M) was by far the largest party and kept the small parties on a leash. The bureaucracy and the police force were all under the CPI(M)'s thumb and did their bidding mostly out of fear and sometimes out of genuine loyalty as the CPI(M) had put their own men in strategic positions.

I had varied experiences of rigging in all the Parliamentary elections I fought. A senior CPI(M) leader had already told a common friend that his party had arranged for at least 40,000 bogus votes to defeat me. Rigging could be of different kinds. First, the same people might cast multiple votes. The ink spot that was put on the nail of a voter after he had cast one vote could be erased with some chemical and so they could go on casting false votes. Second, there could be booth jamming. Voters stand in the sun in long queues. The line is made to move very slowly or not at all, so that genuine voters leave in disgust. Third, there could be straightforward booth capturing. That is, the goons of the ruling party would force their way into the booths, beat up the agents of the rival party, drive away genuine voters, and stamp the ballot papers according to their wishes. This sort of blatant rigging happened usually in booths a little away from the media glare.

The CPI(M) was a past master at what had come to be called 'scientific rigging'. They were a very organized party. The rigging process for them would begin at the stage when voters lists were being prepared. On polling day, certain voters whose sympathy lay with the other side would find that their names had vanished from the electoral rolls. The cadres of a well-organized party would know who the 'dead' voters were and whose names still figured on the rolls. The dead would come alive on the day of the voting and cast their votes. India is acclaimed as a great democracy, but there are serious blemishes in its functioning. West Bengal has not had a free and fair election in a very long time.

Our party workers were not angels. Given the opportunity, they might have resorted to the same tactics as the CPI(M). But unfortunately for them, they did not have the backing of the police force and the administration. It would be unfair to claim that the CPI(M) had been winning the Parliamentary and assembly elections in Bengal by rigging alone. But rigging helped a great deal and was made easy because of the lack of a credible opposition. The rise of the CPI(M) to power in West Bengal coincided with the decline of the Congress all over India. The Congress in West Bengal was in a pathetic state with no leader of stature who could be projected as a future chief minister to replace Jyoti Basu. Many of the leaders of the Congress opposition were beholden to the ruling party, having accepted small favours from them every now and then. And they were leaders because they were willing pawns in the hands of the all-India Congress leadership and possessed no support base of their own.

The best I could hope for in 1996 was to contain the rigging by the CPI(M), not stop it altogether. To give a small example, news came that at Mograhat eight booths had been captured, our agents driven away and all the ballot papers were being stamped on the CPI(M)'s hammer and sickle symbol. I met the District Magistrate and asked for a repoll at the eight booths which accounted for nearly eight thousand votes. The District Magistrate asked me to wait because he said he would have to call the presiding officers at the booths. They must give a report that there were disturbances in the booths—only then could the District Magistrate take action. The presiding officers employed in booths were always strong supporters of the ruling party. Soon faxes rolled out in the District Magistrate's office which said the polling in these eight booths had been extremely peaceful. Of course, it had been very peaceful since only one party was present, to peacefully stamp the ballot papers! The results confirmed that more than ninety per cent of the votes in these booths had gone to the ruling party. The District Magistrate, who was also the returning officer, knew that a farce had been enacted at these and other polling centres, but seemed helpless about taking remedial measures. In many other booths our agents dared not protest against voting irregularities. At the end of the day they could not emerge from the polling centres for fear of being beaten up by the ruling party goons. My election agent had to go personally in many instances to ensure their physical safety.

The day of reckoning arrived. On counting day I got up early in the morning and did a round of as many counting centres I could. This was to give my counting agents a sense of confidence. Counting day also had its hazards of rigging. My counting agents had to be very alert to prevent entire bundles of votes being thrown on the CPI(M)'s scale by partisan officers. As the counting dragged on, our boys in the counting centre became exhausted and sleepy. But the CPI(M) sent in three fresh batches of counting agents. They seemed to know beforehand that there would be an unusual delay in the counting process. Late in the night I came home while Sugata and Sumantra stayed on. During the night there was a lot of trouble at the counting centre. Bombs were thrown near the gate of the building where the counting was taking place. The driver of my car, along with others, took shelter inside the National Library compound opposite the counting centre. Men with revolvers entered the counting room for the Jadavpur assembly segment and threatened my counting agents that they would not be able to return to their homes in Jadavpur. In the battle for the state legislature from Jadavpur, Buddhadeb Bhattacharya, the then home minister, was the CPI(M)'s candidate. He would rise to be the chief minister of West Bengal in 2001.

Early in the morning I was standing on the terrace of our house when I noticed a motorbike at our gate. It was driven by a stranger, but Sumantra was riding on the pillion. He gave me an account of what had happened during the night. He could not find any of our drivers or cars. He had no idea where they had taken shelter. So he had taken a ride on this motorbike. Sugata was holding fort at the counting venue.

Soon the election trends became clear. I was leading very well in Behala West. Behala East had also given me a lead. In Kabitirtha I was winning by a huge margin. Baruipur also gave me a comfortable lead. In Bishnupur I was in a neck-and-neck battle. Even Mograhat, the criminal-infested area, had given me a lead. Altogether I already had a comfortable margin of lead. But everybody knew the story would change soon when counting for the Jadavpur segment would finish. All the nice leads would be eaten up by Jadavpur and an ignoble defeat might await me there.

Another interesting thing that happened was most of my comrades-in-arms who were contesting the state elections fell in battle, one by one. I kept up my lead in the Parliamentary election but the state legislature candidates lost. Kumud Bhattacharya in Behala West, Sonali Guha in Behala East, Mahadeb Nashkar in Bishnupur, all went down by the afternoon. Sobhandeb Chattopadhyay won in Baruipur by a modest margin. Ram Pyare Ram —my bete noir in Kabitirtha—won by a huge majority. Jadavpur counting went on very slowly. The state legislature candidate, Kakoli Ghosh Dastidar, was going down by a huge margin. She had been a very active and aggressive campaigner but that did not seem to have helped. Kakoli was pitted against Buddhadeb Bhattacharya.

Sumantra and I took a taxi and reached the counting centre. Yes, I was trailing at almost all the counting tables. Kakoli had already lost badly. She was in tears. Buddhadeb Bhattacharya arrived with his daughter and was declared elected. I sat in a corner flanked by Sugata and Sumantra but Buddhadeb-babu declined even to glance at us and left in, what used to be his usual haughty manner. After he became chief minister he put on a more polite and amiable face. I had a glimpse of my rival—the woman academic. But she looked despondent and left the centre quietly.

I felt a peculiar sense of detachment and could not care

whether I won or lost. I had taken up the challenge knowing fully well I was fighting a lost seat. I had put in as much effort as I could in the campaign and now I was ready to face the result, whatever that may be. Sumantra was running from one table to another calculating by how many votes I was trailing in this segment. I looked at him as he scribbled on small pieces of paper with a worried look on his face. Suddenly I thought I would not mind a defeat at all, but the children would be really disappointed. Maybe I would have to win for them. After an eternity it seemed the Parliamentary counting came to a stop. Much of my lead in other segments had been eaten up by Jadavpur. But still, it was a victory. The margin of defeat at Jadavpur was reduced to a great extent compared to previous elections. And I had won the Jadavpur Parliamentary seat. For Bengali newspapers the headline was—Congress snatches Jadavpur from CPI(M).

Sisir, Sugata, Sumantra all joined me. Sisir who by nature was very calm and unperturbed, had spent a sleepless night, I knew. He had been listening to the radio throughout the night. The radio was always slow in catching up with news and was also fed misleading news from the official centre at Writers' Buildings. Rankuda was there looking like an exhausted general but happy at victory. Tushar was there, so was Ratan. Someone put a garland on me.

On the way back from the counting centre, I stopped at Mamata's place. There was a crowd at her place—media personnel and also party cadres. Flash bulbs went off as Mamata and I greeted each other. Slogan shouting began: '*Jadavpurer Lal Durga Bhanglo Ke?*'—Who has captured the Red Bastion of Jadavpur? And the crowd responded with '*Krishna Bose abaar ke?*'—Krishna Bose, who else? Some of the Bengali newspapers had my photograph next day as the fall of Jadavpur, a stronghold of the CPI(M), was indeed news. There were victory processions taken out by our boys the next day. I joined the one in Behala East organized by our local councillor Tarak Singh.

It was time to go to Delhi. Sisir and Sugata came with me and we brought Tushar with us. Mamata was on the same flight. This was a short trip and I stayed at Hotel Kanishka. I had to sign many forms asking for accommodation, etc. and eventually I was allotted temporary accommodation at Banga Bhawan until a permanent apartment was found. We came back after the short trip. A few days later I was summoned in the name of the President of India to attend the first session of the eleventh Lok Sabha.

The People's Representative

A new chapter of my life began in the month of May 1996. I had been a professional woman all my life before I entered politics. But public life, of the sort I had to live now, was quite different. I had travelled almost all over the world but it was always with my husband or sometimes with the whole family. Even the Delhi-Kolkata flight, I had never done alone. Now, however, almost every week I had to make the trip to and from Delhi. Sometimes I took the morning flight for a meeting and came back by the evening flight. When Parliament was in session I spent the week in Delhi and came back to Kolkata for the weekend. I had to come back to my family as also to my constituency. Those were the two days when people from the constituency came to see me or I visited them. I adjusted myself to this routine quickly. Sisir and I had never lived apart. This single life in Delhi was somewhat difficult for me. Later on, Sisir tried to come and spend some time with me in Delhi in spite of his busy professional schedule and his work at the Netaji Research Bureau.

On the flight to Delhi, to attend the first session of the eleventh Lok Sabha, I met Jyoti Basu, the then chief minister of West Bengal. He was in his usual seat in the first row, as one entered the plane. My seat was in the first row on the other side. I got up, went up to him and greeted him. He looked up and said: 'Well, I never thought you will win. But since you have won— all right, congratulations.' After this rather grudging expression of congratulations, he asked politely about Sisir. He also mentioned my father whom he knew and respected for his erudition. My father was one of the secretaries of the West Bengal legislative assembly for twelve years from 1948 to 1960. During that time Jyoti Basu was the leader of the two-member communist party in the assembly along with Ratanlal Brahmin.

I remember the day I took the oath as a Member of Parliament. The ritual unfolds somewhat like this. First a protem Speaker of the House is elected. He is usually the most senior member of the Lok Sabha. Indrajit Gupta of the CPI was the protem Speaker for all the three times I took the oath. I came to know him very well and liked him very much. He was one of the old-time Parliamentarians who always upheld the dignity of the House. When the name of the newly elected member is called, he or she goes up to the microphone placed below the Speaker's chair and reads out the oath of allegiance to the Constitution. Then the newly inducted member goes up to the Speaker, shakes his hand, goes around the Speaker's chair and comes down from the other side. Then the member signs his or her name in the register kept on the table.

When my name was called I got up. There were more than five hundred members present in the House, but suddenly I was swept by an utter sense of loneliness. I was about to enter a new phase of my life but none of my near and dear ones were present. Some members had their family or friends up in the gallery. I remembered two persons and paid my silent homage to them before I went up to take my oath. One was my father to whom I owed my education. When I was young, girls were married off early in the midst of their college education. Father was determined that I should finish my university education, which I did. I graduated with honours in English literature and then did my Masters from Kolkata University in the same subject. Father's dream was that I must be an accomplished woman: I must have an interest in diverse subjects. I had learnt classical Indian music. I learnt to play the sitar very well and also trained as a vocalist.

My father wanted me to be someone who could converse intelligently on any subject and encouraged me to read as widely as possible. Father was a lawyer and a constitutional expert and I learnt about the Indian Constitution from him. He would have been very pleased to see me as a member of the Indian Parliament.

The other person to whom I offered my silent homage, as I took my oath, was my father-in-law, Sarat Chandra Bose. I had never known him since he had passed away in 1950 and I got married in the winter of 1955. But I did know a lot about him. My uncle Nirad C. Chaudhuri had worked as his secretary and admired him greatly. My father, Charu C. Chaudhuri, and my uncle, K.C. Chaudhuri, who was a doctor, both knew him well. The reason why I remembered my father-in-law was rather special. Sarat Chandra Bose was the leader of the opposition on the eve of the transfer of power in 1946. He was the leader of the Congress party in the central legislative assembly which was later transformed into today's Parliament. As members of the Congress we sat in opposition on the day we took oath. I looked at the leader of the opposition's seat and thought that he may have sat there.

Sarat Chandra Bose never got the recognition he deserved in free India despite his stellar role as leader of the opposition in the Bengal legislative assembly during the 1930s and in the central legislative assembly from 1945–46. He took a strong stand in 1947 against the Congress high command's call for the partition of Punjab and Bengal. He tried his best to prevent the partition of Bengal and came up with the idea of a united independent Bengal that would be free to determine its relation with the rest of India. He fell out with the Congress on this issue and resigned. Just before his death, he was elected to the West Bengal legislative assembly with a huge margin of votes, in spite of fierce opposition from the Congress. He was a leader of integrity and great stature but he was denied his proper place in independent India. He should have been in the central cabinet or the first chief minister of Bengal. He had a very short stint as minister for power and mines in the interim government in 1946 but was asked by Gandhiji to resign to make room for Muslim League members.

Sarat Chandra Bose and his brother Subhas Chandra Bose were great names in India's struggle for independence. But with the untimely death of Sarat Bose in February 1950 the Boses were completely out of the Indian political scene. So in May 1996, before I took my oath, I remembered the sacrifice made by him for his country's independence and the injustice that did not allow him to contribute to the development of the newly independent nation. I offered my silent pranams to him and got up to take the oath of allegiance as a Member of Parliament.

Atal Behari Vajpayee was the prime minister at the outset of the eleventh Lok Sabha. After the Congress, the BJP was the largest single party but did not have the required majority. He was prime minister for thirteen days. On the thirteenth day only, he addressed the Lok Sabha. He conceded that he did not have the majority and declared he was going to President Shankar Dayal Sharma to put in his papers. But on the first day of the session when Vajpayee was the prime minister, the President of India had addressed the joint session of Parliament in the Central Hall. That was my first experience of a joint session. The President read the English version of his speech. The Hindi version was read by Najma Heptulla, deputy chairman of the Rajya Sabha. When she reached the part mentioning the ban on cow slaughter Mamata jumped up from her seat and shouted, 'No, no!' She sat between me and Vasundhara Raje. We pulled at her sari and tried to make her sit down since any disturbance during the President's speech was considered unparliamentary. But she was irrepressible and staged a dramatic walk-out.

During the early days of the eleventh Lok Sabha, Mamata invited me to come and spend a few days with her instead of staying alone at Banga Bhavan. I had the opportunity to observe her closely. I found her to be a complex character riddled with

contradictions. On the one hand there was a childlike simplicity
about her and on the other hand a politician's shrewdness along
with a deep suspicion of people around her. She could not sleep
throughout the night and only went to bed in the early hours of
morning. A few years ago a CPI(M) goon had struck her a blow
with an iron rod when she was leading a procession at the crossing
of Hazra Road in Kolkata. She suffered a serious head injury.
Mamata told me that incident had disturbed her sleep pattern.
Late into the night as we sat together, I would sing Tagore songs.
'Krishnadi, do you know this song ,' she would ask. 'Yes, I do,'
I would answer and she would join me and we sometimes sang
Jibana jakhan shukaye jaya Karunadharay esho—Tagore's plea
for a shower of God's mercy to relieve the aridity of human life.
After a few songs I would go to bed, but she could not sleep till
dawn. I saw her other side also. She could not brook any criticism
and she would be ruthless towards anyone who invited her wrath.
She would shower favours on undeserving minions. However, I
got on well with her and she was also friendly and caring.

After Vajpayee's resignation, there was a lot of political activity
around the choice of the new prime minister. The Congress was
still the largest party. The former Congress prime minister,
Narasimha Rao could have staked his claim to form the
government. But he had already said he would not, and the
Congress would give outside support to any non-BJP government.
Consequently Deve Gowda, a rather unknown person from
Karnataka, was chosen as prime minister. He was from the Janata
Dal. Deve Gowda formed a coalition government of various
regional and caste-based parties and the Congress pledged to
support it from outside.

I quietly learnt how to negotiate the various Parliamentary
rules and procedures. My party, the Indian National Congress,
did not have any infrastructure to train or help newly elected
members, nor did the leadership really care. So I learnt my
Parliamentary skills the hard way and in the long run that was

probably a good thing. I learnt to submit questions which ministers were bound to answer either orally or in writing. I learnt to ask supplementary questions by raising my hand. I also came to know how to raise important issues during zero hour.

My first opportunity to speak in Parliament came during zero hour. Noon was the time fixed for zero hour when special mention could be made of important issues. I had to give notice by 10 a.m. regarding the issue I wished to raise. That morning I had given a notice about an important issue relating to women's empowerment. Most of the political parties had promised, in their election manifestoes, that they would reserve thirty-three per cent of the seats in Parliament as also in state assemblies for women. I wanted to know when the government would bring in this bill to amend the Constitution.

Sometimes when you gave notice for a zero hour special mention, you had to wait a long time for your turn. Your name may be the last to be called by the Speaker or the more unruly members might speak out of turn. Sometimes you could miss the opportunity if the time was over. That day I was startled to hear my name being called first. I got up and demanded a quick introduction and passage of the Women's Reservation Bill. It was the first time that the matter was raised on the floor of the Lok Sabha. There was general appreciation of what I said both within and outside the House. The minister promised that the bill would be introduced and passed during that very session. That was the summer of 1996. The promise has not been kept even as I write in 2007.

The opportunity for my maiden speech came a little later during the discussion on the general budget. The Congress chief whip Santosh Mohan Dev had asked if I would like to participate in the budget debate and I had said yes. In a departure from the generally unhelpful attitude of the Congress leadership, Manmohan Singh briefed the Congress Members of Parliament (MPs) who were to take part in the debate. The finance minister was P. Chidambaram. I carefully prepared my points for the speech, even though as is the practice in Parliament, I would speak extempore. The budget debate could go on for two or three days and one had to patiently wait for one's turn. It appeared that my turn could come late in the evening on 29 August 1996, the second day of the budget debate. That morning I got a call from Kolkata that Sisir had been admitted to the Centauri Nursing Home and his cardiologist felt he urgently needed a pace-maker. The doctor wanted to wait till I returned. I wanted to take the next flight home, but Sisir wanted me to make my budget speech and then come. I was in tears and did not care about what happened to my budget speech. I bought the ticket for the Kolkata flight which would leave around 7.30 p.m. I packed my carry-on bag and put it in the boot of the car and went to Parliament. The car was parked in the Parliament's parking area. I decided to wait till 6.30 p.m. If my turn to speak came, well and good; if not, I would leave. A good friend Ratan Mukherjee helped me. He tele-checked me in for the flight, which was fortunately a bit late, and waited to take me to the airport. After 6 p.m. Manoranjan Bhakta, a Congress MP, and Santosh Mohan Dev, Congress chief whip told the Speaker P.A. Sangma that I had a medical emergency in the family and I may be allowed to speak out of turn. Sangma agreed. At a quarter to seven, or '1849 hours' according to the Parliamentary records, I got up to speak. I spoke for fifteen minutes and ended saying, 'Thank you Mr Speaker. I am done'.

As I rushed out of the chamber, one member from the north-east said, 'You spoke very well.' Although I was worried about Sisir, I had spoken calmly and forcefully and expressed both my appreciation and disappointment with various aspects of the budget. 'While listening to the variety of poetry in multiple languages delivered by the finance minister in the course of his budget speech,' I said at the outset, 'I was reminded of the rather more sobering lines of our Bengali poet Sukanta which if translated might read: "Poetry, today I give you leave to go; the rule of hunger has turned the world into prose, where the full moon appears to be a warm piece of bread".' 'Well, indeed,' I added, 'when we turn to the cold prose of the finance minister's speech, shorn of all its poetical flourishes, what do we find?' Chidambaram nodded his head now and then. When I suggested that on the revenue side he might have tried to widen the tax net by bringing in the rural rich, he got up to intervene. He waved a fat book at me and said he was forbidden by law to tax farmers. I responded that then at least he should do something on the expenditure side about the subsidies which never reached the poor peasants, but got siphoned off by a host of well-to-do intermediaries. The most glaring inadequacy of the budget, however, was in my view in social sector expenditure. Drawing on comparisons with southeast Asian countries, I called for massive investment in education and also health. Chidambaram had claimed that he had increased expenditure on education from Rs 1,825 crore to Rs 3,388 crore. I pointed out that Manmohan Singh had already increased the allocation in his February budget to Rs 3,383 crore. The budget for health had actually declined from the February allocation of Rs 815 crore to Rs 792 crore. I urged Chidambaram to show real courage by expanding the revenue base and also show true compassion by investing in basic health and education. I concluded with a word about defence expenditure. 'Defence is very important for us,' I said, 'but I would ask the finance minister to be careful about the jingoistic postures that emanate from certain quarters now and then. The best defence of a country is a healthy and educated population.'

I reached the airport just in time to catch the Kolkata flight. Sisir had his pace-maker installed the next morning. The doctors did a good job. He came back home and soon resumed his normal duties. I remember a rather interesting and amusing interaction I had with Chidambaram. On our fortieth wedding anniversary in December 1995, our daughter had sent us a small glass elephant from Venice. It had been shipped directly by the shopkeeper. Nearly a year passed and we had forgotten all about it. One day I got a letter from the customs department in Kolkata summoning me to come with my trade licence to pick up the art object. I explained to them that I was not a businessman. Then they asked me to get a permit from the commerce ministry. I wrote to the commerce minister, but he replied that it was the finance minister who should give me the permit. The whole matter became a family joke and I gave up all hope of getting this present. However, one day as I sat beside Chidambaram in Parliament, I told him the story in a light-hearted manner. Soon afterward I received urgent messages from the customs department in Kolkata. They asked me to send someone to pick up the packet that was lying with them. Kartik, who worked in my office, went and came back highly pleased. He had been treated to tea by the customs officers before the little glass elephant was handed over to him.

Every year the railway budget is presented in Parliament before the general budget. All the states demand that the railway budget address their demands for—more trains, more railway tracks, more jobs in the railways, etc. Ramvilas Paswan, the minister for railways, had presented the budget and naturally favoured his own state of Bihar. Other states felt neglected and there were loud protests. That year West Bengal was treated with disdain. Mamata, as was her wont, shouted and protested, but to no avail. In desperation she threw the black shawl she was wearing at the minister. She missed her target and the black shawl landed on the defence minister, Mulayam Singh Yadav, who was sitting next to Ramvilas. Mulayam took the shawl, crossed the floor and gave it to the Congress chief whip. A visibly embarrassed Santosh Mohan Dev came towards me and delivered the shawl to me. For a moment I did not know what to do. I then took the shawl, folded it neatly and put it in the pocket of my seat. All this drama was published in detail in the newspapers next morning. Meanwhile, Mamata sat in the well of the House and refused to budge. An exasperated Speaker, after repeated requests to her to return to her seat, finally shouted—'Get out!' Mamata left the chamber in a huff and did not come back for the rest of the session.

I was a member of the Parliamentary standing committee on Human Resource Development (HRD) during the eleventh Lok Sabha. I was also a member of the Consultative Committee on External Affairs. The consultative committees were presided over by ministers. But the Parliamentary standing committees were of a more independent nature and more powerful. I enjoyed the work of the HRD committee. I learnt a lot from the meetings and the tours that we took to different parts of India. The chairperson of the committee was S.B. Chavan of the Congress. He was a capable man and I got on well with him. HRD was a multifaceted committee. I served in various sub-committees like education, culture, family welfare, and preservation of national monuments.

The national monuments sub-committee took us to Ajanta, Ellora and other places of historic interest. We had to see how well the preservation work was progressing and also how the places could be made more attractive for tourists. Many of the spots needed eating places, drinking water and clean modern toilets which were essential for tourists and particularly foreign tourists. I felt that the Archeological Survey of India, a great institution founded in British times, was doing good work but needed proper guidance and necessary funds. We said that in the recommendations in our report.

The activities of the national monuments subcommittee needed a lot of physical exertion. One had to walk miles, climb hills and unending steps leading to temples. So the joke was that if you wished to be on the national monuments sub-committee of the HRD Committee you must first go through a stringent medical test. On one occasion we drove from Aurangabad to the

Ajanta caves and found the officers of the Archeological Survey waiting to welcome us. A 'dooli' had been kept on one side. A dooli is a chair borne by men, in which people are ferried up the mountain. The officers said, 'We have kept a dooli for Madam because it will really be very tiring for her to go up the hill and then to visit all the caves.' I brushed them aside and said I could walk up as I had done this before. I started walking up briskly. After climbing for some time I realized I was no longer young. My last visit to Ajanta was when I was a much younger woman. Some of my male colleagues were also panting. They rested for a while and again started climbing. Sheepishly, I agreed to get into the dooli. I apologized to the dooli-carriers because I hated to be carried by other human beings. The dooli-carriers, however, never understood my reluctance to use the dooli because it was their job, their livelihood. They were simple people. They chatted with me throughout the journey and told me many anecdotes. Having reached the office near the first cave they put the dooli down and after that I could manage by myself.

But when they put the dooli down, many of my colleagues protested and said 'Dooli nehi utrega'—the dooli will not be put down. In Bihar and UP, I was told, the bride arrives in a dooli to her in-laws house. The bridegroom has to pay a fee to the friends and relatives, particularly to the womenfolk, for permission to put the dooli down. It was a wedding custom. So my colleagues said, 'Where is Dr Bose? Let him come and give us our due only then the dooli will be allowed to be put down.' Dr Bose was not with me at Ajanta. But this incident became a permanent joke. Whenever they met my husband in the Central Hall of Parliament they would demand their dooli dues.

The family welfare sub-committee was also an experience. We went to Rajasthan and visited interior villages. At a health centre in one such village I met a woman who had come for a check-up. She was expecting her sixth child. I gently asked her, 'Was it necessary to have a sixth child; you have five already?'

She answered, 'I have five daughters, I need a son'. 'What if this one also is a daughter?' I could not help asking her. '*Tab to mar jayega*,' then I will have to die, was the answer.

The apathetic attitude regarding a girl child was very much evident in Rajasthan as it was in many other places of India. We were told that many mothers or grandmothers would take the newborn girl child and bury her or expose her to the elements. Places were found with skeletons of small babies strewn around. We were told of villages where no 'barat' or bridegroom's party had come in recent times because there were no girls of a certain age any more.

It was, however, good to see Rajasthan fighting these superstitions and baleful customs. There were many non-governmental organizations (NGOs) which were doing good work. The state government along with the central government was also trying to help. We were taken to villages where women were more emancipated. They welcomed our committee with singing, dancing, and the beating of drums. We saw how they were struggling to educate their children. They demanded education and immunization for their children. They tried to learn some craft so that they could market products and be economically independent. It was heartening to see such efforts. One officer of the Rajasthan government doing good work was Aparna Sahai who accompanied me on the tour. Since then she has become one of my adopted daughters. I am in the habit of picking up adopted sons and daughters in all sorts of places. I have several such in different states of India, in Pakistan, and even a few in the US. Since the Rajasthan tour Aparna has become my 'Jaipur-wali beti' or my daughter from Jaipur.

In the field of education and culture, the committee tried to do a lot of work. We conducted a study of value-based education, that is where the students learned to discern between right and wrong and are made conscious of the fundamental values of life. We had to devise methods of imparting value-based education without favouring any particular religious community. We did visit some institutions run by religious organizations like the Ramakrishna Mission in Kolkata and Belur, the Sai Baba deemed university of Puttapurti in Karnataka, and the Brahmakumari Educational Institute at Mount Abu.

I had my first and only meeting with Sai Baba during the visit to Puttapurti. One evening we waited with the crowd. There were thousands of people but all very disciplined. Sai Baba arrived and walked through the crowd. He passed very near but did not pay any attention to me. I was disappointed and remarked to Mrs Chavan who sat beside me, 'What sort of a darshan is this!' Early next morning we were again made to sit in the crowd. Sai Baba came and walked past us. But this time he looked at me and said, '*Chala jana mat*'—don't go away. Soon afterwards, a few of us were called to his room. It was a very small room. He sat on a chair, while I sat at his feet. Others sat around him. He asked me, 'Would you like some bibhuti?' and he turned over his right hand on my outstretched palm. White bibhuti rained on my palm and soon it was full of the white powdery stuff. He held a long discourse with us. He told me, '*Tum to griha lakshmi ho*'—you are the goddess of your household. He said he was happy to see I did public work as a Member of Parliament but I must always remember the 'grihalakshmi' aspect of my life. He suddenly asked me, 'What are you hiding under the anchal of your sari?' It was an envelope with a letter from my aunt who had recently lost her husband. She had asked me to give the letter to Sai Baba but I was hesitant and did not know how to give it to him. Now I delivered the letter. He read the letter and talked a lot about death which was inevitable and how to face it. He asked me that as a Member of Parliament I should concentrate on education and drinking water for the poor. I was astonished because those were the two aspects on which I had focussed from the first day of my life as an MP. Before we left, he waved his hand and produced a diamond ring and a navaratna ring which he gave to my two colleagues who were with me. I, however, only had the bibhuti which he himself packed in a piece of white paper and gave to me. On my return to Delhi, Kolkata devotees of Sai Baba clamoured for a share of the bibhuti. But detractors of Sai Baba taunted me and said, 'So you witnessed the magic but ended up with only bibhuti. No diamonds or navaratna for you.'

One of the subjects that came under the purview of the HRD committee was culture and some of the many national institutions of importance that came under this head were the National Museum and the National Library of Kolkata, the Nehru Memorial Museum, the Gandhi Smarak Nidhi and others. I noticed from reports that millions of rupees were spent to keep alive the memories of our freedom fighters like Mahatma Gandhi, Jawaharlal Nehru and others, which I thought was as it should be. But I thought what about Netaji Subhas Chandra Bose? The one authentic memorial to him was Kolkata's Netaji Research Bureau, an institute of history, politics and current affairs situated in the ancestral home of the Boses. NRB had been established by Sisir in 1957 and we had to struggle very hard to keep it going. There was no help from the central government. The state government was indifferent, if not hostile. I raised the issue in the meeting where the secretary for culture and other officers were present. The members enthusiastically supported me. S.B. Chavan knew Sisir quite well. He had been to the Netaji Research Bureau when he was education minister in the Congress government. He was aware of the kind of work that was done there. However, it was decided that on the next visit of the committee to Kolkata we would visit not only the National Library and the Indian National Museum but also the Netaji Research Bureau. This was 1996 and the next year would be Netaji's birth centenary.

Sisir had some time ago, on behalf of the Netaji Research Bureau, submitted a proposal to the then prime minister

Narasimha Rao for the extension, maintenance and modernization of the Netaji Research Bureau. I was present at that meeting with the prime minister. He was very attentive and promised that he would certainly try to get the proposal through the cabinet. It was financially a very modest project compared to what was allocated to other institutions. On Netaji's birthday, 23 January 1996, Narasimha Rao sent his external affairs minister Pranab Mukherjee to Netaji Bhawan. We were celebrating the inauguration of Netaji's birth centenary. At a gathering of two thousand five hundred people in front of Netaji Bhawan, Pranab-babu declared that the prime minister had asked him to say on his behalf, that whatever Dr Sisir Bose had asked for the modernization of the Netaji Research Bureau would be granted. Half of the amount would be immediately released and the other half a little later. All the international media carried the news. We received congratulatory messages even from Japan. As destiny would have it, general elections were announced before a single paisa was actually granted and the Netaji Research Bureau had to carry on its struggle as usual.

After the HRD committee's visit to Kolkata, it stated in its report that the Netaji Research Bureau was doing commendable work for the preservation of Netaji's life and ideals. All the members were deeply impressed and moved. The museum and archives were excellent. Volumes of Netaji's speeches, letters and writings were being published. Audio recordings of his speeches in Hindi, Bengali, English and German had come out. There was a video made on his life from rare film footage collected from all over the world. This institution deserved support, the committee recommended. The promise made by the former prime minister was also mentioned.

I chased the current prime minister, Deve Gowda, regularly to get him to act on this matter. He was always very polite to me. He kept on saying, 'Sister, do not worry. It will be done.' But I knew the Deve Gowda government's days were numbered.

He himself was in a precarious position. But before his government fell he visited Netaji Bhawan in response to my invitation and before the fall of his government he granted half of what the previous prime minister had promised. That is, we got a quarter of what we had asked for. For us at Netaji Bhawan our financial struggle was not over. The Congress president at that time was Sitaram Kesri. That was one of the worst periods for the Congress—the party was in complete disarray. Sitaram Kesri threatened to withdraw support to the Deve Gowda government. Many of us in the Congress never understood what purpose it would serve since the Congress was not in a position to form a government. The alternative was going to the polls prematurely, where the Congress's performance was expected to be worse than before. But Kesri took the conflict course to such a high pitch that it was impossible to back down. He demanded Deve Gowda's head. The Deve Gowda government was defeated on the floor of the Lok Sabha after a debate on a confidence motion. The debate and the voting were televised. The whole process appeared to me to be an exercise in futility. I asked Jitendra Prasad and Sharad Pawar, 'Why are we committing hara-kiri?' Sharad Pawar pleaded helplessness. But Jitendra Prasad was angry with me when I told him that he had two members from UP— Noor Banu and Ratna Singh—and in case of a fresh elections the number from UP would be zero for the Congress. My wicked prophecy later came true and in the next elections there was no Congress member from UP.

I had developed a soft corner for Deve Gowda during my interaction with him about Netaji Bhawan. He was not a very talented or articulate person but he gave the impression of being simple and sincere. The confidence vote ended late in the night. When a division was called, corridors were cleared and the doors were closed till the voting process was finished. The votes were recorded electronically. The results were apparent in a moment. A few votes given on slips of papers were still being counted. I had thought that the TV must have been put off. So I crossed the floor, went over to Deve Gowda, and shook his hand. I was surprised to know that the handshake was watched on television all over India. There was a general sympathy for Deve Gowda so after my demonstration of sympathy, some others also crossed over from the Congress side and wished him. A sort of farewell gesture of good will for the man we had voted out.

Already hectic political activity was on about the choice of a prime minister from within the United Front who would be acceptable to the Congress. No party wanted an election so soon. A few days later I was on a flight from Kolkata to Delhi. I had gone to the toilet and could hear the pilot saying that we were flying at such and such height, wind speed was such and such, that we were flying over the beautiful holy city of Varanasi and so on. Suddenly he paused and said, 'Oh! News has just come that Mr I.K. Gujral has been chosen as the prime minister'.

I came out of the toilet and asked Sisir, 'Did you hear that?' He had not heard the announcement. Both of us were delighted. Of the names that were doing the rounds this was, in our view, the best choice. Next morning in Parliament when I met Prime Minister Gujral and congratulated him, he gave me an affectionate hug.

Gujral had a dinner for Congress MPs after he became the prime minister. At that dinner I reminded him of the Women's Reservation Bill, which was pending. He said, 'You are trying to convert someone who is already converted.' It was true he was a staunch supporter of women's empowerment. However, the day he tried to introduce the Women's Reservation Bill he looked utterly helpless. With the bill in his hand he stood for twenty minutes while members—many of them from his own Janata Dal criticized him severely. Sharad Yadav made his oft-quoted remark that he did not want women with bobbed 'bobcutty' hair in Parliament. When I expressed my disappointment to the prime minister later that day at his inability to introduce the

legislation, he said with a tired smile, 'You know my party!'
Another field in which Gujral tried to take some positive initiatives
was in Indo-Pakistan relations. He unilaterally announced many
visa relaxations for artists, writers and elderly people. I
commented to him that he could have gone further, but he said
even the little he had done had been difficult to achieve. There
were objections to the Gujral doctrine from various quarters
though by and large it was welcomed.

Like his predecessor Deve Gowda, Gujral also visited Netaji
Bhawan. I had requested him to visit and he had enthusiastically
agreed. He was going to Kolkata for a different programme on 1
July 1997 and it was decided he would come to Netaji Bhawan
after that programme. There was a very good gathering at Netaji
Bhawan on that day. Kolkata's elite and intelligentsia were well-
represented. Almost all the members of the diplomatic corps of
the city came. This was his first visit to Kolkata after he became
the prime minister. He was delayed at the first programme but
people waited patiently. He was shown round the museum by
Sisir. He came down to the Sarat Bose Hall and addressed the
gathering. He got down from the stage and shook hands and
exchanged pleasantries with the consular corps and the
journalists. He looked at a small model in one corner and asked
me, 'What is that?' I told him it was a plan for the further
development and expansion of Netaji Bhawan, but we had not
been able to carry that out. 'Why could you not do it?' he wished
to know. I told him the truth, 'We have no money.' He looked
at the gathering and said, 'Now she has extracted a promise
from me. I have to do something.' Unfortunately for us his
government fell before he could do anything about his promise.

The period of Gujral's prime ministership was short but
important. It was 1997, the fiftieth year of India's independence.
It was also Netaji's birth centenary. Sisir was chosen as one of
the members of the Golden Jubilee and Centenary Committees.
The prime minister presided over the committee. There were

several meetings of the committee, but as usually happens with such committees there was a lot of discussion but not much work. One concrete proposal was to have a short but authentic biography of Netaji published in different Indian languages. The task was given to the National Book Trust. They examined several existing books and chose *The Flaming Sword*—a short biography Sisir had written some years ago. The Forward Bloc member Chitta Basu and the CPI(M) member Somnath Chatterjee did not like the idea that Sisir's book was being chosen. Their attitude surprised the other members. Everybody knew Sisir Bose had devoted nearly fifty years of his life to the preservation and propagation of Netaji's ideals. The book was accepted despite the objections of sectarian leftists.

I came to know that on 15 August 1997 there would be a midnight session of Parliament—a joint session of both Houses in the Central Hall. On that occasion recordings of the speeches of Mahatma Gandhi and Jawaharlal Nehru would be played and broadcast to the whole country. Nehru's famous 'tryst with destiny' speech which he gave on 15 August 1947 had been chosen. This would, of course, be appropriate. I wondered which speech of the Mahatma would be played because he was a very sad man on that day. The partition of India, which he had declared could only take place over his dead body, had already happened and he did not celebrate. The speaker P.A. Sangma told me that an earlier speech of the Mahatma had been chosen.

I requested Sangma that a speech of Netaji Subhas Chandra Bose should also be played on this historic occasion. He told me everything had been planned already and it would not be possible to make any changes at this stage. I met the Speaker several times and repeated my request. I told him that after all Netaji had provided the alternative leadership in the freedom struggle. He was twice the Congress president. He had taken part in the non-violent struggle and had been imprisoned innumerable times. And, most important, he had led the armed struggle against the

British Empire. He had raised an army and marched towards India and entered India near Imphal and Kohima. His contribution to India's freedom struggle must be recognized. The suffering and sacrifice of those who did not enjoy state power after 1947 must not be ignored.

All my pleas were in vain. So at last I asked Sangma, 'Please, allow me to raise the issue in Parliament and after that if you cannot do anything it will be all right with me.' He agreed. I raised the issue in zero hour. I said, 'We are very happy that Mahatma's and Nehru's speeches will be heard at that historic midnight session of Parliament. But I feel that Netaji Subhas Chandra Bose's voice should also be heard.' I could barely finish what I had to say. There was enthusiastic desk thumping all around, cutting across party lines. All the leaders of the different parties wanted to make a speech in support. Sangma said, 'I have taken the point that everyone supports Mrs Bose. There is no need to make speeches.'

Days passed. The midnight session was almost upon us but I did not hear anything about the inclusion of Netaji's speech. One morning I sat in my usual seat and saw Mr Gujral. I tore a slip of paper from the day's business agenda and wrote on the back: 'Dear Mr Prime Minister, you saw the enthusiasm of the members when I demanded that Netaji Subhas Chandra Bose's voice be heard at the midnight session. Nothing has happened so far. Now, I need a nod from you.' I gave the slip to a chaprasi and asked him to pass it to the prime minister. When the torn piece of paper reached him. Gujral looked up at me across the floor, smiled and gave a nod! Soon thereafter Sangma called me to his chamber. He showed me a hand-written note from the prime minister saying, 'I fully agree with Mrs Bose's suggestion.'

Things started moving fast. I arranged to send some audio cassettes of Netaji's voice. The government also acquired some from their own archives. I was invited to be present in the Speaker's chamber with the party leaders when the selection was made.

On the night of 14–15 August 1997 the voices of all three leaders were heard. When Netaji's speech was announced there was spontaneous thumping of desks for a long time. Even during the course of the five-minute speech there was spontaneous applause almost at the end of every sentence. My husband and I sat among the audience. Sisir was, indeed, very happy. When I saw the response of the people around me I wondered aloud, 'Why were the authorities wary about playing his speech, what were they afraid of?' Somebody remarked, 'This is exactly what they were afraid of.' Many Members of Parliament came forward and congratulated me. Surjeet Singh Barnala told me, 'So, you had your way. You did not give up.' Outside Parliament on Vijay Chowk A.R. Rahman's rendering of *Vande Mataram—Maa tujhe salam*—was being performed and young people were dancing.

Earlier in the year, Netaji's birth centenary was celebrated at the Red Fort by the central government and the centenary committee. On the eve of his birthday the Netaji Research Bureau published a collection of important speeches and writings of Netaji entitled, *Essential Writings*. It was edited by Sisir and Sugata. I requested President Shankar Dayal Sharma to formally release the volume. The book was released a day before Netaji's birthday at a function at Rashtrapati Bhawan by President Sharma. Sisir, Sugata, Janaki Athinahappan of the Rani of Jhansi Regiment and I were present, among others. Sisir left immediately for Kolkata to join the 23 January morning function at Netaji Bhawan. Sisir and I could never accept any invitation to Netaji's birthday celebrations anywhere since we had to be at Netaji Bhawan. That centenary year Sugata and I were in Delhi and Sumantra and Sisir were in Kolkata. At the Red Fort function, speeches were made by various leaders. Atal Behari Vajpayee, as opposition leader, was preparing his speech and needed some books. I gave him my suggestions. An impassioned and emotional speech was made by Colonel Dhillon of the INA. He made a fervent appeal that Netaji's remains be brought to India from the Renkoji Temple in Tokyo.

Sometime in 1995 the Narasimha Rao government had decided that they would bring the remains of Netaji Subhas Chandra Bose back from Japan and build a mausoleum in Delhi. How they took such a bold decision was not entirely clear to Sisir and myself. It appeared that Narasimha Rao had come to the conclusion that it would be a popular move. It would be welcomed by a majority of the Indian people barring some cranks and opportunists. Pranab Mukherjee was the foreign minister at that time and he also thought on the same lines. They correctly came to the decision that in this matter they would be guided by the opinion of three persons only—Netaji's wife Emilie, his daughter Anita and the man who had devoted his life to preserving the life and work of Netaji Subhas Chandra, that is, Sisir Kumar Bose. Emilie and Anita would give the family's point of view. Sisir was chosen not only as a family member but as a participant in Netaji's movement, a close associate and as an acknowledged scholar for his encyclopaedic knowledge of Netaji and India's freedom struggle. Narasimha Rao sent Pranab Mukherjee to Germany to ascertain the views of Emilie and Anita. Anita had been asking for quite some time that the ashes be brought back. If they were not wanted by India, she was prepared to take them home to Germany although she would prefer to bring them to India, the country for which her father had sacrificed his all. She readily agreed with Narasimha Rao's proposal. Auntie Emilie also gave her assent.

In early 1996 Pranab Mukherjee told Sisir and myself that he was planning to bring Netaji's last remains to India in August. We were in his office in South Block. I interrupted him to say, 'But we have elections in May and you are expected to lose.' He looked a little embarrassed. Sisir quickly intervened and said, 'No you will not be defeated, but Congress will come back with a thinner majority.' 'Yes, yes, with a reduced majority,' Pranab Mukherjee conceded and shook his head. Unfortunately, my wicked prophecy as usual came true. Congress lost the election. But as destiny would have it, I was elected to the eleventh Lok Sabha as a Congress member. However, the plans of Prime Minister Narasimha Rao came to nothing.

In mid-1997, West Bengal politics was taking a peculiar turn. The rift between the Somen Mitra faction and Mamata Banerjee faction of the West Bengal Congress had widened. Mamata was trying to consolidate grassroots workers under her banner Trinamool, which literally means 'grassroots'. Trinamool was still an entity within the Congress. But a split in the party seemed imminent. The All India Congress Committee(AICC) held its session in Kolkata in August, 1997. Congress President Sitaram Kesri told Sisir and myself that he had chosen the city because it also happened to be Netaji's centenary year. The AICC session was held at the Netaji Indoor Stadium of Kolkata, which was temporarily named as Netaji Nagar. Mamata held a huge parallel rally outside in front of the Shahid Minar. She tried to demonstrate that while the official Congress had the 'stamp and pad', as she put it, the grassroots workers were with her. The central leadership of the Congress was uninspiring and lack-lustre. Attempts were made to persuade Sonia Gandhi to join active politics. But she remained non-committal and showed no signs that she would be interested in politics.

Soon after I was elected to the eleventh Lok Sabha I had met Sonia at a Rashtrapati Bhavan lunch. On being told I had been an academic all my life and had just entered active politics, Sonia told me, 'You must be feeling awful.' A couple of years later when she chose to join active politics and became president of the Indian National Congress I met her at another Rashtrapati Bhavan reception. I reminded her of what she had told me then and asked, 'Are you feeling awful now?' She smiled and replied, 'I am trying to adjust.'

In mid-August 1997, the Congress had a serious leadership crisis. Personally for me the situation posed a dilemma. On the one hand, I was present at Hazra Park from where several processions for Mamata's rally started. On the other hand, as a disciplined Congress MP I also attended the AICC Session. In my own way I tried to prevent the split. I spoke to Sitaram Kesri and Jitendra Prasad. At some of the meetings Sisir was present with me. Kesri took great pride in telling us that when Netaji had come to Patna as Congress president, Kesri as a young Congress worker had played the drums in the band. We tried to impress upon him that he should find a way to honourably rehabilitate Mamata into the mainstream of the party. The West Bengal state leadership was against the idea. We were given to understand Pranab Mukherjee also did not want it. Mamata herself also remained extremely adamant. The party headed inexorably towards a crisis.

In the winter session of the Parliament it became apparent that Congress would withdraw support from the Gujral government. The Deve Gowda government as also the Gujral government depended entirely on the support of the Congress. I did not understand why the Congress wished to precipitate a fresh election. There was no way we could do any better at the polls. I again spoke to Sharad Pawar and Jitendra Prasad. Pawar again pleaded helplessness though he said he agreed with me. I told him that if I knew we would get even one seat more in the next election, I would go for it. But the Congress party was in complete disarray. Jitendra Prasad was visibly annoyed with me for telling him some home truths. Who was I—an outsider in politics—to tell veterans what was good for the Congress party and what was not.

I resigned myself to the prospect of my term in Parliament coming to an abrupt end. Instead of a full five-year term, the eleventh Lok Sabha would be dissolved at the end of one and a half years. It had taken me a few months to get settled as a Member of Parliament. As I had occasion to mention before, Congress as a Parliamentary party never took care of its new members. There was no help, no orientation organized by the party. I had to learn the hard way to raise issues in zero hour or ask supplementaries during question hour. I tried my best to leave a mark in Parliament. Some of the important issues on which I could speak were the question of women's representation in Parliament, the serious arsenic poisoning of drinking water in vast areas of West Bengal, the plight of labourers in the sick industries and in Kolkata port, the state of health and education, human rights abuses in Kashmir, and Indian foreign policy. I had also worked diligently to provide funds for schools, roads, electrification and drinking water in my constituency from the Member of Parliament Local Area Development (MPLAD) scheme.

The day I tried to raise the issue of arsenic poisoning, nobody was in a mood to listen to me for quite some time. There had been a murder somewhere in Bihar and the opposition and the treasury benches were excited and kept shouting at each other. I managed to raise my voice and said, 'Hon'ble members are agitated about one murder but I want to tell you about how thousands of people are slowly being poisoned to death. Please, let me be heard.' There was a sudden hush. I took the opportunity to describe the terrible situation in West Bengal—parts of my own constituency were in the arsenic belt. I had met Dipankar Chakrabarty of the Jadavpur University Environment Centre. He had given me a most detailed presentation on the topic. I laid on the table of Parliament some of the horrible photographs he had given me of arsenic poisoned patients. The hon'ble members rose to the occasion. There was a clamour for action from the government. The West Bengal government's reaction thus far had been that the scientists were unnecessarily spreading panic. It took them some time to realize the real threat posed by arsenic poisoning. After that, in later sessions of Parliament the topic of arsenic in drinking water cropped up now and again. But I still remember the commotion it created on that first day.

We were all waiting for the final dissolution of the Parliament.

The government was definitely going to fall. The Congress had decided to withdraw support. A few feeble attempts were made to see if a new government could be formed without dissolution of Parliament. The Bharatiya Janata Party (BJP), which was the main opposition party, tried its best. I sat in the Central Hall where many of the BJP members came up one by one and said they were just short of five or six members. If they could get those numbers, they would be able to form a government. Ajit Panja came and told me that I would be given a cabinet post in an alternative government. I politely declined the BJP's overtures saying that I did not support their ideology. There was a lot of activity going on in the Central Hall. At one point Mamata came to me and said, 'Let us go and see the Speaker.' She had got it into her head that with Sangma as prime minister a sort of national government might be possible. By this time she had forgiven Sangma for telling her to get out of Parliament on an earlier occasion. But no alternative emerged. On 4 December 1997, Sangma adjourned the House sine die and the eleventh Lok Sabha came to an end.

I decided to go back to Kolkata immediately. I missed Sisir. In our long married life we had hardly ever lived separately. But since I became a Member of Parliament I often had to be in Delhi, although every weekend I used to rush back to Kolkata. Sisir was busy with his patients and the Children's Hospital, not to mention Netaji Bhawan. He joined me in Delhi when he could. Ratan Mukherjee informed me that no ticket was available in the executive class. But he had bought an economy class ticket and booked the front seat 7A in economy for me. I stood on the first floor verandah of the circular Parliament building. The trees swayed in the breeze and the statues looked on silently. I bade goodbye to the trees and statues because I thought I might not be back again.

I started for the airport in my old rented ambassador. Midway the car broke down. I hailed a taxi, transferred my suitcase from the car and drove off. The taxi driver demanded a hefty sum which I had to pay. I was somewhat absent-minded and dropped the new *India Today* I had bought, somewhere on the tarmac.

There was a middle-aged gentleman in the seat next to me. He turned out to be a curious George! 'You look very familiar', he said. I smiled politely. 'I am sure you are a journalist,' he said. 'Oh, you are not. Then you must be . . .' He made about five guesses. I asked for a magazine from the stewardess. She brought a *Desh* from the executive class. I tried to take cover behind that. But my fellow-passenger was indomitable. At last I looked up at him and said: 'Well, a couple of hours ago I was a Member of Parliament.' However, the interrogation continued, 'CPI(M) or Congress? Oh Congress! Somen Mitra or Mamata Banerjee?'

Amidst all this I heard the announcement that our plane was about to land at Kolkata's Netaji Subhas Chandra Bose Airport.

Between Region and Nation

The month of December is very pleasant in Kolkata. It is also the season full of interesting events—art exhibitions, flower shows, group theatre, poetry readings, musical soirées. I looked forward to going back to my usual world of books, paintings and music. But it was not to be. I was overtaken by political events.

My constituency workers started to pour in. They were worried about the imminent split in the Congress party. The overwhelming majority sided with Mamata, but promised to stand by me in whatever decision I took. Everyone hoped some last-minute solution could be found and the split avoided. Sonia Gandhi came forward in the role of a facilitator at this late stage. Mamata and some of her lieutenants were called to Delhi. There was a meeting between Mamata and Sonia in Delhi. It was already late at night. Sonia had retired for the night, so Mamata was called inside while her lieutenants waited in the outer rooms. Sonia's formula was that Mamata and Somen would have an equal number of candidates from West Bengal in the next Parliamentary election.

Mamata waited for a formal announcement of the formula by the Congress high command the next day. But no such announcement came. Time was running out. If she wished to register Trinamool as a separate party to take part in elections, she had to act without further delay. She met the election commissioner and had the party registered. She also had the party symbol approved by the commission. The symbol was simple but attractive—two flowers on a bit of grass. It evoked the lines of Kazi Nazrul Islam—'two flowers on a single stem—Hindu and Mussalman'. It was a final parting of ways for Mamata from mainstream Congress.

It was time for me to make up my mind. On the one hand, Mamata was instrumental in bringing me into politics. I felt close to her and believed she was honest and above religious prejudice. On the other hand, I had been elected to the previous Lok Sabha as a Congress candidate. I was by temperament a person who did not change loyalties or opinions easily. I thought hard. I spoke to my political workers who had worked hard for me in my election and also stood by me during the last one and a half years. Most of my workers favoured my joining Trinamool. I took a quick tour of my constituency and sensed that most of my workers were for Trinamool though they dutifully told me, 'Whichever side you are, Madam, we will be with you.' One thing was clear to me: the ordinary Congress workers did not want the split. They wished to remain united. But in case of a split they preferred to be with Trinamool.

Sugata arrived for the Christmas holidays. Some of my workers were more frank with him than with me. They pleaded, 'Please tell Madam to announce her decision that she will be with Trinamool.' After a few days Sarmila and Sumantra also arrived in Kolkata. Our confabulations went on. Sisir was part of the family discussion, but he was, as always, reserved and did not influence me to join any side. Another person who was a participant in our brainstorming was Suman Chattopadhyay, the journalist. He was in our decision-making team, not in his professional capacity but as a close friend of the family. Suman had been a friend of Sugata's from his Presidency College days and was, as a matter of fact, a member of the family. At that point of time he strongly supported Mamata. Like many others he was disillusioned with the jaded, mediocre leadership of the

Congress. Mamata seemed to be a ray of hope for West Bengal. It was thought she might be able to offer an alternative leadership against the CPI(M). Among ourselves we had reached a decision by Christmas Day but did not immediately make it public.

I had been brooding a lot on the matter. I even thought of giving up politics altogether. I was disgusted with the over-centralizing tendencies of the Congress high command and could understand the reason for the rise of regional political forces across India since the 1980s. The central leadership of the Congress did not pay any heed to the aspirations of the regional leaders and workers. The state committees were often not democratically elected but were ad hoc committees imposed on the state from Delhi. But to leave the Indian National Congress and go along with a regional breakaway party was a hard decision. The brooding affected my health. Suddenly I developed an eye problem. I started seeing everything double. The doctors took serious note of it and started treatment. My friends and close political workers said the Congress split had affected their MP and she had developed double vision!

In the meantime I also heard that Mamata had lamented that I was hesitating and had not come over to her side. It was reported to me that she had even characterized me as a 'betrayer'. The Somen Mitra group was paying extra attention to me. I must say they had never shown any disrespect to me at any time. However, I was not to be swayed easily. I took my own decision after weighing the pros and cons and also the wishes of my own workers. I could not care less for Mamata's rather unfair accusations or the extra-friendly overtures of the Somen Mitra group. However, my decision to opt for Trinamool was clinched on my birthday at the Baan Thai Restaurant of Oberoi Grand Hotel.

It was my sixty-seventh birthday on 26 December 1997. Sugata took me for dinner to Baan Thai along with Sisir and Sumantra. We sat on the floor in Thai style and not on chairs.

The waiter who served us was a friendly and pleasant young Muslim. He brought in the food and chatted with us. I do not remember how we drifted to current politics. But when Sugata and Sumantra asked him what he thought about the present political scenario he emphatically said he would support Trinamool. He was disgusted with the CPI(M) who had reigned unopposed for twenty years, made big promises to help the poor and the downtrodden, but had failed absolutely. He was equally disgusted with the Congress who could not even behave like a good opposition. Trinamool could be the answer. He at least would repose faith in the new party. We looked at each other in silence. The man seemed to be the epitome of all anti-Congress and anti-CPI(M) sentiment that prevailed at that point of time.

I called a press conference on 28 December 1997 at our home, Basundhara. Hordes of press reporters and TV crews crowded our first floor drawing room. I announced that I would be joining the Trinamool Congress. I said it was a very difficult and very sad decision but after much deliberation I had decided to abide by the sentiments of my workers and voters. There were questions from the media, which I answered with confidence. My joining the Trinamool Congress was the lead news in the papers next morning.

As soon as the press conference was over, Mamata arrived. While we were talking to each other, the telephone rang. It was Somen Mitra. He said, 'Didi, why did you leave us?' It was an awkward moment. Then Saugata Roy spoke and also expressed his displeasure at my leaving the party. Saugata at that point of time was close to Somen. In fact, he fought the ensuing election against Mamata, although later on he came back to the Trinamool fold. I have often wondered at the ease with which politicians keep changing loyalties. But I really felt embarrassed when the Congress leaders called, although I knew in my heart I had taken the right decision according to my conscience.

Mamata invited me to the mass meeting at Shyambazar the

next day. She asked me to come over to her place so that all of us could go together. We reached Shyambazar in a Tata Sumo. Dr Ranjit Panja, Bikram Sarkar and Nayana Bandyopadhyay were in the car with Mamata and me. We were all to be candidates in the Parliamentary election. Nayana was, however, later replaced by her husband, Sudip Bandyopadhyay. There was a sea of humanity at the Shyambazar crossing where five roads converged. We had to wade through the crowd towards the stage. Near the stage were several bamboo barriers at different heights which gave me an eerie feeling because I was seeing double. I saw so many bamboos in front of me that I did not know whether to jump over them or bend and go under them. I heard Mamata shout from behind, 'Give Krishnadi a helping hand.' Somebody picked me up and put me on the other side and without my volition I found myself on the stage. The view from the stage was really stunning! There were unending streams of humanity in all five directions. The statue of Netaji on horseback dominated the scene somewhat like the Statue of Liberty. People perched dangerously on half-built constructions, roofs and balconies, wherever they got a toe-hold.

Since then I have seen many huge meetings, some even bigger than the Shyambazar one, but somehow this first meeting of the Trinamool at the Shyambazar five-point crossing remains etched in my mind. Besides, if there were one hundred thousand people I saw two hundred thousand because of my double vision! There was something electrifying in the atmosphere.

Lengthy and fiery speeches were made. Ten candidates of the Trinamool for the ensuing Parliamentary election were presented to the huge crowd. Mamata was very proud that she had chosen new and distinguished faces. However, some of the faces left us, even before the election. One was Mani Shankar Aiyar who had briefly joined Trinamool. Another was Amjad Ali who joined and left but came back again the next year.

The stage was crowded with media people, particularly the

electronic media who vied with each other for a strategic position. Just before the conclusion of the rally one of the media persons, perhaps Monideepa of NDTV, thrust a piece of paper in my hand which said that Sonia Gandhi had announced her decision to campaign for the Congress in the election. She did not make it clear if she was actively joining politics but that she would tour the country and campaign. The media wanted Trinamool's reaction. I passed the piece of paper on to Mani Shankar who was known to be close to the Nehru-Gandhi family.

Sonia's entry at that point of time did help the Congress and prevented the total disintegration of the party. The exodus from the Congress did not halt altogether, but the flood became a trickle. I wondered if the split in the West Bengal Congress could have been avoided if Sonia had taken the decision a few days earlier. We had already taken the plunge and there could be no looking back.

All the political pundits prophesied that Trinamool was doomed. The Congress votes, they claimed, would split down the middle and thus the CPI(M) and its Left Front would gain. Some people even predicted that they would win all forty-two seats from West Bengal. The BJP's presence in the state was negligible. But if the Trinamool Congress had not been formed, it might have gained a little from the disenchantment with CPI(M) and Congress alike.

January 1998 was hectic for me, though my eyesight improved and I no longer had double vision. Dozens of young workers gathered at our Basundhara home. I spread a big carpet in our garden. The workers sat there and I sat on a chair. We discussed our campaign strategy. It was the month of Ramzan and at sundown the Muslim workers from Mograhat and Baruipur broke their fast and offered namaz. Sugata and I arranged fruits and sweets for them. The election office was still being run by my twosome—Tweedlededum and Tweedlededee, namely, Rankuda and Tushar. They still regularly fought with each other, made up and continued. I had an open jeep this time and my driver was Anjani.

Finance was as usual a headache. Trinamool had no funds and could not be expected to help. Fighting two Parliamentary elections within the space of two years seemed an impossible task. After a day's strenuous campaign I would sit down late in the night with pen and paper and try to figure out what could be the minimum expenses. Sisir was a solid help once again. He stepped up his medical practice and quietly stood by me. So was Sugata. But every penny we spent had been earned by the sweat of our brows.

The other thing that bothered me was the continuous infighting within the Trinamool. The ordinary workers were fine and full of enthusiasm but the second-rung leaders whom I called the 'gruppenfuhrers' bitterly fought against each other. Every locality had at least three to four aspiring leaders. I had to mediate every now and then though I hated it. The physical strain and the mental worry affected my health.

One fine morning I was informed that some disgruntled cadres from Jadavpur were waiting downstairs to meet me. I was irritated but asked them to wait. Then the telephone rang. It was Rankuda from another part of Jadavpur. Rankuda told me the councillor of that ward was complaining that I had done nothing for him in the last one year or so. I was suddenly furious and said, 'Give him the phone. I will give him a piece of my mind.' Since he was the only councillor from our party in the Jadavpur segment, I always complied with all his requests. It was too much to have disgruntled cadres downstairs and a complaining councillor on the phone so instead of being my usual calm self, I shouted at him over the phone.

After this there was oblivion. No, I did not faint or become unconscious. But the next thing I remember was waking up in a hospital bed. It was like being in a dream which now and then got blurred and again got focused. I asked the nurse the time. It was four o' clock in the afternoon. The nurse asked me if I would like to eat something. I suddenly remembered I had not had any lunch, so I asked for soup and a toast. Did I have that? I am not sure. Next scene: I was being taken down in the elevator on a wheelchair. Two nurses held bottles which were strapped to me. They put me in the ICU which looked familiar to me because in recent times Sisir was admitted there and I had been a regular visitor.

I thought, but what am I doing here? Is it a dream? It is Sisir who used to be in the bed and I used to sit in the single chair provided specially for me. But now I was lying in the bed. Why? I suddenly spotted Sarmila standing outside the main door to the ICU. I pleaded with the nurse, 'You see that lady outside—that is my daughter. Please call her. I have to ask her why I have been brought here.' The nurse said, 'Soon it will be 5 p.m. and visiting time. Your family will come to visit you.'

I lay down helplessly and wondered what I was doing there! Nothing seemed to be wrong with me. It had been late morning at home where disgruntled politicos had been waiting downstairs to meet me. Another cantankerous one was on the phone. But after that I could not remember anything.

Only one visitor at a time was allowed in the ICU. The first visitor was Sarmila. I asked her anxiously, 'What am I doing here?' She looked irritated and tense. She said, 'You have asked the question fifty times already and I have told you why. But you keep on asking again and again. That is why you are here.' What! When did I ask her? What was she talking about? I was in total confusion. Surely I had never asked her anything.

The next visitor was Sugata, who was his usual gentle self. To my query he said, 'You see, after speaking to Gopal on the phone you felt unwell. Do you remember the telephone call?' 'Of course I do!' Sugata was delighted that I remembered every detail up to the telephone call. 'Was I able to scold Gopal as much as I wanted?' I asked. 'You did,' said Sugata, 'But after that you looked unwell. We rushed you to Centauri Nursing Home and consulted Dr Debal Sen. He checked you. You are a low blood pressure patient. Your blood pressure had shot up abnormally. On Debal's advice we rushed you to the Kolkata Medical Centre where another doctor saw you. He had an MRI done and checked you thoroughly. He asked you your name, address, telephone number. You answered correctly and promptly. He asked you to give answers to some oral sums which you did very promptly and correctly.' I did not know whether I should feel amused or scared because I did not recollect my interaction with the two doctors at all. I had lost four hours of my life completely from just before midday till 4 p.m. in the afternoon of 31 January 1998. The doctors had decided I was perfectly all right. Only my short-term memory had been slightly affected but it would be restored soon. Sugata said, 'You told the doctor—I am in the midst of an election campaign. I cannot afford to fall ill.' The doctor then asked, 'To which political party do you belong?' I had replied confidently, 'Indian National Congress'. The short-term memory failure had played its trick. I had completely forgotten Trinamool Congress!

After Sugata, the next visitor was Sisir. He was calm and collected as ever. He had no idea about the drama that was being enacted regarding my brief loss of short-term memory. He had finished his work at the Institute of Child Health, had gone to Netaji Bhawan and worked there till two o'clock. When the car did not come to pick him up, he went home in a taxi and lunched alone. Because of the election campaign, our home life was often disturbed. After admitting me at Centauri, Sugata called his father and explained everything. I can still see him in my mind as he stood by the bedside. He wore a black jacket, a ruffled shirt and no tie. He did not betray any signs of extraordinary anxiety on my account. But I knew deep in his heart he was worried. I also tried to pretend as if nothing much has happened. 'Our roles have changed,' I told him. 'It is you who are a frequent visitor to this place.' I had caused a lot of anxious moments to my husband and to my children on that day. Sugata and Sarmila, who had witnessed my loss of memory, were quite distraught. The youngest one, Sumantra, was away in the US and in continuous touch over the phone. Although I was all right by evening, I have an uncanny feeling whenever I look back and think of the lost four hours of my life. After the visiting hour was over, a doctor came to my cubicle and said in a rather familiar manner, 'How are you feeling, Mrs Bose?' I replied, 'All right, thank you!' But in my mind I wondered who the hell is this fellow and why is he trying to be so familiar! He said, 'Do you recognize me?' I said, 'No,' and looked blank though the voice seemed to ring a bell somewhere. Much later I came to know he was the neurologist who had examined me and had asked me to do all the oral sums—which I got right.

My doctor Debal Sen said that I would be under observation for three days. The fourth day was the last day for filing nominations. I asked Sugata to tell Mamata to look for someone in case the doctor did not permit me to contest. Many people did not know about my sudden illness. But one Bengali newspaper came out with the front page news that I was in a serious condition and nearly dying of a brain haemorrhage. My doctor was annoyed. 'Why could not they get the diagnosis right at least?' he asked.

On the fourth day I was discharged from the nursing home. I came to Netaji Bhawan and went from there to the District Magistrate's office in Alipore, to file my nomination papers. Dr Debal Sen said he was amazed at himself. How could he allow a patient just released from the ICU to go straight into an election campaign? At the DM's office a sizeable crowd was waiting for me. There was a lot of slogan shouting when I went in and signed the forms. Flash bulbs went on frequently. The media was somewhat intrigued as to what had actually happened to me.

The campaign for the 1998 election to the twelfth Lok Sabha

was very exciting. Ours was a new party. Trinamool Congress was just a month old. Every day, I opened the newspaper and read that my seat was particularly vulnerable. This time with the Congress votes split between Trinamool and the mainstream party, it was seen to be a hopeless situation. But my own experience on the ground did not match that prediction. Wherever I went in my constituency, there was tremendous enthusiasm among the people. Our first task was to acquaint people with the new symbol. I remember Sonali who accompanied me on some of my trips would be shouting from the jeep, 'Dada, *mone rakhben, jora phool*'—brother, remember the twin flowers. We found people had already accepted the twin flowers. Many did not express their opinion publicly, but there was a feeling people had made up their mind to support me. The slogan that was doing the round those days was '*chup chap phooley chhap*'— quietly, quietly, stamp the flower.

There was another prediction from media persons that because we had made a seat adjustment with the BJP the Muslims would leave us. My experience told me that was not true. My day began early in the morning and went on till midnight. Even at midnight in the Muslim villages women waited patiently at the crossroads. They would offer me flowers. In the dark electricity-less villages women stood with kerosene lamps in hand. When I stood on the jeep they would lift up the kerosene lamps to have a look at my face. They would clamour to touch my hand. I had to make many an unscheduled stop on the way. My driver Anjani, driving precariously along the narrowest of roads, would say, 'Tonight we'll not be able to go home at all if this goes on.' I was deeply touched by the affection of the people. I mention women in particular because Muslim women were traditionally conservative and would not generally come out of their homes at all sorts of unearthly hours. Not that the men were any less enthusiastic.

At Mograhat I found the drinking water that I had promised and also had sanctioned from my MPLAD funds was yet to be implemented, thanks to the lethargic state government agencies. It took ages to move one file from one table to the next. But the village women reposed their trust on me. 'Ma has given us drinking water. It may be delayed, but it will come.' The Jadavpur segment seemed to have gone through a transformation since the last time. It was no longer a hesitant individual or two who came out to listen to me. Hordes of people came out on to the streets and cheered. Women formed a large section of the crowd.

The two Behalas, Behala West in particular, were supposed to be my stronghold. Wherever I went to, either Behala East or West, there was increasing enthusiasm everywhere. Due to lack of funds I was unable to spend much on publicity and I was envious of the CPI(M) candidate whose campaign was full of splendour. Most of the minibuses of Behala had huge boards fitted at the back where the name of the CPI(M) candidate, Malini Bhattacharjee, was painted in many colours. The buses overtook me as I looked on from my old and worn-out jeep. But the driver of the minibus and the young helper who hung precariously from the footboard waved at me lustily and shouted, 'Didi, we are with you.' It boosted my spirits.

In Muslim-dominated Kabitirtha I had a reasonable number of Muslim youths working for me. But my greatest help came from the slums of the Dalits. I had a loyal and dedicated worker in Jai Jai Ram who was their local leader. I sat with him in the sweepers' colony and discussed campaign plans. I was struck by his sincerity. He was uneducated but had a love for education and had opened a school for children, which he ran with the help of some NGOs.

The Congress had put up the MLA of Kabitirtha, Ram Pyare Ram, as their Parliamentary candidate against me. They were hoping that he would be able to split enough votes in this segment so that the CPI(M) candidate could defeat me. Days before the election there was a huge story in the *Anandabazar Patrika* on the front page that I was going to be soundly defeated. 'Malini *joyer mala gaanthchhen*' was the headline—Malini (the feminine form of gardener or mali) is stringing her victory garland. The report was effusive in its praise for the rather disreputable Congress candidate, who the reporter claimed would take enough votes in Kabitirtha to let Malini through.

There is hardly any time to read newspapers during an election. So the next day on a campaign trip to Kabitirtha when I heard people standing in verandahs and rooftops chanting '*Bhoy nei, amra aachhi*'—have no fear, we are with you—I was taken by surprise. After some time I asked someone in the jeep, 'Why are they saying bhoy nei?' I was used to hearing 'we are with you', but had never heard the new addition, 'Bhoy nei'. Were they going to stand up to the usual rigging by the CPI(M)? I was told that the people were responding to a particular report in that day's edition of the Bengali newspaper *Anandabazar Patrika*. I passed through Muslim localities inhabited by Urdu-speaking non-Bengali Muslims. I passed the mosques and heard the usual thunderous roar which I associate with these areas of Kabitirtha: '*Jitega, jitega*, Krishna Bose *jitega*.'

That particular election of 1998 was both exhilarating and exhausting for me. My son Sugata and daughter Sarmila were glued to me throughout the campaign. They did not leave me alone for a single minute. The youngest one, Sumantra, arrived a little later and relieved them somewhat in the final stages of the campaign. I stood on the jeep and was driven miles and miles. There was a spare tyre on the floor of the jeep. I stood on it so that people could see me better. I did not realize it then, but this caused incalculable harm to my knee joints. While I addressed huge gatherings from make-shift stages, either Sugata or Sarmila or both would position themselves just behind me. They had gone through a scary experience during those four days of my strange illness. Sometimes extravagant demands were made on me by my workers or even close aides as they did not realize the

Krishna cycling, Delhi, 1947.

Krishna with her husband, Sisir Kumar Bose,
12 December 1955.

Krishna with her parents, Charu Chandra Chaudhuri
and Chhaya Devi, and son Sugata, 1957.

Krishna with Sisir, Sugata and daughter, Sarmila, 1959.

Krishna with Emilie Schenkl,
Vienna, 1971.

Krishna with Sisir, Annecy, 1993.

Krishna filing her nomination, 1996.

Krishna addressing election rallies, 1998.

Wall graffiti in Calcutta, 1999.

Krishna with the then prime minister Atal Behari Vajpayee, 2000.

Krishna with the then French foreign minister Hubert Vedrine, 2001.

Krishna with (L–R) Zubin Mehta, and Martin and Anita Pfaff.

Krishna with Hillary Clinton, Washington, 2003.

Krishna in Kashmir, 2003.

Krishna with her sons, Sumantra and Sugata, 2004.

Krishna with Mamata Banerjee, 2010.

seriousness of my illness. Once, at 2 a.m., my election agent Rankuda informed me that one of my workers had been picked up by the police and a large number of our young workers were sitting in protest on the main road of Behala. My presence there was imperative. Sugata put his foot down that I could not go. There was some argument and both sides thought that the other was being unreasonable. In the end Sugata went instead of me to the demonstration.

The popular response in 1998 was unbelievable. On one occasion I was in the jeep in the narrow lanes of Behala. About two dozen young men followed me in a procession. Trinamool being a new party and a breakaway group from the Congress, we did not even know who were with us and who were not. But interestingly, the procession kept growing in size. There were gradually one hundred, two hundred, three hundred young men following the jeep. At one point I looked back and the narrow lane looked like a river of humanity. I could not see the end of the procession any more.

The slogans were most interesting. The leader would say— '*Shamne kara?*', the rest of the procession would roar in unison— 'Trinamool, Trinamool.' '*Daine kara?*' Trinamool. '*Bayen kara?*' Trinamool. '*Pichhane kara?*' Trinamool. Who goes in front? Trinamool, Trinamool. Who goes to the right? Trinamool. Who goes to the left? Trinamool. Who is at the back? Trinamool. Hundreds of people clapping hands and chanting slogans followed the jeep. There were other slogans as mesmerizing. In Behala someone gives the lead—'*Ei behalay* Trinamool'—up goes the roar 'Trinamool, Trinamool'; followed by: '*Ei* Jadavpure Trinamool', with the response, 'Trinamool, Trinamool' (since Jadavpur is the whole constituency)—and finally '*Ei Banglaye* Trinamool' culminating with a roar of 'Trinamool, Trinamool.' Translated it would mean Trinamool in Behala, Trinamool in Jadavpur, Trinamool in Bengal, victory to Trinamool.

I was tiring towards the end of the campaign. My lips smiled but I did not smile. I folded my hands, looked at people on both sides of the road, I looked up at balconies and terraces and windows. I gave short speeches. It felt as if someone else was doing all this. I looked forward eagerly to the rest day before polling. On the last day I was again in Behala with young workers and followers. Amidst shouts of 'Trinamool, Trinamool' the campaign drew to a close. I went home, crashed on to the bed and fell asleep. I whole-heartedly agreed with my eldest grandson Tipu who said, 'I think I have had quite enough of this election.'

Downstairs in the office, preparations went on for voting day and counting day. There were the usual arguments between my two campaign managers, Rankuda and Tushar. But they did not have much time to fight. Rankuda on voting day was very busy doing the rounds of election booths. Tushar had to get food packets ready for our workers on both polling and counting days. Sugata and Sarmila set up a sort of control room in the upstairs sitting room. Throughout polling day the phone kept ringing. Complaints from various booths poured in. There was an eagerness on the part of voters to vote. 'We are not being allowed to vote'—someone shouted on the other side of the telephone line, 'they are harassing us'. Sugata and Sarmila kept on faxing complaints to the District Magistrate. They tried to telephone the election observers who had been sent from Delhi. The rigging machinery of the communists was functioning in full force and we tried to counter as best as we could.

Sumantra and I went to some of the booths. We chose what was known as 'sensitive booths'. As I got inside a booth I heard whispers—the candidate has come, careful. These were cadres of the CPI(M). They had tremendous manpower. I did not even have agents in some of the Jadavpur booths. And God alone knew what was happening in the rural booths of Baruipur or Bishnupur or Mograhat. At the Dhalipara booth in Jadavpur our agents were threatened. I asked my young agent, 'Are you afraid?' He replied, 'No I am not but I can tell you a lot of irregularities are going on here.' At the end of the day I received a telephone call that he was unable to come out of the booth. His life was being threatened. Rankuda arrangeed a police van to escort him home.

It was counting day at last. I always felt a kind of detachment to my surroundings on counting days. I was never tense. I could not care very much whether I won or lost. I felt like the epitome of the philosophy of the Gita—'*Dukheshu Nirudbignamona, Sukheshu Bigataspriha, Beeta rage bhoya-krodha.*' I am not anxious about sad experiences—I am unattached to good experiences of life. I am indifferent to attachment, fear, anger . . . But for my workers it is different. For them it appears to be a life and death question. They are ever alert and vigilant. Some malpractices are possible from the other side even during counting.

On the home front, a very calm person like my husband Sisir was somewhat tense. He sat by the telephone throughout the day and night and into the next morning. Sugata and Sumantra were at different counting stations and kept him posted on what was happening. Counting stations are many and far apart. I made a quick tour of all of them. So did Rankuda, my election agent. Only the two of us were allowed to go in. We therefore took different routes. It was a very slow and tedious process. We did not have electronic voting machines at that time. By evening I was leading in both Behalas—East and West—with sizeable margins. Kabitirtha, the Muslim segment, was giving me a big lead.

I slept peacefully at night to be woken up now and then by Sisir's voice. He was speaking on the phone. I trailed in Mograhat, Bishnupur looked to be neck and neck, I had taken a lead in Baruipur. I was not disturbed and slept on. Early in the morning I made another tour of the counting centres. I went into the centre where counting of the Jadavpur segment was going on. This was our most difficult segment. We usually go down here

by thousands of votes. I approached the first table. The young
Trinamool cadre there held my hand, tears in his eyes. I was
alarmed. 'What is the matter?' I asked. He replied in a choked
voice, 'Didi, we are winning!' It was, indeed, amazing. At every
counting table I was in the lead, however small the lead may
have been. It was a kind of history being created in Jadavpur. In
the end I had a handsome lead of over 15,000 votes in that
segment, something unheard of since independence. The MLA
from Jadavpur was Buddhadeb Bhattacharya, a very important
member of the West Bengal cabinet who held the portfolios of
home and police. He later succeeded Jyoti Basu and became chief
minister. All this made my lead in Jadavpur very significant.

It was late morning when Sumantra called me from the main
counting centre at Alipore. 'Can you guess by how much you are
leading now?' 'No, I have no idea. Is it twenty-five thousand?'
He said, 'You are leading by nearly eighty thousand votes at this
moment.' I was summoned to the centre by my workers, all mad
with joy. I got down from the car at the gate and was mobbed
by the crowd on the street. Green abir powder and flowers were
strewn over me. I could hear Sarmila pleading with the police at
the gate to rescue me from the enthusiastic mob. What can a few
policemen do? There was a huge crowd on the street, hysterical
with joy. Someone took a photograph. I was in a yellow sari, my
hair was green with abir and I held a bouquet of red roses.

Trinamool raised great hopes in the minds of the people of
West Bengal. They thought that after a very long time a party
had emerged that could provide an alternative to two decades of
communist rule in the state. There was no doubt that the people
hankered for a change of government. In Delhi there was a lot of
curiosity about the two-month-old party which won seven seats
in and around Kolkata. The mainstream Congress was reduced
to irrelevance with one seat from Malda.

We arrived with a lot of fanfare in Delhi. The press was after
us all the time. There was a lot of curiosity about Mamata, the

leader of Trinamool. Here was a woman who had come up in politics on her own. She was not the wife, widow or mistress of any well-known political leader but a simple worker of the Congress party. In the 1984 Parliamentary election she had won Jadavpur in the wake of the Indira Gandhi assassination, but lost it next time in 1989. It fell on me in 1996 to win back the Jadavpur seat. But Mamata, who had won from south Kolkata in 1991, never looked back. There was a legend woven round Mamata. She lived in a tiny hut in the slums of Kalighat. She always wore inexpensive, cotton saris, white in colour with unobtrusive checks or stripes. She wore a pair of cheap rubber slippers, often torn and put together by a safety pin. At a time when politicians lived in opulence, she cut a different image. And now she was the leader of a new party in West Bengal, the Trinamool Congress. The national and even the international media found her to be a most intriguing phenomenon in Indian politics.

In the days when we were in the Congress, the BJP was looked upon as an untouchable party. We agonized at the thought of Trinamool Congress having to ally with the BJP. In terms of ideology we were poles apart. But the BJP had accepted the rules of coalition politics and unlike the Congress, seemed more accommodating of regional political parties. They agreed to put the question of a Ram temple at Ayodhya, their earlier demand for the abolition of Article 370 in Kashmir, and the issue of a uniform civil code on the back-burner and hammered out a common minimum programme. On our arrival in Delhi we were received by Vajpayee, the prime minister in waiting. Trinamool was being courted as an important ally.

In spite of overtures from the BJP, we decided not to join the cabinet but offered support to the government from outside. The Telegu Desam Party of Andhra Pradesh also did the same, but got the Speaker's post. All the regional allies sent letters to the President pledging support for the Vajpayee government. For some time Jayalalitha's AIADMK caused some trepidation as her letter of support arrived a few days late. We were present at a huge gathering at the courtyard of Rashtrapati Bhawan when Vajpayee was sworn in as prime minister on 13 March 1998.

I was a second-term MP now and was offered a spacious apartment on Baba Kharag Singh Marg. I was quite happy in my North Avenue first-floor apartment, but it had to be vacated for a first-term MP. I moved to my new apartment. It was on the first floor of a multi-storeyed building and Mamata lived on the fourth floor of the same complex. Sudip was a first term MP and entitled to a North Avenue or South Avenue flat. But he was a close confidant of Mamata and his actress-wife Nayana was a very close friend of hers. Mamata wanted them to be near her. So Sudip and Nayana moved to the apartment next to Mamata's on the same floor. Akbar Ali Khondkar, Ranjit Panja and Bikram Sarkar settled down in their respective North Avenue flats. Ajit Panja remained in his bungalow where he had stayed since his days as a minister in the Congress government. The story doing the rounds was that Ajit-babu was unhappy at our decision not to join the ministry. He was looking forward to becoming a minister again. Our Congress colleagues joked with us: 'What have you done! You have laid a sumptuous spread on the dining table and asked Ajit-babu not to touch the food!'

My life as a second-term Parliamentarian started in all earnest. I asked questions and supplementaries on a host of issues, big and small. I once asked a question about why we named our airports with such fanfare if our airlines did not bother to use these names in their announcements. The civil aviation minister gave an assurance that henceforth the names of airports would be mentioned in the announcements before landing. I was a member of the Consultative Committee on External Affairs (CCEA). The committee was headed by Vajpayee himself. He was prime minister and in charge of external affairs as well. I again joined the Parliamentary standing committee on HRD.

Chavan was still in the chair. I was happy to be back with my work on education, culture and family welfare. I was also involved with the sub-committee on national monuments. This gave me a chance to see the old, beautiful churches of Goa and to report on the preservation and maintenance of such monuments.

In Parliament I took up the question of women's representation very seriously. The bill for legislating thirty-three per cent reservation of seats for women was pending since 1996. I had my doubts about the bill then, but had deferred to the consensus among women MPs at that stage. I was of the firm opinion that the bill in its present form would never be passed. So I started to put forward the view that it was the duty of political parties to see to it that they sent a certain percentage of women to the policy-making bodies of the nation. I suggested that while choosing candidates, each party must see to it that neither gender received less than forty per cent of the nominations to Parliament and assembly in each state. Since no party would voluntarily do this, I proposed a two-line amendment in the Representation of People Act to say: first, each party must give at least forty per cent of its nominations to either gender and, second, if any party did not, it would lose the recognition of the election commission and thereby its symbol and, therefore, could not participate in elections.

There was another attempt to introduce the Women's Reservation Bill in Parliament. We women, cutting across party lines, huddled together in seats near law minister Ram Jethmalani, who would get up and introduce the bill. When the Speaker called him, he stood up. But from the other side members of Mulayam's Samajvadi Party and Laloo's Rashtriya Janata Dal (RJD) descended like a swarm on us and rushed towards the Speaker. Some of the members snatched the bill from the minister's hands and tore it into shreds and scattered the bits of paper in the well of the House. I was in the front row and suddenly found that the shawl which was on my shoulder had disappeared. I had also lost one of my shoes. I looked around for my shawl and shoe. But I found a physical scuffle going on in the well of the House. Mamata had rushed into the mêlée. She took one of the members by the collar. I was afraid Mamata was going to be physically hurt. I spotted Akbar, one of our members, who was hefty and strong and shouted to him, 'Akbar, look after Mamata.' But she needed no looking after.

Ram Jethmalani was very clever. He had not been holding the bill in his hands when he stood up, but another piece of paper. Now he brought out the real bill and declared he had introduced the bill. After that the Speaker adjourned the House. Some of the members of the other side threatened to bring a privilege motion against Mamata for catching another member by the collar. Some others sympathized with Mamata.

When Mamata and I reached her flat, I told her in no uncertain terms that I did not approve of her behaviour. I told her, 'Look, you are now the president of a party, leader of a Parliamentary party, you have to think twice before you go in for such things.' Mamata sometimes has a child-like disarming attitude. She told me: 'Look Krishnadi, what could I do? That man pushed me and tripped me. I was about to fall. I raised my hands to hold on to his hair. But the fellow was bald. So I put my hand on his collar. When you see the TV film footage you will find it was he who assaulted me first.' I still remained disapproving of the whole drama when the telephones started to ring. There were calls from unknown persons and they said: 'Mamata, you have done the right thing. This is how these men should be treated.' So I gave up my argument with her. It appeared that people had given her brownie points.

The Telegu Desam Party (TDP) had got the post of the Speaker in the twelfth Lok Sabha. I remember I had suggested to Mamata that she might ask for the Speaker's post for our party. But she did not take me seriously. The BJP had initially agreed to have

Sangma, the previous Speaker, continue in his post. But at the last moment in order to please the TDP they had to dump Sangma, who remained very bitter about this rejection.

Balayogi, the TDP Speaker, was very inexperienced. Whenever the House descended into pandemonium, he kept on saying, 'Not good, not good.' Later he graduated to saying, 'Nothing will go on record.' In spite of initial problems, Balayogi learnt from his experiences and improved a lot. He was a nice man and soon came to be liked by all of us. I also came to know him well and developed a rapport with him. But early in his tenure I wrote a strong letter to him. For a number of days I had been raising my hand till my arm ached, but was unable to attract his attention. He was either guided by the turbaned marshal or more often by members who could shout and get his attention. There were some members who by sheer exercise of lung power got to speak out of turn. 'Mr Speaker, Sir Adhyakshji'—they would shout, drowning out the more civilized attempts by other members to speak.

Frustrated, I wrote a strong letter to the Speaker and said, 'Those of us who abide by rules, raise our hands, keep quiet and wait for your permission, never get to speak. The ones who are unruly and shout always get your attention. And in the process the worst sufferers are the women members.' The Speaker at once called a meeting of the Business Advisory Committee of the House. This is the committee where the leaders of different parties meet and decide on how the business of the House should be conducted. I was asked to be present by invitation. My letter was discussed. Mulayam Singh Yadav, Laloo Prasad Yadav, Somnath Chatterjee and others were present. Somnath Chatterjee was trying to leave midway. I told him, 'Somnath-babu, do not leave. Please, sit down.' He promptly sat down. I also commented that senior leaders always usurp most of the time during discussion. The newcomers and backbenchers should be encouraged and accommodated. Everyone agreed with me and said I had raised valid points. But I really cannot say things changed or improved very much.

The Speaker usually takes delegations of MPs abroad and I went to Morocco with Balayogi. During the tour I came to know him well. He was a very likeable person. I remember he asked me in Morocco what he could buy for his wife. I said, 'Moroccan leather is very good. Maybe you should take a leather handbag for her.' He at once telephoned her and said, 'Madam suggests I take a handbag for you.' And he went on, 'Do you know who Madam Bose is? She is a very active Parliamentarian and she belongs to the illustrious family of Subhas Chandra Bose.'

The Morocco visit was quite interesting. King Hassan was still alive. We were invited to the Parliament on the inauguration day. The members of Parliament or deputies as they are called, were in white gowns—all looking alike. This led to a discussion among us about whether we should also have a uniform dress code for our Parliament. The King arrived in a procession cheered by the people. He blew kisses at them. We had an audience with the King and shook hands with him. When I came back to the hotel the maids came to me and wanted to touch me because King Hassan was their religious leader as well. 'He has shaken hands with you, he has touched you,' they said awestruck. 'Let us touch you, we will feel his touch then.'

Morocco is a beautiful country. Apart from Casablanca and Rabat, we went to Fez and Marrakesh—two very ancient and beautiful cities. The cobbled lanes and bylanes of Fez with small shops on both sides charmed us. But it was Marrakesh I liked most. I told Sisir over the phone that after Weisbaden in Germany, which was our favourite city, Marrakesh in Morocco could be another one in which to retire. A Moroccan family friend came to the hotel and took me out to dinner. He was a very interesting and colourful person with his longish hair in a ponytail.

Whenever I went out on these official tours abroad or even within India, I left a part of me in my Kolkata home—the two-storeyed house that I had named Basundhara and my husband Sisir whom I had to leave behind. Sisir was himself a most busy person professionally and otherwise, though he was not in very good health in recent years. In Morocco I remembered him very much because on the day I left for Morocco I received news that one of our long-time and very devoted workers at Netaji Bhawan had passed away. His name was Naga Sundaram. He had been a soldier in Netaji's Indian National Army and was Sisir's trusted assistant at Netaji Bhawan from 1946 to 1998. I knew Sundaram's passing would hurt Sisir very much. On my way to Morocco I spoke to him from Geneva. He sounded his usual calm self. He said, 'Sundaram's son has arrived. He is very upset. I have told him, "Do not weep for your father, be proud of him".' I repeated this comment to my children when Sisir passed away a couple of years later.

On my last day at Rabat, I went down for dinner to the main restaurant of the hotel. A quartet of two stringed instruments and two small drums was playing. The tune sounded very much like our boatman's tune 'Bhatiali'. The manager came up to me and said, 'Madam, don't leave. We are just about to start a belly dance.' They wanted the Indian lady in a sari to be present for that. That evening I realized how graceful the dance could be and how difficult to perform. The performance was accompanied by a mournful tune. I have the tendency of getting into a shell, detached from my surroundings. I am basically a loner. I thought, what am I doing here far away from my home in an alien land? The music wailed on. I felt like Ruth in Keats' poem *Ode to a Nightingale*, homesick for Kolkata.

Back home I got involved in my developmental work in the constituency. The urban areas were in a somewhat better condition than the rural ones. From my MP development fund I gave grants to schools and colleges, especially girls' schools. Next on my priority list was drinking water and roads. In the rural constituencies, the demand was for electrification which I tried to address.

In May 1998, the village level panchayat elections took place in West Bengal. It was the height of summer but I went in for a gruelling election campaign for our candidates. I had to go into villages in the interior and address small gatherings. Some of the villages could be reached only on foot. At one place I had to row in a canoe-like narrow boat. It was a canal full of weeds—*kachuri pana*. So one man walked in front of the boat in waist-deep water and pushed the weeds aside to make way for the boat I was in. It was difficult to ensure a free and fair election in villages and particularly the remote ones. Even so, in and around Kolkata and south Bengal, Trinamool did fairly well. We were still riding on the popularity of our new-born party.

The election of the Deputy Speaker of the Lok Sabha turned out to be interesting. The BJP proposed the name of a woman member of their party, Rita Verma, for the post. The Congress came up with the name of P.M. Sayeed. Mamata decided to support Sayeed. The prime minister was looking for a consensus so he called a meeting of the leaders of allies. I do not know why Mamata sent me to the meeting to represent our party. 'Why me?' I asked surprised. She gave a peculiar answer. She said, 'I have noticed that whenever you get up in Parliament to speak on Kashmir or Pakistan or whatever, the prime minister looks at you from the corner of his eyes and listens carefully. He will listen to your point.' My brief was that I must go on fighting for P.M. Sayeed. In that meeting, Nitish Kumar of Samata and Maneka Gandhi were somewhat aggressive from the beginning. Maneka said, 'So you want a Muslim. In that case instead of Rita Verma I propose the name of Abdul Gafur of Bihar. Will that do?'

I remember I was very calm and refused to be provoked. I said quietly, 'It is not at all a question of having a Muslim. I am sure Rita Verma will be a very good Deputy Speaker. It is a tradition to let the Deputy Speakership go to the opposition. We only ask for that convention to be respected. The Congress has requested the prime minister to consider P.M. Sayeed for the post. If the BJP agrees to that it will only enhance the respect for the BJP.' Someone said the Speaker's post is not ours, that is why we want the Deputy Speaker's post. I said, 'How can you say that? The Speaker is very much ours. We the allies have chosen him.' The TDP was also present in the meeting. They vigorously shook their head since Speaker Balayogi belonged to their party. BJP leader, L.K. Advani at once stepped in and said, 'Of course the speaker is ours.'

I told the prime minister that after the meeting, he should announce that the decision would be left to him. And then he should make the announcement that in response to the Congress party's request he was accepting P.M. Sayeed. Vajpayee in a rather despondent mood said in Hindi—'*Hamare upar mat chhorna*'—please, do not leave it to me anymore. '*Jo karna abhi kar dijiye*'—do whatever you wish to do now. So it was decided that P.M. Sayeed would be the Deputy Speaker. When the meeting broke up I went over to the prime minister and said, 'I am sorry.' He smiled.

The year 1998 turned out to be that of our nuclear summer. When the news of our nuclear tests in May became public, there was jubilation among large sections of the people. Many overseas Indians also rejoiced. There was a widespread feeling that India had at last arrived. However, the intelligentsia expressed its concern and reservations. Pakistan responded with a series of nuclear tests of their own. The international community criticized India severely. Japan put an embargo on all aid projects, excepting humanitarian ones and the US came down heavily on us and clamped sanctions which hurt India economically. Prime Minister Vajpayee assured the world there would be no 'first use' by India. He also emphasized that we had done this as a 'minimum deterrent'. The opposition in Parliament demanded a debate and the Speaker fixed a date.

That weekend I was going to Kolkata. Upon my return on

Monday, I was supposed to take part in the debate. Sisir and I waited in the lounge of the airport. I did not usually go to the VIP lounge to which I was entitled because I always preferred the ordinary executive lounge. That Friday afternoon as I waited in the executive lounge a short, dark-complexioned man walked in. He had long grey hair falling on his shoulders. I recognized him because his photographs had been on the front page of newspapers—he and Vajpayee standing at Pokhran, our nuclear test site. In some of the photographs where he was without his helmet, his flowing grey hair covered half his face. This was A.P.J. Abdul Kalam, the scientist.

I put down my newspaper and walked straight to him. I introduced myself. I said, 'I am a Member of Parliament. I have to take part in the nuclear debate next week. What do I say?' He looked up at me and said, 'Look, please remember that if you are powerful, the whole world looks up to you. If you are weak, no one cares for you and does not pay any quarter to your views. Keep this in mind and then express whatever is your opinion.' He chatted with Sisir and me for some time. With Sisir he talked about his uncle Netaji Subhas Chandra Bose. I had no idea, on that day, that this scientist would become the President of India in future. And that one day I would welcome him at Netaji Bhawan as President.

The Indian and Pakistani prime ministers—Vajpayee and Nawaz Sharif—met for the first time after the nuclear tests at the SAARC summit in Colombo in July 1998. I took part in the debate on foreign policy on 3 August 1998, soon after Vajpayee's return. I had to manage a difficult balancing act. Personally I had strong reservations about the nuclear tests. But I belonged to a party that supported the government. I noted that the tests had 'done away with that very unequal nuclear regime that the nuclear haves wanted to impose on us'. But I urged the prime minister to act on his declared promise of 'responsibility and restraint' and avoid the dangerous course of nuclear weaponization in Asia. I argued in favour of pursuing the path of diplomacy with both Pakistan and China. As for the prime minister's ringing slogan 'Jai Vigyan'—Victory to Science—in the aftermath of Pokhran II, I had this to say: 'When we shall have a useful partnership between politics and science which will eradicate poverty and hunger from this unhappy land, on that day, the Jai Vigyan slogan our Prime Minister has given, will become truly meaningful.'

By late 1998 all was not well at the centre in Delhi. The fragile coalition led by Prime Minister Vajpayee was having problems with one of its partners—the All India Anna Dravida Munnetra Kazhagam (AIADMK) led by Jayalalitha. The BJP always paid extra attention to her and tried to keep her in good humour. Once when she visited Delhi, the local BJP MP Vijay Goel threw a big reception in her honour. I was introduced to her there and she spoke to me in a friendly way. As a matter of fact, she was extra friendly, saying to my surprise how much she had heard about me, read my articles and so forth. I took all this attention with due caution.

Subramanyam Swamy of the Janata Party—a one-member party—had been elected to the Lok Sabha that term. He was at that point of time very close to Jayalalitha. Stories began to circulate that Swamy was plotting to bring this government down. Sonia Gandhi would lead the new government and Jayalalitha would join the cabinet. She also had the ambition of becoming the prime minister in the not too distant future.

Some argued that Swamy would not go the way of the dissolution of Parliament and fresh elections. After all, he had been able to get elected after a very long time. He would not want to take the risk of another election. What he was planning to bring about was a regime change. Jayalalitha would withdraw support from the Vajpayee-led coalition and support a Sonia Gandhi-led Congress government which was expected to be supported by all the opposition parties like Laloo Prasad Yadav's

RJD, Mulayam Singh's Samajvadi Party (SP), the communists from West Bengal and Kerala. Swamy, of course, would have a berth in the cabinet and most probably the finance portfolio. Whenever Swamy entered the Central Hall, the question on everyone's lips would be 'Whom does he wish to destroy?'

Events started to move fast. Jayalalitha arrived in Delhi, we were told, with a large number of trunks which contained the innumerable saris that she would need for the swearing in and other ceremonies. There was a famous tea-party where Sonia and Jayalalitha met. They were the two women who dominated the Indian political scene at that time. But there was another powerful woman politician who was to play a significant role in toppling the government. That was Mayavati of the Bahujan Samaj Party (BSP). The party had a small number of MPs on whose votes much depended.

When Jayalalitha withdrew support from Vajpayee's government, the President of India asked Vajpayee to go in for a confidence vote. Many criticized President K.R. Narayanan for insisting on this. During the debate on the confidence motion, Mayavati declared on the floor of the House that she thought both sides were equally unacceptable and so her party will not take part in the voting. That meant they would abstain. This was good news for the ruling coalition. It meant the government would not fall. When an MP announces something on the floor of the House, it is usually taken to be sacrosanct and inviolable.

The vote took place next morning. I was about to enter the chamber when I was face to face with Sangma who told me – 'Didi, did you hear that Mayavati will vote with the opposition, so the government's fall is imminent?' I was taken by surprise. I went in and told Mamata the news. She could not believe it and said the opposition was trying to spread panic. Even this morning Vajpayee had spoken to Mayavati, she told me.

Just before the vote, there was an exciting and tense moment. Among the Congress members sat a member from Orissa who had just been asked by his party to take up the post of chief minister of Orissa. He had been sworn in as chief minister. Technically he could retain his membership of Parliament for six months if he so wished. The question arose if he could at all sit in the chamber and vote. The Speaker went through rule books and precedents. On a similar occasion when Siddhartha Ray, who had become the chief minister of West Bengal had entered the chamber, the then Speaker of the House had ordered him to leave the chamber forthwith. The chief minister of a state is part of the state legislature and should not be inside the Parliament at all.

The Speaker gave the ruling that he would leave the matter to the conscience of the member. The member sat through the proceedings and took part in voting. His party, if not his conscience, instructed him to do that. We voted electronically. The red and green lights came up on the board. The government fell by one vote. Mayavati and her block had of course voted with the opposition. But the clinching vote was from the chief minister of Orissa.

The Members of Parliament still hoped that the Lok Sabha would not be dissolved and no fresh elections would be necessary. Sonia Gandhi claimed at Rashtrapati Bhavan that she had the magic number to form the government. But she had spoken too soon. The numbers did not add up. She asked for more time. The President agreed and gave her time. This made some members comment that President Narayanan was being partisan because of his long association with the Congress party. Mulayam Singh's Samajvadi Party did not agree to have Sonia as prime minister. The question of her foreign origin was brought up. After a tussle for a few days Sonia Gandhi had to announce that she did not have the requisite numbers to form the government.

The Speaker adjourned the House sine die and we faced another Parliamentary election. The twelfth Lok Sabha had lasted all of thirteen months instead of five years. Members were upset.

They demanded that in future when confidence or no confidence motions were brought, the House must be assured that the movers of the motion are ready to provide an alternative government.

For a second time I bade goodbye to the trees and statues around the Parliament House. It was April, spring time. The trees looked beautiful with flowers in blazing red and subdued violet. There was no certainty that I would come back for a third time.

Sunset of the Century

The sudden fall of the government created an unexpected difficulty for me. Sisir and I were supposed to leave for Pakistan in a couple of days. We were part of an unofficial delegation of the Bengal Initiative going to Lahore. Both of us had diplomatic passports but I was no longer an MP and the diplomatic passports ceased to be valid. I was rendered stateless. Anyway, hurried trips to the passport office resulted in new passports and we were able to join the tour.

I always looked forward to trips to Pakistan. For historical reasons we had close family friends there. Most of the officers of Netaji's Indian National Army came from Punjabi Muslim families. After the partition of India, they settled in their homes in Pakistan and served the newly created nation to the best of their ability. But these officers in their hearts remained forever loyal to the memory of Netaji Subhas Chandra Bose under whose leadership they had fought for the independence of the subcontinent. These families were like part of my own family. In Lahore there was Colonel Arshad and his family, but we usually stayed with the daughter and son-in-law of General Zaman Kiani who also lived in Lahore. Mrs Kiani was in Rawalpindi. Colonel Dara's family was split between Islamabad and Lahore. Colonel Dara, apart from his INA background, was a famous hockey player. There were friends in Peshawar as well. It was good to meet them whenever the opportunity came. Besides, Sisir had a historical connection with Lahore. We had last visited the city in

1994 on the fiftieth anniversary of his solitary confinement in the Lahore Fort by the British government on the charge of assisting his uncle Subhas Chandra Bose.

On the political side, we were going to Pakistan at a time when there was a general thaw in Indo-Pak relations. This was late April 1999. The prime minister, A.B.Vajpayee, had undertaken his famous bus journey to Lahore in February. The Lahore declaration had been signed between Vajpayee and Nawaz Sharif. The outlook on the Indo-Pakistan front looked reasonably bright.

On our arrival in Lahore we were received by G. Parthasarathy, our high commissioner. In Lahore Sisir and I met all our Pakistani friends and their families. This time we did not stay with Zahida and Farid because we had to move around with the delegation. Many came to meet us at the hotel. Sisir and I went to the Human Rights Commission of Pakistan to meet old friends Asma Jahangir, I.A. Rahman, Mubashir Hasan, and others. Some meetings with political personalities were set up including Nawaz Sharif and some cabinet ministers. But inscrutable are the ways of God. I fell ill in Lahore. Pakistani doctors treated me and family friends came to see me. I could not take part in some of the important political events. Later I thought that whatever happens is for the good. No sooner were we back from Pakistan than the Kargil war broke out. Friends in Kolkata asked us, whatever did you do? You go to Pakistan and start an Indo-Pak war!

The prime minister's Lahore initiative thus came to naught. The hawks in Vaypayee's own party and his opponents criticized him. They said while the prime minister extended his hand of friendship, the Pakistani leadership conspired behind his back and attacked us in Kargil.

The elections for the thirteenth Lok Sabha would be held at the end of September or beginning of October, we were told. There was a general sense of election fatigue among all. Voters and candidates alike felt that to go through the process of a general election every year was really too much. There was an awkward gap of nearly six months between the fall of the twelfth Lok Sabha and the election for the thirteenth one. It seemed to be taken for granted that I would stand again from Jadavpur. If I won for the third time in a row, it would indeed be a remarkable performance in a communist stronghold like Jadavpur.

Meanwhile, in early June, Sisir and I decided to take a week's holiday in Mumbai because it would be our eldest grandson's sixth birthday on 2 June 1999. We always tried to be together on his birthday and travelled to London if he was there. Our elder son Sugata also made it a point to come for his nephew's birthday. Sugata arrived from Boston on 1 June. Sumantra was away in Turkey and could not make it. The birthday went off very well. But the next day Sisir complained he was not feeling well and soon his condition became critical. We moved him to the Breach Candy hospital. He suffered a heart failure in the hospital and was removed to the ICU. The five-day holiday we had planned turned out to be a three-week sojourn. Sugata and I became permanent fixtures at Breach Candy hospital. I preferred to sit out on the corridor and watch the changing colours of the Arabian Sea, from morning to evening, going inside the ICU whenever allowed. A long-time friend, Dr Erin Broacha, who was Sisir's student in her younger days, was a great help. She also kept vigil with us. Dr Udwadia of the Breach Candy hospital called Sugata and me one day. What he said made us aware that we did not have much to hope for.

Every morning I had a call from the Prime Minister's Office (PMO) asking me if I needed anything and if the prime minister could help in any way. Sudheendra Kulkarni was usually the person who phoned from the PMO. I told them I would like to shift Sisir to Kolkata and I would need help at that time. I was thinking of taking him on a stretcher on the flight but the doctors did not allow that. When he recovered somewhat he was moved to a hospital room. After keeping him under watch for a few days they decided to release him.

The PMO instructed the Maharashtra government to give me any help I needed. I only asked for a good ambulance. A cabinet minister arrived with the ambulance. There were a large number of police officers. They wanted a police jeep with a siren to precede the ambulance so that we did not get stuck in a jam. But I refused the police escort. Sisir, who was very weak and pale, smiled and said that the presence of so many policemen reminded him of his prison days. At the time of his first imprisonment Sisir had nearly died of typhoid fever in the Presidency Jail in Kolkata. He was removed as a prisoner to the Kolkata Medical College hospital where he was kept under armed guard.

It was a hospital to hospital transfer. Sugata and I brought him to Kolkata and admitted him in his usual Centauri Nursing Home. The flight from Mumbai to Kolkata was fine. But the journey from Kolkata's Netaji Subhas Airport to Centauri in a very poor non-AC ambulance was a nightmare. The arrangements at the Kolkata end were not satisfactory. His doctor friends lamented later that they had not been informed in time about his arrival. Sisir suffered a setback due to the journey and took quite some time to recover his strength.

I had to resume my political work gradually. Visits to different parts of the constituency started. Workers and cadres also started to throng the downstairs office. My two election managers—Rankuda and Tushar—were back in the office.

Sisir came home from the nursing home. It was heartening to see his gradual recovery. He wanted to get back to work. But we stopped him. He was allowed to go for a short while to the Institute of Child Health and Netaji Bhawan in the morning. In the evening he was allowed to see two patients. As a doctor he was in great demand so to restrict patients to two was extremely difficult. It took a lot of argument and persuasion to explain the state of his health to his patients. Sisir looked very well and in two months nobody could guess how seriously ill he had been. He always looked ten years younger than his real age. On our return from Pakistan after the last trip, the immigration officer had looked at him and his birth date on the passport and exclaimed—'*Etna umar me etna achha sakal*'—such good looks at this age. The lady standing in the queue behind him said, '*Kya aap nazar lagate hani*'—don't say that because an evil eye may fall on him.

It was I who was not feeling exactly well that summer. Sisir's critical illness had been a mental strain. Then I had severe pain in both knees. It was arthritis made worse by two gruelling election campaigns and now I was going into a third one. The jeep that I had for this campaign was fitted with an improvised chair so that I did not have to be on my legs all the time. Somehow I never used the chair. I kept standing on the seat and sometimes sat on the back of the seat.

From August the campaign started in earnest. My long time housekeeper, Gomma, rendered single-handed service. She looked after Sisir and saw to it that he had his medicines and meals at the proper times. She also took care of two grandchildren—one six and the other three years old since their mother was away in London and their father in Mumbai.

In September it rained a lot. Every day I came back drenched. Then there were floods in different parts of the state. Even low-lying areas in Kolkata got flooded. Our workers had to rescue slum-dwellers and poor people and house them in temporary shelters. Altogether it was a difficult campaign. I went through a replay of the first two elections. An arduous campaign standing on my jeep preceded voting day followed by counting day. The CPI(M) changed its candidate. In place of Malini Bhattacharjee, who had lost to me twice, they put up a tough party man, Kanti Ganguly, well known for his strong-arm tactics. He knew how to manipulate the election machinery. But at the same time he was media savvy and got on well with people. A few weeks before the election there was a big fire in the *Anandabazar Patrika* office. *Anandabazar* was the most powerful newspaper in West Bengal. Pictures of Kanti Ganguly at the forefront of the fire-fighting operation appeared in the press. The newspaper naturally was very sympathetic towards him. For other reasons also my cadres felt somewhat crest-fallen. Kanti Ganguly would hug anyone on the street or in the wayside stalls and say, 'I am Kanti Ganguly. Please, remember me!' I was not in the habit of hugging anybody and everybody. The cadres knew that. When just before the election, Kolkata got flooded—there was Kanti Ganguly wading in the flooded areas with a towel wrapped around him. No, I could not be expected to match that though I did visit all the temporary camps and shelters where these unfortunate people were put up. From my meagre election funds we had to buy rice and lentils to feed them khichhuri for days.

Kanti Ganguly conducted an aggressive campaign. There were more violent clashes in 1999 than there had been in 1996 or 1998. He behaved as if he had already won. This was good psychological warfare meant to demoralize the other side. On counting day he even started bursting crackers, in anticipation of victory, when the counting had barely begun. At the counting centre their boys told our boys—this time Trinamool faces sure defeat. So when I started to lead by leaps and bounds our boys asked them—'So what now!' The CPI(M) cadres answered it is not a Trinamool victory—it is Krishna Bose winning because of her personal pull. Our boys retorted, 'So when we lose Trinamool loses and when we win even that is not a Trinamool victory.' They nearly came to blows.

I had never met Kanti Ganguly before. Even during the campaign our paths never crossed. After my election victory I had gone to a Durga Puja pandal in Jadavpur to inaugurate the puja. A man with a dancing gait came over to me and said, 'Didi, I am Kanti Ganguly. I am your younger brother. You have defeated me.' I looked at him, smiled and said, 'If my younger brother had won the election, Didi would have been truly happy.' There was a rush among the photographers for a picture.

My election results this time came out late in the night. My constituency did not have electronic voting machines though three Kolkata seats were given these machines. So for the third time I went through the tedious counting process. Day rolled into night and morning. It was about 2 a.m. when I was called to the Alipore counting station. I had won by a margin of nearly 70,000 votes, taking forty-nine per cent of the total votes polled for all candidates to the CPI(M)'s forty-three per cent. Sisir said he wanted to come with me. 'At this time of night?' I hesitated, considering his recent illness. But he insisted.

At that hour of the night there was a huge crowd of supporters on the street. There were the usual scenes of jubilation. I can see in my mind Sisir happily clicking away his camera while Sugata and I moved around. The boys clamoured to be in the photographs and jostled for a place near me.

Mamata decided to join the cabinet this time. She was given the railways portfolio, a very important portfolio in India. The railways budget was prepared separately and was placed by the railway minister in Parliament even before the general budget. The railway network is huge in India and it is a large employer. There were problems in the railway ministry as well. The old worn out rail lines needed repair and continuous maintenance. The innumerable railway bridges across the country were in a dilapidated condition and a threat to railway safety. In order to increase revenue, passenger and cargo fares had to be hiked. This was always looked upon as an unpopular measure. So observers were curious to see how Mamata would handle the problems.

After our 1998 victory, some industrialists had approached me and offered to help Mamata. They wanted to talk to her. They approached me because to them Mamata was an unknown quantity. They knew me, even if superficially, from my pre-politics days. Some of them knew me as the wife of Dr Sisir Kumar Bose, a very respected name in West Bengal. The communist rulers in West Bengal had some pet industrialist houses of their own which they patronized. But other independent-minded industrialists were keen to forge a relationship with Mamata. She was not even a minister at that time. But every time I tried to broach the subject I found Mamata totally disinterested in long-term planning and economic policy. She was only interested in immediate populist measures. Even so, I tried to tell her that just to say that we must get rid of CPI(M) rule, is not enough. We have to tell the people what we can offer them, what our policies are. We need to be clear about our alternative policies in the industrial, agricultural and service sectors. But Mamata preferred agitation and populist gimmicks to constructive work.

When Mamata became railway minister, the Confederation of Indian Industries(CII) approached me again. They wanted to offer their suggestions for the coming railway budget. Mamata did not respond. The railway ministry was housed in a huge building called the Rail Bhavan. There was a cute little engine in front of the building. We went to see her in her new office. In one of her childlike gestures she said to me, 'Krishnadi, see how nice the bathroom is.' It was nice, I agreed. Whenever we went she would order tea or coffee or, may be, soup for us. And as soon as it was brought she put her hand inside the cloth bag which usually hung from her shoulder, brought out some money and paid up promptly. She made it a rule that even when she herself had a cup of tea, she paid. Mamata's honesty was admired by everyone. She stood apart from the corrupt politicians of the day. But there were soon whispers that the people she gathered around her were not that honest. Some of them were making money in an underhand manner. If it were so, it was always difficult to either prove or disprove such allegations.

We all knew that she was against any kind of fare hike. It will hurt the people, she argued. But to gather revenue was extremely urgent. She came up with all sorts of ideas. She wanted to lease unused railway property and raise money. She said, 'In India a very large number of people travel ticket-less. Even if the ticket collectors and ticket checkers were a little more vigilant, there should be a rise in ticket collection money'. So at railway stations tickets began to be checked vigorously. I told Mamata one day, 'Do you know what my maid who comes to work for the day was saying?' The maid had demanded a raise in her salary from me. The maid's argument was since Mamatadi initiated vigorous ticket checking, she had to buy tickets every day. That cost a lot, while before she used to travel ticket-less. There were a large number of women who came from villages every morning to work as maids in city homes and went back at night. I had no idea that Mamata had taken a mental note of what I said. In her budget she introduced an inexpensive three-month pass for women who came to work in the cities, the vegetable vendors who brought vegetables to the markets, the workmen who came to work for building houses. So the daily workers could use the pass. The MPs or MLAs could issue a certificate saying that such a person came from a poor family and is eligible for the pass.

My sister-in-law Anita, daughter of Netaji Subhas Chandra Bose, was visiting me in Delhi that winter. On the day Mamata presented the budget, Sisir and Anita sat in the Distinguished Visitors enclosure and watched the proceedings. This was February 2000. Sisir had turned eighty on 2 February 2000. Anita had decided to come and join in the family celebrations but she could not make it on time. She was delayed and joined us in Delhi in late February. In Kolkata we had a dinner for Sisir's birthday. We put up a shamiana in the rear garden of Basundhara and the trees were strung with colourful lights. We had all our close friends with us. Sugata, Sarmila and Sumantra had ordered a huge birthday cake which was a replica of Netaji Bhawan and was admired by everyone. There was no music that evening. But it was decided that Sarmila would give a recital of Sisir's favourite

D.L. Roy songs later in the year. That was one of the last happy family celebrations that we had. Anita could not join us then. But here she was with us in Delhi.

Mamata had become the railways minister and Ajit Panja the minister of state for external affairs. He was happy to be a minister again. Sudip Bandyopadhyay had become our chief whip. Mamata kept on saying that she wanted me to be on the panel of chairpersons. When the Speaker or the Deputy Speaker was not present someone from the panel of chairpersons conducted the proceedings of the House. Everyone from the panel took a turn. I was not at all enthusiastic about this and pleaded with Mamata to spare me. But she kept on trying to include my name on the panel.

One afternoon in December 1999 we were about to order lunch in the Central Hall. For some reason Sugata was with me. My other party colleagues, except Mamata, were also there. Suddenly we found Mamata rushing in. She came towards me and said, 'Give me your hand' and vigorously shook my hand. To the others she declared, 'Today's lunch will be on Krishnadi. Let us all congratulate her.' My heart sank. I thought, now she must have got me into the panel of chairpersons! But no! She announced, 'I have just heard Krishnadi has been appointed the chairperson of the parliamentary standing Committee on External Affairs (CEA).' Thus began my new responsibility in the thirteenth Lok Sabha.

This was indeed an onerous task. The committee system in our Parliament had started only from 1994. My predecessors as chairpersons of the CEA were Atal Behari Vajpayee for four years and then I.K. Gujral for one year. I found my committee to be a star-studded one with all the who's who of the two chambers represented in it. There were Karan Singh, L.M. Singhvi, Ranganath Mishra, T.N. Chaturvedi from the Rajya Sabha; R.L. Bhatia and Sushil Shinde from the Lok Sabha. Each year the composition changed slightly. And I had more and more veteran

Parliamentarians as members of my committee. At various times I had Natwar Singh, Fali Nariman, Kuldip Nayar, Arun Jaitley, Suresh Prabhu, Jana Krishnamurty, Maneka Gandhi, Jaya Prada, Venkaiah Naidu and so many others. It was my good fortune that they accepted me with warmth and affection. And I had full cooperation from all the members cutting across party lines.

One of our tasks was to scrutinize the budget of the external affairs ministry, write a report and have it adopted by the committee. Our other job was to interact with the large numbers of foreign delegations that descended on Delhi from time to time. My job as chairperson of the committee was not only to have discussions on bilateral issues but also explain India's foreign policy stand on various issues of international importance. I enjoyed my job and tried to do my duty to the best of my ability.

One of the most important delegations that arrived in early 2000 was the one that accompanied President Bill Clinton. Nearly all the Indian Members of Parliament were charmed by Clinton. After he had addressed the joint session of the two Houses, there was a rush of MPs anxious to shake hands with him. Members jostled with each other and jumped over benches to do so. I did not quite like the way my colleagues were going overboard. The current joke was that if President Clinton had asked the Indian Parliament to sign any agreement, CTBT or whatever, at that moment, the Parliamentarians would have been ready to sign then and there.

I took care of the US delegation that sat at one side in the Central Hall. This included Gary Ackerman, Jan Sckakowsky, Shiela Jackson Lee, Jim McDermott and others. Next morning some newspapers commented that while everyone's attention was on President Clinton and while some of the women members of the Congress party were more interested in attempting to attract Sonia Gandhi's attention, it fell on the 'conscientious Krishna Bose' to look after the foreign delegates. The CEA had an interactive session with the delegates the next day where a variety of issues were discussed. The visit of President Clinton marked a turning point in Indo-US relations.

Since our independence, India had pursued an independent foreign policy. In the days of the cold war, India had decided to remain non-aligned. Some other countries were attracted by India's policy and NAM or the Non-Aligned Movement was born. India was a leader of the non-aligned movement and had exercised a moral authority over the international community. However, India was always perceived to be tilting towards Soviet Russia which indeed had helped India in moments of crisis. Indo-US relations, however, remained problematic. But the world had changed with the disintegration of the Soviet Union. We were faced with a unipolar world in a military-strategic sense where the US was the only super-power. Under the changed circumstances India started cautiously to establish a closer relationship with the US. President Clinton's visit brought the two countries closer. India's then foreign minister, Jaswant Singh carried on long confabulations with Strobe Talbot. As chairperson of the CEA I closely observed the transformation in Indo-US relations between 1999 and 2004.

I was taken to be a rather unconventional chairperson of the CEA since I was determined to make the committee stronger in its role of overseeing the conduct of India's foreign policy. The Senate Foreign Relations Committee was my model, even though I did not succeed in making my committee as powerful as its American counterpart. I did things which were not usual and raised some eyebrows in the bureaucracy. At every meeting a written welcome speech was placed before me. I found these very stereotyped and boring so I started to speak extempore. The welcome speech became much more spontaneous.

After I assumed office, the high commissioners of African countries expressed a desire to come and meet me. I thought it was an excellent idea and at once fixed a date and a committee room for the meeting. There were immediately a lot of questions from the ministry of external affairs as to why all of them wanted to come together. If they wanted to call on me, it could be one at a time or in smaller groups. In order to bypass all this I announced that the committee will have an informal meeting with all the heads of African missions in Delhi. That term 'informal' came to my aid many a time afterwards. All the African high commissioners turned up—some in suit and tie and some in their colourful national dresses. A few of them were women. We had a very free and frank conversation about national and international issues over tea, coffee and snacks. Some of their local problems also came up for discussion. For example, they needed more space for their diplomatic missions as Delhi's main diplomatic area—Chanakyapuri—was already fully occupied and a new diplomatic enclave for Delhi was becoming necessary. I came to know many of these diplomats quite well. The high commissioner of Senegal had been in Delhi for a very long time and was currently the dean of the diplomatic community. He confided to my son afterwards: 'When we first met your mother in that meeting we were very much surprised. She appeared to be a very unusual woman. We discussed among ourselves, who is she? Where has she come from?' I do not know what they had expected and why they were so awestruck.

The Arabs came next. Again there were the initial protestations from the external affairs ministry. Again I took recourse to an informal tea meeting. Again there was a free and frank exchange of views. The Arab diplomats implied that they were apprehensive because India and Israel were at that time building a close relationship which they thought would harm India's friendship with the Arab world. We assured them that there may be new friendships, but never at the cost of old ones. The only drawback of the meeting was that the Arab diplomats could not eat anything because it was Ramzan. We decided to have another meeting later when they would be able to accept our hospitality.

I was fortunate to have the cooperation of successive foreign secretaries and that of the other senior officers of the MEA. Lalit Mansingh was the foreign secretary when I took over as the chairperson. It was a pleasure to work with him. Sisir and I came to know him very well and liked him very much. The next foreign secretary was Chokila Aiyar. At that time Nirupama Rao was the spokesperson for the MEA. I had an excellent rapport with these two women who came frequently to testify before the committee. Kanwal Sibal was the third foreign secretary I worked with. I had first met him in Paris when he was the ambassador there. He too was an efficient foreign secretary.

Early in the year I was asked to join the Inter Parliamentary Union delegation that was going to Jordan. Speaker Balayogi was leading the delegation. A Royal Jordanian flight brought us to Amman. Najma Heptulla was still the chairperson of the IPU. Margaret Alva was also in the delegation. I did have a chance to participate in the deliberations but what we spoke was prepared by the officers. I felt better when I could intervene in the middle of a discussion where I could make my own points. I had to put up the wooden plaque with India written on it to be recognized by the president of the meeting.

Margaret and I found out that there was a place in the Committee for Women which was designated for Asia. These things are usually negotiated beforehand in behind-the-scenes parleys. Nobody from India had taken care of it until the morning of the election. Margaret was interested in the committee so I hurriedly spoke to the representatives of Nepal and Bangladesh who agreed and Margaret was elected. Next day another place in the committee on the West Asia peace process had to be filled. Margaret suggested that I join that committee and other Asian countries readily agreed. However we got a message from Najma Heptullah that we should not do this since India, that is Najma, was the current president of the IPU and people might think she was keen to have Indians on all the committees. That seat remained vacant as other Asian countries had not put up any name because they had agreed on India. Most Indian members of the delegation were not happy with the argument put forward by Najma. I was told that she was not happy that Margaret had got into an important committee without her knowledge.

King Abdullah of Jordan addressed the inaugural assembly of the IPU. Later we, the delegates from India, had an audience with him. He was young, smart and spoke well. At an evening reception we also met his beautiful Palestinian wife. During this tour I started to feel sharp pain in my knee joints. Climbing stairs was proving to be difficult but I put on a brave face. The German delegation to the IPU invited us for lunch one day. Many of the German delegates knew my brother-in-law, Martin Pfaff, who was an SPD member of the Bundestag. I met Angelika, a German MP, who not only knew a lot about India but also knew a few Tagore songs.

There was a gala reception on the shore of the Dead Sea one evening. The area was covered with huge tents and enormous quantities of fruits and other delicacies were laid out on tables where we ate and chatted with friends from different countries. Angelika was at my table and I asked her what Tagore songs she knew. And she sang softly—*Mone ki dwidha rekhe gele chole…*

The sun set over the Dead Sea. Across the sea was Jerusalem. As darkness descended, fireworks began. The sound of crackers shook the sand dunes at the back of the beach and the sky lit up with the dazzling display. I am from India—the land of Diwali, the festival of lights, but even I was charmed by the beautiful fireworks that went on for quite some time.

Some of us decided to go to Jerusalem. We were told we would need new passports to do so because from Amman we were to go to Dubai but we would not be able to enter Dubai with an Israeli stamp on our passports. Overnight we got new passports which were marked 'for Israel only'. We were driven to the border and crossed into no man's land. Another car came from the Israel side and drove us into the city. Jerusalem looked very green and

I wondered how they kept the city which was in the middle of a desert so green. I went to the Wailing Wall and prayed there. Just beside that was the beautiful golden mosque. We climbed through the narrow lanes towards the hill where there was a majestic church. We were shown where Christ was crucified and the place where his body was kept. When we walked back down the narrow lane I bought a small wooden cross as a memento. I placed it in my corner of worship at my Delhi home along with pictures of Goddess Kali and Lord Krishna. We drove further to Bethlehem and here we saw Christ's place of birth. Jerusalem and Bethlehem looked so peaceful that it was hard to believe they existed in an area where violence would erupt every now and then. Back in Amman I had one more engagement to keep. King Abdullah had ascended the throne after his father King Hussain's death but there had been a general belief, until the last moment, that King Hussain would nominate his brother Hasan to be the next king. The brother was loyal to the king and looked after the kingdom but the king finally chose his son. As uncle of the present king, Prince Hasan was still powerful and active. He had addressed one of our IPU meetings and spoken very well. However, I had asked for a separate appointment with his Pakistani wife, Princess Savath-el-Hasan. I knew her mother Shaista Suhrawardy whom I had met in Karachi and in London. Whenever I met Shaista she asked me about Kolkata and the Suhrawardy family house on the road now named Suhrawardy Avenue. She was very nostalgic about Bengal and spoke a lot about her brother H. Suhrawardy. She had brought Suhrawardy's son to meet me and my husband Sisir in London. We tried to bring her to Kolkata once to attend an international seminar at Netaji Bhawan but she said though she lived with wonderful memories of Kolkata she had lost any wish to go back again. After our meeting with her she said she again had an urge to return because she felt she had a home there with us. In her Karachi home she showed us photographs of Netaji Subhas Chandra Bose and Suhrawardy

standing in front of their Kolkata house. In one of our long
conversations I had asked Shaista how come after so many years
of independence both India and Pakistan remained so poor, so
backward in health and education. She recited an Urdu couplet
in reply. Soon after independence, power went to the hands of
people who were not participants in the fight for the liberation
of the subcontinent. '*Manzil unko mile, jo sharike safar na the*'—
they went past the post who were not in the race at all. Shaista's
poor health and age made it impossible for her to travel to
Kolkata. She used to tell me about her daughter Savath and the
days she sometimes spent with her in Amman. I was invited to
the palace to meet Savath-el-Hasan. The Indian ambassador in
Jordan accompanied me. I had a very pleasant conversation with
her about her mother and also about current politics.

On my return from Amman I found Sisir had arrived in Delhi
to spend a week with me. So I poured out to him all my
experiences, all the stories of Amman and Jerusalem. I had written
two poems while in Amman. One was written while I passed
through the Arab refugee quarters of the city. At the IPU that
year we were specially discussing refugee issues. India had tried
to make terrorism the main topic, but the consensus was for the
refugee problem to be the main item on the agenda. I read out a
poem to Sisir that I had written on *The Refugee Camp at Jabal*
and another on *The Ruins of Jarosh*. The day I visited Jarosh,
my colleagues and other delegates walked around the ruins. With
my arthritic knees I decided to sit alone in the shadow of a ruined
column and muse rather than walk around. The result of the
musing was this:

On the Ruins of Jarosh
The desolate rows of ionic columns
Look on in silence reminding
You of bygone days of glory
The city square of cobbled

Stones once full of life and celebration
Now stare at the azure sky

From the roofless temple of Zeus
The gods send a message
Forget your pride, man
See the futility of strife
Violence, conflict.
Where have they disappeared?
The Emperors of yesteryears
The invincible army that
Held the world to ransom?
Where are they?
Power and pride are transitory
Bow your head to the
Eternal Being.

I could never rest until I had shared with Sisir and my children all that happened around me. It had been a long-standing habit of mine. All my children left home early for higher studies abroad. Sugata went to Cambridge in England, and Sarmila was in her undergraduate college in Bryn Mawr, and later at Harvard. I wrote long letters to them twice a week. I wonder now how I managed. It would be the same letter to all so I used carbon paper to make copies. I saw to it that each received originals in turn. I wrote about little things that happened at home, about social gossip doing the rounds as also important political events in Bengal and in India. I always felt the children must not feel they were away from home although physically they were thousands of miles away. I must say they kept up the flow of correspondence reasonably well, if not as vigorously as I did.

By the time my younger son, Sumantra left for higher studies abroad, telephones had become much more efficient and e-mail had come into vogue. I still think the art of letter-writing cannot be replaced by short e-mails. I still have the heaps of letters stacked away somewhere. Sometimes we joked among ourselves that if any researcher ever had to study and use the letters there would be family phrases nobody could decipher. If I wrote 'there was a stone thrown at the crows' nest and all the crows are crowing', what did it mean? If I wrote 'all the lost sons of Haradhan are coming out of the tiger's belly'—it was indeed a puzzle. Only the family would know what I meant. So there I was telling Sisir all about my Amman visit and incurring huge telephone bills talking to the children.

Soon after I came back from Amman I was summoned to Delhi in June 2000 and asked to go to the UN with a women's delegation. I had an enduring interest in issues relating to the empowerment of women. One of the first things I had done in the thirteenth Lok Sabha in late 1999 was to take up the question of enhancing women's representation in Parliament and the state assemblies. I had come to the firm conclusion that the Women's Reservation Bill in favour of which I had first spoken during zero hour in the Lok Sabha in mid-1996 had no prospect of being passed. I, therefore, decided to concentrate on the alternative that I had been advocating since 1998—of amending the Representation of the People Act. I wrote about my views in the print media. The *Indian Express* published an article by me and the *Times of India* did a long interview. Many in the media and the intelligentsia thought my proposal was very sensible. It would be easier to pass since it needed a simple majority unlike the Reservation Bill which, being a constitution amendment bill, needed a two-thirds majority. My idea took care of the flaws in the Reservation Bill whereby women were treated as a separate species and women would fight women in all elections within the protected walls of reserved constituencies. In my proposal women were put on par with men and given a more honourable way of entering Parliament and state assemblies than through the demeaning route of quotas. The Reservation Bill was based on the principle of rotation of seats. A particular seat is reserved for women for one term and then it becomes a general seat for the next term. If that were to happen, the bond between the elected representative and the represented—a key feature of Parliamentary democracy—would get disrupted and the incentive to serve one's constituency would vanish. Some political parties like the Samajvadi Party demanded reservation within reservation for women of the backward and scheduled castes. They were afraid elitist women would otherwise take all the women's reserved seats. My proposal took care of that danger. I told Mulayam Singh that he had the liberty to choose the kind of women he wanted to nominate as under my proposal parties could choose the seats for which they would nominate women. All his women nominees could be Dalit or backward women if he so wished. A veteran politician was on record saying he did not want women with short hair taking advantage of women's reservation. I told him my proposal gave him the freedom to give all the nominations of his party to women with long hair.

My alternative to the Women's Reservation Bill created a lot of interest. It shifted the emphasis from reservation to enhanced women's representation. On 20 December 1999, I was interviewed by Rajdeep Sardesai and Sonia Varma on Star TV's *News Hour*. I spelt out the details of my alternative proposal. I found an unexpected ally in the election commissioner, M.S. Gill. He happened to have listened to the interview. He himself came to *News Hour* on the same channel the next day, 21 December 1999, to say he fully supported my proposal and thought this was the only realistic alternative. I carried on my campaign on Star TV's *Breakfast News* on 22 December 1999, and spoke to other TV channels and the print media as well. Gill called various political parties for consultation, but was unable to persuade them. I met him several times. He jokingly used to say, 'We are a two-member party. If the political parties would listen to us there would be so many women in Parliament in no time.'

Unfortunately, our political class is unthinkingly wedded to a reservations culture and is incapable of understanding or acting upon innovative ideas. The old Women's Reservation Bill was introduced once more in the midst of utter chaos on 23 December 1999, the very last day of the session, so that it could again gather dust.

I eventually introduced a Private Members' Bill in the Lok Sabha on the lines of my proposal. It is Bill No. 62 of 2000 dated 28 February 2000 and is called the Representation of the People (Amendment) Bill, 2000. I was able to have it introduced in the Lok Sabha by voice vote on 20 April 2000. The object of the amendment was to give women 'fair representation in the legislatures' by making it 'obligatory on the part of political parties to give fair representation to both genders to qualify it for registration' and 'to cancel the registration of a political party if that party does not field candidates at elections to Lok Sabha/Assemblies from both the genders proportionately'. I added a sub-section (5A) to Section 29A of the R.P. Act saying that every registered political party 'shall ensure that there shall be not less than forty per cent of the candidates belonging to either gender out of the total number of candidates contesting elections to the House of the People or the Legislative Assembly of a State in the name of that association or body'. After section 29A I inserted a section 29B which read: 'If any association or body which has been registered as a political party does not comply with provision of sub-section (5A) of section 29A, the registration of such political party shall be cancelled by the Election Commission forthwith.' I still believe that my bill is the best way to enhance women's representation in the Lok Sabha and the state assemblies. How I wish the government of the day would adopt it instead of chasing after the mirage of the doomed Women's Reservation Bill or pursuing cumbersome, unimaginative and unsatisfactory alternatives of the sort floated by the home minister Shivraj Patil in 2005!

After introducing my alternative bill on women's representation, I was totally engrossed in my work as chairperson of the CEA. Being a member of the delegation of women Parliamentarians to the special UN session on women in June 2000 enabled me to combine both my interests. We were supposed to evaluate how far we had progressed with women's empowerment since the Beijing Convention of 1995. Before I left for New York I decided that I could not leave Sisir behind. The flight to New York would, however, be too much for him in his present state of health. So I decided he would go half-way to London and spend some time with Sumantra while I attended the UN special session at New York. Sisir left for London one day before I did. I saw him off at the Delhi airport. The security officer of the airport was very helpful. He sent an officer with me and allowed me to go inside the airport up to the gate leading to the aircraft. I could not sleep well that night as I was worried about how Sisir would stand the night-long journey. I was relieved when Sisir called in the morning to say he was all right. It was Tipu's birthday. Sugata would come for his nephew's birthday from whichever corner of the world he might be in, so he arrived from Boston for the celebration. Sugata and Sisir checked into a London hotel where the birthday party was to take place. I was on my way to New York via Paris and Sumantra was in Bosnia.

We were a bunch of lively women who travelled together to the UN. We were on an Air France flight, so we arrived at Paris and spent a day there. Some of the delegates had never been to Paris before so we were taken for a tour of the city. I had been to Paris before and was not interested in the tour but I accompanied the group because I liked the drive around the streets of Paris. I remember I had difficulty climbing on to the high van since my knees were getting worse and worse. We were invited to tea by Kanwal Sibal, who was our ambassador then. I came to know Sibal better when he later became our foreign secretary.

Our delegation to New York included Sumitra Mahajan, Mayavati, Najma Heptulla, Margaret Alva, Bhavna Chikalia, Bharati Roy, Sharda, Girija Vyas, Abha Mahato, Jayashree Mahanto, Phoolan Devi and others. Phoolan Devi, the bandit queen, was a great attraction for the media in New York. Many had seen the film made on her. The story of the humiliation of a poor low-caste girl who turned into the leader of a gang of dacoits and took revenge on the upper-caste men of the village, had caught their imagination. She had spent years and years in prison. Once out of prison she was elected to Parliament. Men used to look upon her with some awe. Behind her back they also joked with each other—'Beware, there comes Phoolan Devi, she may just whip out a revolver and start shooting at us.' I came to like her quite a lot. She could not read or write. When she had to read out the oath as a Member of Parliament, an officer of the Parliament stood by her at the mike and she repeated the oath after him. After she had delivered her maiden speech in Hindi, I went up to her and congratulated her. She smiled the child-like smile that she had and said, 'I have never spoken to such an audience. You know I was scared'. '*Dar lag raha tha*', she said to me in Hindi. I was amused that such a fiery person could be scared to deliver a mere speech. I was shocked when she was later assassinated in front of her bungalow at a stone's throw from the Parliament.

At the special session of the UN there were many speeches on women's empowerment, women's position in society and such topics. However, it was a comment by Phoolan Devi which still rings in my ears. One day some of us were discussing women's issues. Phoolan was listening quietly. Someone asked, 'Why don't you join us?' She suddenly burst out in Hindi and said, 'Such big things are spoken about women, but what is the real position of women in our society?' In a shrill voice she said, '*pitai karta, pitai karta*'—women are beaten up. Everyone fell silent. She brought out the stark reality of the situation while we were discussing women's issues only theoretically.

We stayed at the UN Plaza Hotel also known as Millennium Hotel just across from the UN. During this visit to the UN I came to know many of our officers at the permanent mission to the UN quite well. Satish Mehta and his wife Priti looked after us very well. Kamalesh Sharma, our Permanent Representative, called on me at the hotel on my arrival. Sugata had flown in from London to spend the evening with me before returning to Boston. Both of us came to know Kamalesh well. I met Satyabrata Pal for the first time on 44th Street. I was on my way to the UN when he approached me and spoke to me in Bengali. It was a pleasure to discuss politics and current affairs with him. He struck me as a scholarly and intellectual person.

I loved my hotel room, which was big and open on two sides with glass windows. On one side it overlooked the East River and the bridges; on the other side were the twin towers of the World Trade Center with their majestic beauty. After 9/11 I often remembered the towers framed in my window. Every evening when I came back from work the red light on my telephone blinked to indicate messages. Calls from Sugata in Boston, Sisir and Sumantra from London, Lenny Gordon from New York, Amitav Ghosh from Brooklyn. I never felt lonely.

On my way back I stopped over in London. I was received by Sumantra and officials of the Indian high commission. I can still see Sisir's happy and smiling face when we met. He went into the kitchen and made a cup of tea for me. I was pleasantly surprised. 'Since when have you started to make yourself useful in the kitchen?' I asked. I spent a very pleasant and relaxed week with Sisir and Sumantra. Sumantra had a well-lit sitting room with a shelf full of English literature books. I read Wordsworth's *Immortality Ode* after a long time:

> Our birth is but a sleep and a forgetting;
> The soul that rises with us, our life's Star,

Hath had elsewhere its setting,
And cometh from afar;
Not in entire forgetfulness,
And not in utter nakedness,
But trailing clouds of glory do we come
From God who is our home . . .

Our English sojourn came to an end. Sugata arrived from Boston to chaperone us home. We left Sumantra behind and left for Kolkata. Vasundhara Raje and I were in first class and went across to see Sisir, Sugata and Amita Sen—Amartya Sen's mother —who were just behind us in business class

The monsoon session of Parliament started. July and August were the months for the monsoon session. Sisir and I spent most of our time in Delhi but went back for the weekends to Kolkata. Sisir caught up with his work at Netaji Bhawan and the Institute of Child Health. I did the rounds of my constituency. At home the three grandsons were a source of perpetual joy. Little did we realize that the happy days would soon be over and that the sunset of the century would also signal a sunset in my personal life.

In that month of August Sisir, now and then, made one or two remarks which in hindsight strike me as having been very significant. He asked me one evening in Bengali, 'Tumi ki korbe?' —What will you do? I looked up at him somewhat puzzled. He added slowly, 'It is only for you that I still live on.' I understood. He asked what I would do when he would be no more. He said he was unable to leave this world because of me. My eyes filled with tears. I tried to remain calm. I said I could not imagine a world where he was no more, he would leave me bereft. So I could not envisage how I would feel. Then I tried to be brave and to break the seriousness of the conversation I smiled and said, 'Well, I will commit sati.' Subsequently, I have gone through this conversation in my mind again and again. I felt I had made him a promise when I said 'I will commit sati.' I did not mean I would jump into the funeral pyre. But I did mean I will follow him soon enough. I wait for that day.

On Independence Day, 15 August, both of us were in Kolkata after a couple of years. In previous years we had joined the reception at Rashtrapati Bhawan, Delhi. This year at Kolkata's Raj Bhawan we met many friends and acquaintances after quite some time. Many commented on how young and how well Sisir looked in spite of his recent illness. On returning home Sisir was just taking off his silk kurta when I said, 'Just a moment, let us take a photograph'. As the two of us sat down on the sofa, the three grandchildren came and cuddled up and soon we were immortalized in a frame.

August rolled into September. Durga Puja was early that year, in the first week of October. It was our custom to buy gifts for each other for Puja. Sisir was always very unmindful of such mundane things. I had to remember what to give to friends, domestic servants and others. I asked Sisir if he could spare some time. I wanted to take him to the shop to pick up a couple of shirts for him. He badly needed some shirts. So we went to a shop on Rashbehari Avenue. I picked up a white and a lemon coloured shirt for him. We stepped out of the shop on the pavement when he suddenly said, 'Let us go and buy a sari for you'. I was a bit surprised. He would never mind if I bought a dozen saris. But he never consciously thought that he might buy one for me as a gift. He was like that and I liked him that way. We did buy saris together quite often, but that would be for our daughter. It could be Bengali New Year's day, it could be Puja or her birthday. She would be in her college in the US far away from us. But we would trudge to Bhojraj, my favourite sari shop, on Rashbehari Avenue, and buy one for her. I would bother friends and acquaintances going to the US to carry these for her or wait for the long summer holidays when she would be home.

But this was different. He took a turn to the right and entered

another shop, Tularam, and asked to see saris. He quickly chose
a pale pinkish silk with a maroon border and maroon dots all
over. That was his last but one present for me. The last one was
posthumous. It arrived a few days after he was no more.
Bhowanipore Art Framing—our art framing shop—sent me a
photograph of myself speaking, may be at the UN or was it at
an IPU conference abroad? There I was speaking and the 'INDIA'
nameplate stood on my table.

The last week of September 2000 is an album in my memory
with different kinds of pictures in it. I had been included in one
of the groups going to the UN for the General Assembly. That
would be in first week of October. But I heard from Delhi that
the Russian prime minister, Putin was arriving in the first week
and so it would be better if I stayed on and joined the later
group to leave in the third week of October. So I got ready to
leave for Delhi and asked my office to convene a meeting of the
External Affairs Committee in the first week.

But destiny had other plans for me. One night in that fateful
last week of September I woke up in the middle of the night. I
found the light was on and Sisir's side of the bed was empty. In
those days Tipu, our eldest grandson, used to sleep with us. There
he was sleeping peacefully by my side. The electric light hurt my
eyes, so I closed my eyes and dozed off. It could have been five
minutes or half an hour, I do not know, before I opened my eyes
again. Sisir was still not there. Taking a long time in the toilet, I
thought. I covered Tipu with a sheet which he had kicked off.
The third time I opened my eyes there was Sisir sitting on the
edge of the bed. He held a glass of coke in his hand and munched
chocolates. That was a sure sign that he had had a 'hypo'—a
sudden drop in sugar level because of the insulin injections he
took. I rushed to his side and sat down beside him. A kind of
poignant affection filled my heart. In Bengali the word would
be 'maya'. I have no translation for that. My heart ached for
him. I gently massaged his back and asked him, 'Why did not

you wake me up? You should not go alone to the bathroom when you feel so unwell'. He said, 'I was not unwell. I was perfectly normal. I went to the toilet and closed the door. Then suddenly everything became dark. I was about to collapse. I held on to the edge of the sink and somehow became stable.' I had no idea that death had performed a dress rehearsal for us.

Next morning he went as usual to his hospital. He felt fine, he said. The doctor colleagues told me later that he had an ice-cream with them and told them he had a 'hypo' last night. My daughter had been suffering from an earache for the last couple of days. I nagged Sisir about not taking her to a proper ENT specialist. So Friday, late morning, he took her to the doctor. They had to wait in the doctor's clinic. He was late for lunch. I had put an apple and a bottle of mineral water in the car. He munched the apple on the way home but said one apple was not much of a help. That evening Sisir and I were invited to a big dinner party at the Bengal Club. Sisir took out the new white shirt I had bought for him. He wore it with the dark suit and a matching tie that Sugata had given him some time ago. He looked radiant. I still remember when dinner was announced. I got up and looked for Sisir. His oval face was rounded and full as it used to be when he was in his thirties. What was it that people say about the lamp flickering bright before it is blown off?

Saturday, 30 September 2000, began as any other day at Basundhara. Sugata was away in the US. He had said goodbye to us in Delhi in late August and gone to Turkey on his way to America. But the rest of the family was in Kolkata. Sisir went to the Children's Hospital and did his rounds. He came to Netaji Bhawan where a staff member behaved with him somewhat impertinently. He was irritated. But because of that he spoke at length with some of the other staff. He spoke of his struggle to build the institution at Netaji Bhawan against heavy odds. He spoke about the devotion and loyalty of some of the men who worked here but were no more. Kartik and Manohar recalled later that he spoke to them about the bygone days, as he had never spoken to them before. He was hurt by the errant behaviour of the person whom he had rescued from dire poverty and retained in the job out of compassion in spite of his utter inefficiency. Sumantra and Tipu came to pick him up. He was still talking so Tipu had a coke and sat at his table. He finished his work, signed some papers and got up to leave. In December 1940 his uncle Subhas Chandra Bose had called him to his side in that Elgin Road house and asked him to do some work for him. He did not stop doing Netaji's work until 30 September 2000.

That afternoon Sisir and I stood on our first floor balcony, the middle one, and waved. My daughter and grandchildren got into the car to go to the airport. They were leaving for Mumbai. Sumantra went to see them off. Back in our sitting room we sat down side by side on the double sofa. Sisir said, 'Let us go and spend a weekend at Tolly Club. I need a break from my patients and you need a break from your constituency and cadres.' He had expressed the wish a couple of times before. The quiet and the lush green of Tolly were always alluring. The last part of his book *Basubari* and some part of my *Charanarekha Taba* were written on our early morning trips to Tolly. We sat under a tree, drank undrinkable coffee and worked on our manuscripts. People go to Tolly to play golf, tennis, squash or to swim. I do not know of any people other than us who wrote books there. But his wish to spend a quiet weekend there with me was not to be.

The afternoon news was that the price of petrol, diesel and kerosene had been hiked by the central government. There were voices of protests here and there. It was almost a routine thing, and then people usually accepted the hiked prices gradually. Sisir went downstairs to his chamber and saw two patients. His doctor had said he must not overwork, so we were trying to restrict the number of patients But it was a difficult job given the trust and popularity he enjoyed among his patients' families.

I can see Sisir climbing the staircase very slowly. He disappears into one of the rooms. I am busy with some papers—a trifling job of some sort. Sisir emerged from the TV room and said, 'Have you heard the news?' He had been listening to the 7 p.m. news. He sounded somewhat amused. He looked rather tired though and I was about to ask him if he was all right when I got totally distracted by what he said. He said, 'Mamata has again created a problem for the Vajpayee government. She has threatened to resign if the price hike of petrol, diesel, and kerosene is not rescinded.' 'What!' I said unbelievingly.

There was Sumantra going out in a hurry with a pile of books in his arms. When did he come back from the airport? I had not noticed. I called him back, 'Did you hear what Baba said?' Sumantra stopped, looked back at me and said, 'Star TV will be after you any minute now.' He was gone and the telephone started to ring. It was Barkha Dutt from NDTV New Delhi. 'I have only just heard the news of Mamata's threat to resign,' I said, trying to avoid an interview. I called Mamata. She responded excitedly over the phone. She had protested, yes. 'Nobody will think of the poor people who use kerosene and the middle class housewives who use cooking gas,' she said in an agitated manner. The telephone rang again. It was Monideepa from the Kolkata studio of NDTV. I tried to avoid them a second time. I put the phone down and it rang a third time: Vikram Chandra from Delhi. 'Could we send you the car to bring you over to Kolkata Studio?' he asked. I relented.

I had a second telephone in my hand. Why? I have no idea. But I was connected to Sumantra at Netaji Bhawan. Amala, my long-time housekeeper, came to me and said, 'Ma, will you come this way? Sahib is in the bathroom. We can hear the shower running but he has not come out. It has been quite some time.' I felt as if I had an electric shock. And I knew everything was over. He was brought out from the bathroom where he lay on the floor and put on the bed.

Four telephone calls mean fifteen minutes. I had lost precious time. If only if I had known earlier, I thought. The doctor said I could not have done anything. He said it was not that he fell and died. It was the other way about. He died and fell. I remembered the dress rehearsal about a couple of nights back. Did he try to hold on to the edge of the sink as he did that night? There was no way of knowing. It was not the shower but the sink tap that was on and water was flowing from it. Sumantra rushed back from Netaji Bhawan. Within a few minutes our Basundhara house was full of people. Some TV channel had already given the news. There were press reporters and electronic media. I begged them not to photograph the body. I do not know why. I wished to remember him as he was in life. I saw Mamata had taken charge of the situation, ordering people about in her usual manner. At one point she came to me and asked for permission on behalf of the TV cameramen to take photographs. She said, 'Krishnadi, the whole nation is watching, people want to see him.' I had to agree. Things were not in my hands any more.

But at the outset I had made two telephone calls. One to the doctor and told him everything was over, but I would still like him to come at once. The other one was to Sugata at Boston. I do not quite remember what exactly I told him. I asked him much later—what did I tell you? He said you told me, 'Try to remain calm. We have just lost Baba.'

I saw George Fernandes the defence minister, walk into my room. He was accompanied by Sudheendra Kulkarni, Officer on Special Duty to Prime Minister Vajpayee. They offered condolences and left the room. The night wore on. Mamata said, 'Krishnadi, there is a crowd downstairs. You remain in your first floor sitting room and let visitors come up and meet you.' Subrata Mukherjee, the Mayor of Kolkata, was there. He suggested, 'Let me take Sisirda to the Town Hall. With the news spreading the crowd will grow bigger. We cannot control the crowd here.' I said calmly that I would spend the night downstairs in the room where Sisir had been laid to rest. We had spent forty-five years together. This was the last time I would be with him. To Subrata I said that the only place he would go is Netaji Bhawan, nowhere else.

Arrangements were made that he would be taken to Netaji Bhawan the next morning so that people could come and pay their last respects to him. So there I was sitting on the beautifully crafted antique bed beside Sisir. He was covered with flowers, white flowers as was the custom. I said I wanted some colourful flowers. The bleakness of white hurt me. Mamata overheard my comment. Soon there was a garland of red roses adorning him.

In the next room an important political meeting went on throughout the night. The prime minister wished to resolve the crisis that had resulted out of Mamata's threat of resignation from the cabinet. Mamata said she had no time for anything else that night. She had to make funeral arrangements for Sisirda and also wished to remain with me. So there was the defence minister George Fernandes, the envoy of the prime minister, Kulkarni, and some of our important Members of Parliament in the next room. All night confabulations went on. Mamata dropped into the meeting now and then while she kept herself busy with funeral arrangements.

In the other room where I sat the atmosphere was totally different. Pramita Mallick, whom we called Moni, had arrived. She stood beside Sisir's bed and sang Tagore's songs of puja and prem, devotion and love, one after another. These were not mere songs but were an affirmation of faith. I kept on telling myself, I must not grieve. And why should I grieve? My heart was full of gratitude for a life of bliss, a perfect partnership of shared experiences for forty-five long years. It was a day of thanksgiving for me. I was ever grateful to the Almighty for the life we had had together. I looked at Sisir lying peacefully covered with flowers. I uttered the Irish prayer in my mind, 'May God hold you in the palm of his hand till we meet again.'

The night ended. The sun rose as usual. There was no sign of any loss. It was dawn, beautiful and clear. Sisir left Basundhara to the accompaniment of music. Sarmila sang—*Oee maha shindhur opaar hote*—the call has come from the other side of the great ocean, come along, come fast to the land where there is no death. Later that day he began his last journey from Netaji Bhawan. His funeral procession departed by the same driveway of 38/2 Elgin Road along which he had driven his uncle Netaji Subhas Chandra Bose on the night of 16–17 January 1941, during his 'mahanishkraman'—the great escape.

Between Home and the World

Sugata wished to take me to Boston with him. I was supposed to take part in the UN General Assembly that October but I had decided to cancel the trip. We rescheduled our plans and after two of the most difficult weeks of my life I left for the US. Those two weeks were full of agony but at the same time I experienced a strange calm.

We decided not to have the formal, religious funeral rites for Sisir. Instead we had what Sugata termed 'a celebration of his life'. Sugata, Sarmila and Sumantra worked on the idea and came up with a beautiful multimedia presentation. There was a large gathering on the rear lawn of Netaji Bhawan. I sat among the crowd with my two grandsons, seven-year-old Tipu and four-year-old Tunku, on either side. But in my heart of hearts I felt terribly lonely and lost. This was the first time I was at Netaji Bhawan without Sisir. The morning after his death I had followed the cortege and arrived at the portico of Netaji Bhawan, but he had still been with me in that glass-covered carriage.

A few more duties had to be done before Sugata and I could leave for the US. We had a small puja at our home on the tenth day after Sisir's death. The three children and I also went to the Dakshineswar Kali Temple and offered puja. Sisir was an agnostic but he had a weakness for the divine mother goddess of Dakshineswar. On the eve of his great escape from the Elgin Road house, Netaji Subhas Chandra Bose had sent Sisir and his cousin Ila to offer puja at the Dakhineswar Kali Temple.

The idea behind going to Boston was two-fold. One, Kolkata was full of memories; Boston might be an escape. Second, once I went to New York the busy schedule at the UN might keep me from brooding over my recent bereavement. It did not quite work out that way. Boston was the first home for Sisir and myself and I had learnt my household skills in Boston. I had arrived here as a young woman with my husband and two-year-old son in 1958. Boston was as full of memories as Kolkata. My outward calm masked an inner struggle. One evening in Boston I broke down. I felt I should have been in Kolkata in my home with all the memories of bygone days. 'What am I doing here?' I wondered. How do I face the crowds of friends and strangers at the UN? All my courage gave way to panic. At that time of crisis Sugata stood by me like a rock. He accompanied me to New York and commuted daily between Boston and New York. Every morning he took the shuttle to Boston, gave his lectures, and returned by the evening shuttle. In my prevailing state of mind I could not have survived alone in a New York hotel suite.

All our UN officers were extremely kind. Without making it obvious they took special care of me. Vijaya Singh Thakur was always there whenever I needed something—medicine, doctor or just someone to sit with me. Apart from her, our ambassador and permanent representative to the UN, Kamalesh Sharma, Satyabrata Pal, the deputy permanent representative, Satish Mehta and all other officers stood by me and tried to keep me occupied. I was a member of two committees. I also addressed the Security Council. Satyabrata Pal and I sat in a Chinese restaurant opposite the UN and discussed my topic—'Women, Peace and Security'. Just before I was to speak, the permanent representative of Pakistan delivered his speech. As usual he somehow dragged Kashmir into it and abused India. Our officers sent me a note asking if I wished to respond. I thought for a minute and then wrote back, 'I would rather ignore him.' I was told later, that this was, indeed, a good decision. Pakistan was peeved at being ignored; they had hoped for a confrontation. After I finished my speech, the Bangladesh permanent representative sent me a note. Bangladesh was at that time a non-permanent member of the Security Council. The note said in Bengali—'As a fellow Bengali, we are so proud of you!'

I addressed a seminar at Columbia University in New York and related how I had stumbled into politics after a long academic career. Gayatri Spivak and Lenny Gordon were in the audience. It was during this trip that Dr. C.R. Ranawat examined me at the Lenox Hill Hospital and recommended total knee replacement surgery. A junior doctor at his clinic asked me the usual questions. Name? Address? Age? Married? For a moment I looked blank then I heard my own voice—as if it was someone else speaking— 'I am a widow.' I was still coping with my new status.

On my return journey home from Boston via London to Kolkata I took a sheaf of papers and started to write down the memories of my life with Sisir. Words flowed from my pen freely. The steward told me, 'You have been writing throughout the journey. How many letters did you write?' I could not tell him these were not letters but tears that I poured out. The book was later published under the title *Je Tarani Khani,* a phrase from a beautiful song by Tagore.

The year 2001 began with the terrible Gujarat earthquake. It was 26 January, India's Republic Day. It was a holiday. But I was called to Delhi to meet Chris Patten who was visiting India. He was to meet me in my office. I had asked my staff to arrange for a bigger room and to inform those members like L.M. Singhvi, Karan Singh, Ranganath Mishra, and T.N. Chaturvedi, who were ordinarily resident in Delhi, to come for the meeting. A few members did come. It turned out to be a very fruitful meeting and Patten's view of India struck me as very positive. We continued our discussion in the private dining room of the Parliament House annexe over coffee and snacks. But I was also somewhat distracted since the early morning TV news had broken the news of Gujarat earthquake. We had even felt mild tremors in Delhi. At first nobody realized the enormity of the destruction. But as the day wore on, it became clear that it was a terrible calamity. My daughter happened to be in Ahmedabad on that day. As soon as my meeting with Chris Patten was over I came home. Sugata and I started making calls to locate her and to find out if she was all right. Telephone links with Ahmedabad, Gandhinagar and Baroda had snapped. Close to midnight we got the news that she was safe. The terrible destruction caused by the Gujarat earthquake evoked national and international sympathy. We were also struck by the way the people of Gujarat started the work of rebuilding and in a short time normal life was restored. Unfortunately, Gujarat was struck by a calamity again next year—but this time it was a man-made one.

Earlier, in the month of January, an important Chinese delegation led by Li Peng, chairman of the standing committee of the National People's Congress of China had come to India. I felt a little squeamish at having to welcome someone widely known as 'the butcher of Tiananmen Square'. A delegation of German parliamentarians, led by Angelika Kostar Lossack, whom I knew well, followed soon after. I had the good fortune of interacting with a number of other German visitors and delegations which included Wolfgang Thierse, President of the German Bundestag and a delegation led by Gernot Erler, vice-chairperson of the parliamentary group of the Social Democratic party. Finally, in November 2001, Chancellor Schroeder came with a group of seven German MPs. I was introduced to Chancellor Schroeder at Ambassador Richter's place. The Chancellor told me he had already got the report of the wonderful meeting the German MPs had with me. I had developed a very good rapport with German diplomats and political leaders. On another occasion, in April 2002, I met a high-powered delegation of representatives of the Bavarian state assembly. In addition to the marked improvement in Indo-US relations, Indo-German relations were also on an upswing during these years. I also had the opportunity to interact with delegations from several African countries. These included one led by the speaker of Uganda, Francis J Ayume; another from Tanzania led by Speaker Pius Msekwa, a Nigerian delegation led by Ibrahim Mantu, Deputy President of the Senate, and a delegation from Morocco led by senator Mustaphe Ogacha. During my tenure as chairperson of the CEA I had the opportunity to meet several very interesting individuals. Chris Patten, the European Commissioner, was one. Then there was General Philip Morillon from the European Parliament who came in October 2002. General Satish Nambiar sent me a message that Morillon wanted to meet me so I asked some of my senior colleagues like Natwar Singh and L.M. Singhvi to join me. I was invited again and again to visit my counterpart in Brussels. Elmer Brok wrote to me inviting me and the committee. I felt we should develop closer relations with Europe because stronger ties with the European Union would be to our advantage in a unipolar world. But I was not able to break through the red tape of either the ministry of external affairs or the Speaker's office although I got a detailed reply from the ministry which tallied with my view. On a later visit a delegation from the EU lamented, 'You did not accept our invitations to visit.' I felt awkward but could not give the real reason for being unable to go to Brussels.

I had occasion to interact with many a foreign minister from all over the world. Among them were the foreign ministers of France, Netherlands, Oman and Bhutan, as also many other dignitaries from all corners of the world. The ambassador of the Netherlands, Peter Koch, lived in a very interesting house. This was the house where Jinnah had lived when he was in Delhi. Apart from being a historic house, its high-ceilinged dining room was quite impressive. Sometimes there were lighter moments in my meetings with foreign dignitaries. The day the French foreign minister, Hubert Vedrine, was to come to meet the committee, I came to the conference room early and found a large number of mineral water bottles placed on the table for the members. Then one of the security staff came in and started to pick the bottles up. Surprised, I asked him what the matter was. He replied dryly that according to security rules only the chairperson is allowed a bottle of mineral water. So the other bottles must be removed. I was annoyed at such a stupid comment and said, 'If my guest cannot have drinking water then take mine away as well.' The man at once happily obeyed my order and took away the bottle. I was about to give him a piece of mind when my secretary Pushpa rushed in and said Monsieur Vedrine and other members of French delegation had arrived. I was supposed to welcome them in the corridor outside so I suppressed my anger and went out. The meeting went off very well. There were questions and answers following which Vedrine spoke for forty minutes. At the end of his speech he looked around and asked for a glass of water. Just imagine my embarrassment! There was not a drop of water anywhere in the room. However, there were arrangements for high tea in the next room.

My telephone started ringing. The press, to my utter surprise, asked me if there was anything amiss at the meeting. I said, no, Indo-French ties remained as strong as ever. But next morning the report in one newspaper was, 'Not to speak of wine, the French foreign minister was denied even a glass of water.' The chief of the security staff came to my house to apologize for the gaffe. The foolishness of one of their colleagues was responsible for the fiasco. From then on during all such meetings, there were so many bottles that we were drowning in mineral water.

There were innumerable diplomatic lunches and dinners to attend during my tenure as chairperson of the CEA. A strict protocol was followed on these occasions. If the guest was a head of state, then the President of India was the host and the venue for the meal was the Rashtrapati Bhavan. The guests were lined up in formation. The President and the visiting head of state arrived and took position. There was a roll call of invitees—from the prime minister downwards—and each one went up and shook hands. A sit-down dinner followed. Apart from a beautifully printed menu, details of the music to be played during the meal were given on another card. Two formal speeches were made by either side. Toasts were proposed but, mind you, only with fruit juice.

The prime minister would entertain only his counterpart. And that would usually be at Hyderabad House. That was a building I admired for its architectural beauty and I always cherished a secret desire to reside in that house some day. But the beautiful house was only used for official functions. For the prime minister's dinner we were again lined up in a formation. But the two prime ministers walked past us and shook hands instead of the guests going up to them. By some mysterious protocol I found my seat was usually quite near the centre—so I had a close view of the guest and the host. According to etiquette, you have to keep up a conversation with people sitting on either side. It was a bit difficult sometimes when it was a foreigner who did not speak English. The prime minister or the President would have interpreters who sat behind them. I always liked to watch Prime Minister Vajpayee at meals. He enjoyed good food and all his attention was fixed on his plate when he was in the middle of a course. I almost thought he was neglecting the wife of the head of state who sat next to him. But it was not so. In between courses he chatted with her and exchanged pleasantries. But as soon as the next course was served, his attention was once more devoted to the food.

The foreign minister entertained his counterparts generally at Hyderabad House but also sometimes at the Maurya Sheraton. The Speaker entertained big delegations in the convention hall of Ashoka Hotel. The speaker once asked me to take charge of the dinner for a parliamentary delegation from Israel led by Amnon Rubinstein. I arranged this at the main dining hall of the Parliament House annexe. It was complete with speeches and toasts proposed with orange juice. It dawned on me that dinner diplomacy was an important part of our interaction with other nations of the world. Even the menu may have some message. At the end of a dinner with Tony Blair in January 2002, I asked him if he had noticed that the cuisine from soup to dessert was from the Kashmir region. He said he had, indeed, noticed it down to the tea that was served last.

While on this subject, let me mention an important state banquet given by Vajpayee. It was a lunch for the President of Pakistan, Pervez Musharraf in July 2001, on the eve of the Agra summit. Both Prime Minister Vajpayee and I had gone through knee operations in early June. At the Taj Palace Hotel all the guests were asked to reach the dining hall via the main entrance which entailed climbing a lot of steps. Only two persons were allowed to come through the gate where there would be no steps to climb. One was Prime Minister Vajpayee, while I was the other exception. As one entered the hall, the first table was marked for Prime Minister Vajpayee. It was done so that he did not have to walk the length of the whole hall. The table was named 'Ganga'. To my surprise and relief I found my seat was at the next table called 'Jamuna'. I was grateful to be spared long walks. The Prime Minister's office and the security personnel treated me with a bit of special care because they knew of my recent knee operation. Having been a fellow patient with Prime Minister Vajpayee at the Breach Candy Hospital also made me a member of, what we jokingly called the 'exclusive knee club'. About two weeks earlier we had an important meeting at the prime minister's house in the panchabati complex to discuss the impending visit of Musharraf. When I got down from the car at the prime minister's residence a wheelchair awaited me and I was wheeled in. At least this time I walked into the dining hall. At our table we had a lot of good conversation and a lot of fun. Sonia Gandhi was with us as were a Pakistani general and the well-known elderly Pakistani journalist, Ardeshir Cowasji. Mr Cowasji kept teasing Sonia Gandhi all the time. He said, 'I have heard you are always grim and you never smile.' At this, Sonia smiled. And there went Cowasji. 'My goodness, you look so beautiful when you break into a smile. Now, now, don't look stern again.' Just before dessert was served I got up and went up to the prime minister's table to greet Musharraf. Like a chivalrous knight he jumped up from his chair and I had a chance to talk to him for a few minutes. All of us had reposed a lot of faith in the Agra summit. But it was not to be.

I know personally how sincere Vajpayee was in his peace initiative. I mentioned earlier that both of us had knee replacement operations in June. He was having his second knee operated on but for me it was the first time that I was undergoing any operation. Dr Ranawat was the doctor who had come from Lenox Hill Hospital, New York. I was mighty nervous. As I was about to be taken to the operation theatre, my phone rang. It was Atalji who had gone through the operation a day earlier. In a rather weak voice he told me over the phone, 'Don't be afraid, go ahead.' His family was with him. His foster daughter Namita, her daughter Neha and Sudheendra Kulkarni had come to see me. They told my son Sugata that he should join them for lunch while the operation was on. But Sugata chose to sit outside the operation theatre. We all knew Vajpayee loved good food. An elaborate kitchen functioned for him so Namita used to send various tasty dishes to my room for Sugata and myself.

The day before I was discharged, Prime Minister Vajpayee sent word through the doctor that he wished to see me. I was in a wheelchair. I was wheeled into his room where he was lying on his hospital bed. I had met him on different occasions, but this was indeed a special meeting. He spoke about the impending visit of President Musharraf. I could see how sincerely he was trying for a breakthrough in Indo-Pak relations. He was getting mentally prepared for the Agra summit while trying to recover physically as quickly as possible. We agreed that we must not let Musharraf make Kashmir the focal point of the talks, but should be prepared to discuss it as one of the more important issues. Vajpayee was anxious to garner broad-based multi-party support for his peace initiative with Pakistan. I had a sense that he felt this was what could get him a place in history.

There was a lot of security in the hospital because of the presence of the prime minister. In spite of that I had lots of visitors, flowers and cards. One of my first visitors was the then home minister, L.K. Advani. He had come to see the prime minister but did not forget me. The security men had a tough time the day my three grandchildren came to see me because the younger two, aged five and two, carried some sophisticated modern war toys. After a lot of scrutiny they were allowed in with their toys. The story of my Breach Candy days would make a good novel. My constant companion in hospital was my son Sugata. Another great help was a long-time family friend, Dr Erin Broacha. Sugata slept on the narrow sofa-cum-bed provided for him in the room. My day began very early when the nurse woke me up for a sponge at 6 a.m. All the family members were thrown out of the room at that unearthly hour. With a paper cup of coffee in hand, all of them loitered in the corridor. Sugata complained that he was the only male member of the early morning coffee club because the other patients like the prime minister and the wife of the Human Rights Commission chairman, Justice Verma, had daughters in attendance.

I was discharged from the hospital after seven days and recuperated in Mumbai for another week. My faithful housekeeper, Gomma, was there with the two younger grandchildren. Sugata left with Tipu for Kolkata since his school had started. It was eight months since I had lost my husband and I sometimes felt lonely and sad. One morning my five-year-old grandson, Tunku, came up to me and said, 'Don't be sad. You will meet dadubhai (grandfather).' I was startled and asked

'When?' He replied, 'When you grow really, really, really very old and disappear.' When I asked him 'Where do I meet him?' He said, 'Up, up, up (ten times) there', pointing his finger upwards and concluded, 'in heaven.' I was struck by the child's sensitive mind.

It was not just recuperating and brooding I did in Mumbai. I took part in official work also. The CEA was meeting in Mumbai to discuss the Haj Bill. I was unable to take part in the meeting that was held at the Taj Mahal Hotel. But one afternoon the members came to the apartment where I was staying and apprised me of the proceedings. Sushil Kumar Shinde and Prabha Rau of Maharashtra were there among others.

Back in Kolkata I hardly had a week's rest. I presided over a Haj Bill hearing at the Taj Bengal Hotel. I had an important conference on UN peacekeeping forces to attend in Potsdam. The doctor told me I could travel three weeks after my operation. I was extremely nervous. But Sugata said he would accompany me. I was still in a wheelchair. In Mumbai, a physiotherapist used to come and help me but in Kolkata I did my exercises on my own. Sugata lent a hand if I needed help. Gomma had to look after my three grandchildren and could hardly give me time. In any case, I had to learn to be self reliant. So I decided to attend the conference in Potsdam. I was operated on 9 June and on 28 June Sugata and I arrived in Berlin. Now when I look back, I am amazed at what I did.

At Potsdam the conference was fortunately held at the same hotel where we stayed. I was happy to see that the two other Indian representatives were Kamalesh Sharma and General Satish Nambiar. I felt reassured. I was dependent on a wheelchair and walker. The conference went off very well. We discussed the Brahimi Report on UN peace-keeping forces. The German Members of Parliament invited me to the Bundestag to meet them where arrangements were made for my wheelchair to be put in an elevator so that I could go directly into the conference room. It was a pleasant and productive meeting. My brother-in-law, Martin Pfaff, who was a member of the Bundestag, sat across the table from me. Anita had also travelled to Berlin so that we could spend some time together. She took me around in the wheelchair, so Sugata had some respite. Sugata and Martin even went sightseeing in Potsdam. Ronen Sen was India's ambassador to Germany at that time and invited Martin, Anita, Sugata and myself to a wonderful Bengali lunch at his residence.

On my way back I stopped at London for a few days. Sugata and I checked into an Irish hotel near Sumantra's place as it would have been impossible for me to climb the steps to his flat. Sumantra camped with us. Lenny Gordon came to see me in London. Our high commissioner in London, Nareshwar Dayal, arranged a meeting with some of the officers at the High Commission. I always made it a point to interact with the staff and officers of our embassies abroad so that if there were any problems we could bring them up at the CEA meetings. After a trip back from the UN I had told the committee that our UN mission needed more officers. Innumerable meetings went on simultaneously and our officers had to hop from one room to another for lack of personnel. The CEA was supposed to look after the activities of our embassies abroad but we were not allowed to go abroad for such inspections. So whenever I was visiting I took the opportunity to meet and speak with our officers and staff abroad and try to understand the problems they faced.

I left London for Kolkata all by myself in the first week of July while Sugata stayed back for a conference in England. When I look back I am surprised at my own will power. How did I manage the travels and conferences mostly in a wheelchair or with the help of a walker! Back home there was hardly any rest. I was continually getting into planes, going to Delhi, coming back to Kolkata, and again leaving. The month of July 2001 was extremely busy. It was the monsoon session of Parliament. There was a meeting at the prime minister's residence to discuss the imminent visit of Musharraf. Then Musharraf arrived. The Agra summit failed after unprecedented media hype. There was the usual debate on the failure in Parliament where I spoke on 1 August 2001. I argued that the prime minister had been right to invite the Pakistani President to Agra and right not to sign any joint declaration. I suggested that there should have been far better media management. I also warned that Jaswant's Singh's claim that Kashmir was the core of Indian nationhood ran the risk of being exploited by Pakistan for the entirely different purpose of pushing its own single-point obsession with Kashmir. I reminded him that all states made an equally important contribution to our nationhood. The process of re-engagement must continue but its timing had to be contingent on a clear display of goodwill from across the border. Meanwhile, the government would be well-advised to move forward on the internal track of talks with all those prepared to negotiate in Jammu and Kashmir. Peace, like the Taj Mahal, I concluded, could not be built in a day. We should make certain that India should not be accused of not trying its level best to build the edifice of peace in the subcontinent.

On 20 August 2001, I was back in Delhi taking part in the debate on the saffronization of education. I made a strong plea that education should be left to the educationists. I argued in favour of academic independence and against over-interference by agencies of the state in shaping the curriculum. While opposing attempts at saffronization by Murli Manohar Joshi, I also took issue with the communists who had painted the educational system of West Bengal in flaming scarlet. I did not want Indian education to be painted in any particular colour. I was also careful not to preach secular uniformity, but wanted our young generation to learn something of the multi-coloured spiritual heritage of India that could not be confined to any one religion.

In between my parliamentary work I had to take care of the Netaji Research Bureau which had been orphaned after Sisir's death. I spoke to P.A. Sangma and asked him to deliver the Annual Sarat Bose Memorial Lecture at the Netaji Research Bureau in September. Sangma spoke on the sensitive subject of 'Understanding the North East'. It was a very well-attended lecture. But the whole world was shaken by one particular event of September 2001, the terrorist attack on the World Trade Center and the collapse of the famous twin towers of New York. 11 September had been a very busy day for me. The CEA had a meeting at the Ghaziabad passport office since we had received a lot of complaints from there. Then I received a French delegation led by Andre Lajoinie, chairperson of the Committee on Production and Trade, of the French National Assembly. In the evening I went to a reception at the Japanese embassy. The Japanese Ambassador, Hirabayashi, asked me 'Have you heard the news?' I had not. The news of the attack was just coming in. 'Is it an accident?' someone asked. Hirabayashi said, 'No, it looks like a deliberate attack.'

The next few hours we were glued to the television. Sugata called from Boston, Sumantra from London. I worried about friends in New York—Maarij, Lenny, Snigdha. Maarijuddin had been driving to his office and saw the whole disaster happen. Lenny was on his way to the university using the subway. I had telephone calls asking me if Sugata and Sumantra were safe, although they were nowhere near the spot. We heard the terrorists had boarded the plane from Boston's Logan Airport.

After a couple of days I was in Trivandram. There as I sat on the Kovalam beach, the world looked so peaceful. We were supposed to go to Kanyakumari, the southernmost tip of India, where Swami Vivekananda had meditated, but I could not make that trip. Somewhat disappointed I wrote in my diary:

Kanyakumari Unvisited
It brings to mind the image
Of the great monk who sat
Erect on the rock at the end

Point of India, bodhi dawned
On him, we hear the clarion call
To serve the poor, the downtrodden.
It was not for me to see the place
Where you have left your mark.

But I will cherish in my mind
The thought that there is a place
In India unvisited, a place to
Visit, perhaps in unknown future
I live in hope and draw
Solace from Kanyakumari unvisited.

Sisir's first death anniversary was drawing near. Death anniversaries are not observed at Netaji Bhawan. Only birthday celebrations are held there. I decided there would be no death anniversary but a book release ceremony so that friends and admirers could come together and remember him. My short book *Je Tarani Khani* was released by a good friend, the poet Nirendranath Chakrabarti. Sumantra was the compere and conducted the meeting, while Sarmila read excerpts from the book. I had also asked Dilip Roy (not to be confused with the senior Dilip Roy), a long-time friend of the family and a noted singer, to be present with us. It was a poignant mourning ceremony.

From that evening I started a truly lonely life in Basundhara. My daughter and the three grandchildren had been staying with us for the last four years ever since they arrived from abroad. They had been looking for a house to buy or to rent and now at last they decided to move to a place of their own. The choice of the day was not a particularly good one. I put up a brave and smiling face. Late in the night, Gomma came and spent the night on the floor of my bedroom and left in the morning.

My parliamentary work kept me going. I had to visit people

all over my constituency. The CEA meetings and tours also kept me busy. I went with the committee in Jaipur. After the meetings we went out sight-seeing. At Amber I went to the Joshoreswari Kali temple. Maharaja Man Singh had brought the deity from Jessore in Bengal. We were asked to a high tea by Maharaja Bhawani Singh at Chandra Palace. Aparna Sahai, who was like an adopted daughter to me, came to see me with her two children. The palace-turned-into-hotel where we stayed was beautiful. I had a gorgeous suite with a colourful swing in the verandah. One afternoon when dark rain clouds gathered in the sky, I sat on the swing and sang the Tagore song—*Emono dine tare bola jai, emono ghana ghor barishay*. Thus life went on. That winter I was busy with a continuous flow of foreign delegations. As an individual MP I did all I could and had a sense of fulfillment. But so far as my party Trinamool was concerned, things started to go from bad to worse.

The last three years had seen the phenomenal rise of the Trinamool Congress. From the beginning of 2001, however, started an irremediable decline, which no one was able to control. Mamata, the party's greatest asset, also turned out to be its greatest liability. In February she had presented the railway budget—her second one in Parliament. But in the middle of that session she resigned from the ministry and withdrew from the NDA coalition. Why she did that remains an enigma to me. The ostensible reason was the Tehelka scandal and her demand for the resignation of George Fernandes who had been implicated in it. That day I was at a banquet for the prime minister of Czechoslovakia. At the end of the dinner as the guests started to leave I found myself walking beside Prime Minister Vajpayee. He told me in a soft voice, 'Mamata is creating difficulties for me again. Please speak to her.' I promised to speak to her at night. I did, but to no avail. Once she made up her mind, it was impossible to get her to change it. Next morning there was again a call from the PMO. I confessed my failure to sway Mamata.

But I still called up other friends in Kolkata whose words she might heed. But all our efforts came to naught. That very evening on 15 March 2001—the ides of March—there was a meeting. Mamata announced to the assembled press that she was pulling out of the NDA. We, the other Trinamool MPs, were asked to sign on the dotted line. At first we thought Mamata and Ajit Panja were resigning from their respective ministries and that was all. Bikram Sarkar, who was drafting the resolution said that was what he had written. Nobody seemed to be sure when and how the line regarding leaving the NDA crept into it. I have no idea if before she took the decision, Mamata held any parleys with the Congress, with whom we were about to forge an alliance. I presumed she might have consulted Sudip and Ajit Panja who were politically close to her. In those days Sudip and his wife Nayana were the closest to her.

Ideologically, Trinamool was undoubtedly closer to the Congress than to the BJP. Thus the alliance could have had a positive impact if the proper groundwork had been done. But the decision was sudden and haphazard and the two Congresses remained suspicious of each other. With just two months to go before the assembly elections it was impossible to explain our party's volte face to the general public. All that happened was that the exodus from the Congress to the Trinamool was halted.

The inevitable happened. The Trinamool fared very badly in the assembly elections in West Bengal. On 13 May when the results came out, I found myself standing next to Biman Bose of the CPI(M) in front of the NDTV crew trying to explain our defeat. All the other leaders had disappeared. I confessed to our organizational weakness. Many people had hoped that at long last there will be an alternative to the CPI(M) rule in West Bengal. But Trinamool got a mere sixty MLAs in a house of 294 members.

From the choice of candidates to polling day strategy, Trinamool had gone about the assembly election in a most unprofessional manner. I had told Mamata to look for a strong

candidate for the Jadavpur segment of my constituency. I
reminded her that it was the constituency of the chief minister,
Buddhadeb Bhattacharya. I had led by nearly sixteen thousand
votes in this segment in 1998 and by nearly six thousand in
1999. No non-communist had ever got a majority in this red
bastion since independence. Even when I won in the other
segments of the Jadavpur Parliamentary constituency in 1996, I
had trailed in the Jadavpur segment. I had suggested that Mamata
herself should contest from that seat. We were projecting her as
the chief minister. Let there be a straight fight. And if I could
lead there by a few thousand votes, she could surely win. She
looked at me somewhat puzzled and then asked who would
look after the rest of Bengal! I still rue the fact that she did not
agree to my proposal. To my great dismay one morning, I opened
the newspaper and saw that our candidate would be the actress
Madhabi Mukherji. I am a great admirer of her as an actress, but
as a candidate she would be a disaster. The party workers of
Jadavpur were extremely upset by the choice. I rushed to Mamata
to see if this farce could be stopped even at this late hour. But
Nayana who was there with her told me, 'Madhabi auntie will
give a good fight,' and Mamata agreed. Journalists congratulated
Buddhadeb-babu and said he should be very grateful to Mamata
Banerjee for having handed over Jadavpur on a platter!

What was behind Mamata's sudden decision to quit NDA
and forge an alliance with the Congress was not clear to me.
Wild speculations were doing the rounds. One was that she did
it for Nayana who was contesting from the Bowbazar seat in
northwest Kolkata and needed the Muslim votes of the area
which Congress could deliver. She had lost the by-election from
the same place after her husband Sudip vacated the seat on
becoming an MP. This was an absurd explanation but I did hear
it from many people. The other common explanation was that
Mamata in any case wanted to have an alliance with the Congress
and used the Tehelka scam as an excuse. Whatever the reason,

the net result was a sharp decline in the credibility of Trinamool. Matters were compounded even further when she decided to return to the NDA fold. She never recovered the full trust of the BJP leadership or that of the allies. Then there was the humiliating wait to be taken back into the cabinet. Vajpayee was willing to take her back, but she insisted on reclaiming the railways portfolio. In the meantime Nitish Kumar of the Samata Party had become the railways minister. It would have been both awkward and unfair to remove him. Mamata was offered many good portfolios. Since she had returned to the NDA, I asked her to accept rural development. She could do a lot for our state of West Bengal and it would help us in the coming panchayat elections. But she remained adamant.

The winter session of 2001 kept me very busy. A stream of foreign dignitaries and delegations kept descending on Delhi. Chancellor Schroeder and German MPs came at the end of October. Then I had the American ambassador, Robert D. Blackwill, come and address the committee on the situation in Afghanistan. The Afghan ambassador, Masood Khalili, came next. He was still recuperating from the grievous injuries he suffered from the blast which killed his leader, Ahmed Shah Masood. I had met him earlier and I remember we discussed Sufi poetry for more than an hour. The Indian ambassador to Kabul, Satish Lamba, followed soon after.

The prime minister, A.B. Vajpayee, went on a state visit to Japan. I had requested him to visit the Renkoji Temple in Tokyo where the remains of Netaji Subhas Chandra Bose had been kept since 1945. I had specially reminded his principal advisor, Brajesh Mishra about this. On 9 December Vajpayee visited Renkoji Temple and paid tribute to the memory of Netaji. This was his second visit. He had earlier visited the temple when he was foreign minister during the Janata rule in the late seventies.

The most dramatic moment of the winter session came on 13 December 2001. The Indian Parliament was attacked by five

Pakistani fedayeens at about 11.35 a.m. Our session started at 11.00 a.m. That day Parliament got adjourned within five minutes. Many members left. Some were in the Central Hall and I was there too. Friends from different corners called me to join them for coffee. I declined. I decided to work at my committee office in the Parliament House annexe which was just opposite the Parliament building. I stood on the steps of the Parliament and waited for my car. I heard the usual announcement, 'Krishna Bose MP *saheba ki gari* gate number one *par le aiye...*'—send the MP's car to gate number one. It was 11.30 a.m. The car usually took some time to come. To my surprise it arrived quickly. I got into the car, crossed the street and entered the PHA (as we called the annexe). On entering I found there was a commotion. People rushed around excitedly. All the doors and windows were being shut. 'What is the matter?' I asked, puzzled. 'There is a shoot-out in Parliament,' I was told. 'Impossible, I have just come from there, it is not even two minutes!' I tried to go near a window and pulled the heavy curtain to peep out. There were shouts from behind. 'Don't do that, don't go near the window.' Some one put the TV on and we saw the most amazing scenes there— a live telecast of the terrorist attack. I called my Kolkata home and asked them not to worry. On the steps where I had stood a little while ago, waiting for my car, there was now the dead body of one of the fedayeen attackers.

It was an attack on democracy. One shudders to think what might have happened to the nearly three hundred MPs inside the premises if even one terrorist had managed to get into the building. But our security men showed extraordinary courage and saved democracy. We lost nine of these men. The security guards inside Parliament were not allowed to carry arms. They only had walkie-talkies. But they warned each other and even when injured, managed to close the heavy doors of the building. It was 3 o'clock in the afternoon when we were allowed to get out of the PHA. I had two commandos in my car to escort me home.

Indo-Pak relations dipped to an all-time low. There was a wave of anger against our neighbouring country. There was heavy deployment of the Indian army at the border and the Line of Control. We recalled our ambassador to Pakistan, Vijay Nambiar. Just before taking up his assignment in Islamabad, he had come to see me in my office and we had discussed how to improve Indo-Pak relations. Now it looked as if we were on the brink of an imminent war.

At the end of the tumultuous winter session I returned to Kolkata. January 2002 was a busy month as it usually was for me and Sisir and the family. I attended constituency functions like the Bishnupur Gramin Mela and the Car Mela at Behala. The Bishnupur village fair had an exhibition of an immense variety of vegetables and fruits, while the Behala fair displayed a variety of motorcars. In between I had to make several trips to Delhi to meet foreign delegations and for VIP visits like the visit of the UK prime minister Tony Blair. We also had the first committee meeting of the year to select subjects to be pursued for discussion during the year. In Kolkata, preparations for the Netaji birthday celebrations were on. Sugata had invited Ranajit Guha to deliver the Netaji Oration. He came all the way from Vienna and delivered an impressive lecture on Netaji's autobiography. We had a wonderful time conversing with this erudite scholar during the few days that he was in Kolkata. In Delhi I had been charmed by a dance performance by a group of Afghan students so I invited them to perform at Netaji Bhawan during the birthday celebrations. Sixteen young Afghans arrived in Kolkata one January morning. They were students of Jawaharlal Nehru University, Delhi University and Jamia Milia. I arranged an interactive meeting for them with students of Kolkata University, Presidency College, and Jadavpur University. Afghanistan was at that time very much in the news. The dance performance by the young Afghan boys was a great hit. The morning function at Netaji Bhawan on 23 January always brought back memories of

Sisir. Tears came to my eyes when Sugata welcomed the guests on behalf of Netaji Research Bureau and in the name of Dr Sisir Kumar Bose, the guiding spirit of this institution. On 2 February we observed Sisir's birthday and the next day Sugata and I set off for Mumbai. Dr Ranawat had arrived from New York and I had total knee replacement surgery on my second knee. All our friends stood by me as they did on the previous occasion—Erin, Dr Laud, Mr Ghorai of Indian Airlines, and my physiotherapist Kavita Mendon. Of course, Prime Minister Vajpayee was not there. 'The PM does not have a third knee,' someone said. Some one else retorted, 'Of course he does, it is Advani.'

Shyam Benegal and his script-writers Shama Zaidi and Atul Tewari came over to discuss their film project on Netaji Subhas Chandra Bose with me and Sugata. Sisir and I had known Shyam Benegal for quite some time. He had come to Netaji Bhawan when he was working on his Nehru documentary. He had shot a long interview with Sisir at that time. We promised to help him with books, photographs, film footage—whatever he needed from the archives of the Netaji Research Bureau. Sugata and I knew Sisir would have been very happy to see a good feature film on his uncle's life.

I rested in Kolkata for about two weeks. Our local cable operator specially telecast the film *Lagaan* on their channel one evening for my entertainment and Sugata and Tipu joined me in watching the climactic cricket match. Hectic days were ahead. After the two knee operations I felt much better. On 15 April, 2002—the Bengali new year's day—I find an entry in my diary. I have written that I had decided to stop writing diaries at the end of 2000 after Sisir's death. A new chapter in my life had begun. In 2001 I occasionally wrote some comments in my diary, but I totally stopped in 2002—I did not even buy a diary that year. But on 15 April 2002 I wrote in my fat Lok Sabha diary that I felt like resuming my diary writing habit. That I was able to walk by myself gave me confidence and may be a desire to live, which I had lost. It was my public work which had kept me going.

At the end of May I went to Boston. This was more or less a private visit but I went to attend a conference at the UN as well. In Boston we had a happy time because my three grandchildren were there. Tipu's birthday was an important annual event in our lives. We figured out he would not be in Boston on his birthday. So we advanced his birthday by a few days and held his ninth birthday party. Sugata, Ayesha, the children and I enjoyed the party. Back home Indo-Pak tensions reached fever pitch and western countries got alarmed. I consulted Lalit Mansingh in Washington and Ronen Sen in London and tried to convince people in the USA and the UK that there would not be a war.

A memorable event later that year was my visit to the temple of Tirupati. We had a committee meeting in Chennai and decided to drive to Tirupati from there. It was a long and tiring drive. It took us more than four hours. But when we reached the small, peaceful pilgrim town we felt it was worth the effort. Unlike usual pilgrimage centres it was so neat and clean. Most people walked barefoot. Next morning we had a darshan of the Lord. It was a Vishnu image with shankha, chakra, gada, padma (conch shell, wheel, mace, lotus). But a piece of cloth was tied over the eyes which did not allow us to see the expression. I was told the cloth was taken off only on special occasions. There was a firm belief that the deity at Tirupati always fulfilled devotees' prayers. For a moment I did not know what to ask from him. Welfare of the world? Knowledge and bhakti? No, like all foolish mothers I prayed for my three children.

The year 2002 was, however, the year of the terrible Gujarat riots or, more aptly, a state-abetted anti-minority pogrom. It went down as a defining moment in India's history. From 28 February onwards violent riots erupted in Gujarat following the attack in Godhra on the train carrying karsevaks from Ayodhya.

Muslim homes and shops were looted and set on fire by rioting mobs. Thousands fled from their homes and took shelter in relief camps. As a member of the Committee on Empowerment of Women I visited the relief camps with a group of my colleagues. What I heard and what I saw there shocked me and broke my heart. Gujarat was, indeed, a 'national shame'. The term was first used by Prime Minister Vajpayee when he visited Gujarat soon after the riots broke out. He asked the errant chief minister, Narendra Modi, to practise 'Rajdharma', the duty of a ruler in whose eyes all citizens are equal. The implication of what he said was clear. He agreed with what was by then common knowledge—the utter indifference of the government of Gujarat to the threat faced by Muslims—if not active connivance in these attacks. We, the allies in the NDA coalition, expected Vajpayee to sack Modi. I repeatedly demanded in television interviews that the prime minister should assert himself. Unfortunately, he retracted from the position he took in Ahmedabad as soon as he arrived at a party meeting in Goa. Vajpayee's flip-flop on Gujarat was the lowest point in his tenure as prime minister. I visited a number of relief camps in Vadodora and Ahmedabad including the Shah Alam Camp and the Panch Mahal. I saw at first-hand the miserable plight of the women and children who had gone through horrible experiences

Apart from my visits to the relief camps I privately visited some Muslim families who belonged to the educated upper middle classes. These families had left their homes and were staying with relatives and friends in comparatively safer parts of the city. They were touched that I had come to see them. Some of them told me that I was the first Hindu who had come to enquire about them. What hurt them most was that they had lived for years together with Hindu neighbours. But when violence broke out, overnight they became strangers and no one helped them. Usually in a riot the poorer people suffer the most. There was a difference this time in Gujarat, in that, well-to-do families were targeted.

There were businessmen, professional persons, even former Members of Parliament, who suffered. A well-known former MP was killed by a mob in his own house. Gujarati surnames do not always reveal a person's religious identity. A 'Gandhi' could be a Hindu, a Muslim, or a Parsi. But the miscreants knew exactly who was Muslim and who was not.

On 23 July 2002, I made an impassioned speech in Parliament on the subject of relief and rehabilitation in Gujarat. Rehabilitation, I said, did not mean giving somebody a shelter and a bowl of gruel or a bowl of rice. Rehabilitation meant bringing people back to normal life, to the mainstream and giving them the security which had been shattered for them. The women in the refugee camps did not want to leave the camps because they were too scared to return and their homes had not been rebuilt. Referring to my conversations with educated Muslims, I told the House that they said that in the last four months none of their Hindu friends had come to see how they were doing. 'I am hearing of Gujarati ashmita,' I said in the course of my speech. 'They are also part of that. They are very proud to be Gujaratis. They have been born and brought up there. Now, they felt alienated. I felt very unnerved when I spoke to them because I could feel the deep suppressed anger and the deep alienation in the minds of these people. Now rehabilitation means that we have to give them back their sense of dignity and sense of security because alienation is the breeding ground of future terrorism.'

The Gujarat riots posed a personal dilemma for me. I was utterly disgusted with the BJP stand on the issue. But in my own parliamentary party mine was a lone voice. I was disappointed and somewhat puzzled by Mamata's ambivalent attitude regarding the Gujarat crisis. She was always known to be secular and even pro-Muslim. But why she failed to see or chose not to see the implications of the Gujarat crisis was a mystery to me. In our party Mamata usually took the decisions while others were informed and nodded their assent. However, on Gujarat she did call a meeting of our Parliamentary party just before a debate and a vote. We met in the small office we had on the second floor of Parliament House. She asked everyone individually, 'Yes, Sudipda, Ranjitda, Dineshda', she went on. By then everyone knew her mind and nodded accordingly—let us criticize the government, but vote for it. I was the only dissenting voice. I demanded that the party vote against the government on this issue. On a previous occasion, I had raised my lone voice and forced my party to abstain in the voting on POTA (Prevention of Terrorism Act) even after a whip had been initially issued directing us to vote in its favour. I believed POTA constituted an unacceptable abridgement of our civil liberties. I was once again brutally frank the day we discussed our stand in the Gujarat debate. These were times when speculation was going on whether Mamata would be taken back into the cabinet and be given the old portfolio. I asked her, 'Could you do a Mayavati act?' Could she demand what she wanted and extract it and in exchange give support? If not, why was she going out of her way to defend something truly indefensible? Mamata knew I was upset. She kept on telling me, 'Krishnadi, don't be so upset. You will see how I criticize the BJP when I speak in the Gujarat debate. I will aggressively criticize BJP, I will demand Narendra Modi's resignation.' I could not make her understand that after doing all this if you go and vote with them your credibility would be totally lost.

I was issued a whip to vote with the government. Under the anti-defection law in force, I would lose my seat in Parliament if I defied the party whip. I considered the idea of defying the whip and getting disqualified, it sounded melodramatic. My friends and well-wishers advised against such a move. All that would happen, they said, is that we will lose a good MP without making any real difference in Gujarat. I thought about my great peers, my in–laws who never compromised and paid the political price for that. They were great men but by resigning or getting expelled they often found themselves in the political wilderness. Sarat Chandra Bose took a principled stand in 1947 but could not prevent the vivisection of India or the partition of Bengal. He lost all voice in political decision-making in free India. Subhas Chandra Bose, the Congress president in 1939, could not bring the high command to agree with his view that with the Second World War the opportune time had come for the final confrontation with British imperialism. His resignation meant political marginalization within India, even though he went on to greater deeds after his great escape. I agonized over the question of whether to defy the party whip. The debate went on till late into the night. In the evening I asked permission from Mamata and chief whip Sudip to go out for an hour. There was consternation. I left my cell number with Sudip so that he could contact me.

I went to a diplomatic gathering. I was off mood. I sat in one corner and sulked. Some of my diplomat friends sympathized with me. Gujarat had become an international scandal by then. If only the BJP would remove Narendra Modi from the chief ministership, it would give a positive signal to the international community and help to bring back the confidence of the minorities. The BJP would not lose anything. There would be some other BJP chief minister, I mused helplessly. One of the diplomats brought a small crystal glass full of sake for me. He gave it to me and said, 'Drown your sorrow in this.' Looking back, I wish I had defied the whip and left Parliament in 2002. This crisis certainly gave me a very different perspective on the anti-defection law introduced in Rajiv Gandhi's time. It simply does not allow any room for an individual MP to vote according to her conscience even on critical issues without losing his or her seat in Parliament. This is not the case in Westminster. Not being able to vote according to one's conscience, I felt, was a worse calamity than the evil of horse-trading and defection.

In August that year I visited Taipei and Tokyo. I was invited to take part in an international academic conference on democracy in Taipei. India did not have full diplomatic relations with Taiwan and ministers were not allowed to visit. There was, however, no restriction on Members of Parliament visiting Taiwan and even Vajpayee had visited as MP. My case was somewhat ambiguous because of my position as the chairperson of CEA. After a consultation with the foreign secretary, I accepted the invitation.

I enjoyed the conference. Sugata accompanied me on this trip. We stayed at the Grand Hotel. This was my second visit to Taipei. Twenty-three years ago Sisir and myself had visited Taipei and stayed at the same hotel. I always had a soft corner for Taipei in my heart for a very special reason. At the end of the Second World War Netaji Subhas Chandra Bose had boarded a Japanese bomber in Saigon. On 18 August 1945 the plane had stopped at Taipei airport for refuelling. When it took off again the plane crashed on the runway. Grievously injured, Netaji was taken to the Nanmon Hospital along with other victims. The only Indian accompanying him was Habib-ur-Rahman who was also injured. Japanese doctors at the hospital treated him, but he died of third degree burns that night. He was cremated at the Taipei crematorium and his remains were kept at the Nishi Honganji temple nearby till arrangements were made for Habib-ur-Rahman and a Japanese companion, Hayashida, to take the remains to Tokyo.

The conference, academic though it was, was inaugurated by President Chen Shui Bian. I met Eugene Chien, minister of foreign affairs, vice president Hsiu-lien Annette Lu, and the prime minister Yu Shyi-Kun. I tried to keep a low profile, keeping in mind the fact that we did not have formal diplomatic relations. But I cannot say I was successful. I found my photographs splashed on the front pages of Taiwanese newspapers and my comments reported in all newspapers. I stressed the need for economic and cultural ties between India and Taiwan.

While I was busy with the conference, Sugata went round and visited the spots which were connected with Netaji's last journey. On my previous visit I had seen the old one-storey Nanmon Hospital. Now in its place was the new modern building of the Ho-ping or Peace Hospital. Sugata also managed to see the Nishi Honganji temple where the urn containing the remains of Netaji was kept for two weeks. He also went to the site of the old crematorium where there now stood a petrol pump. On the day we arrived, the officers of Taipei's domestic airport took Sugata and me in a car and drove us round the runway of the airport so that we could pay our homage to the departed leader. Sugata could see the spot where his grand-uncle had met with the fatal accident.

From Taipei, Sugata and I flew to Tokyo. We stayed at the Four Seasons hotel. Our old friend Shigemoto Okuda, one of Netaji's last surviving Japanese associates, came to see us. We were also delighted to meet Mr Shibusawa. Netaji had lived with the Shibusawa family in Tokyo during his visit in 1943 for the Greater East Asia Conference. Shibusawa junior, whom we met now, was a sixteen-year-old boy at that time. But he distinctly remembered Netaji's stay with them. Sugata arranged a lunch for Shibusawa, Okuda and others at the hotel. We went to Renkoji Temple to pay our homage to Netaji. The priest Mochizuki and his wife welcomed us. Many of our Japanese friends including Mrs Matsushima joined us. We offered incense, fruits, flowers and other offerings before the urn. I met my counterparts at the Japanese Diet and the two chairpersons of their foreign affairs committees from the upper and lower houses respectively. In India we have a combined CEA chaired by one person. Our discussion on Indo-Japanese relations and world affairs went off well. Our ambassador in Tokyo, Aftab Seth, was out of town but his deputy in the embassy threw a dinner party for me where some members of Japanese Parliament as well as the priest, Mochizuki, and his wife were present.

On my return I fell into my usual pattern of work. There were visits to the constituency and I made recommendations for various development projects. My frequent trips to Delhi to meet foreign delegations continued. A delegation of French legislators arrived, led by Mr Fauchon. Another delegation of members of the European Parliament led by Mr Crespo MEP came soon after. I visited Chennai and Mumbai with the committee on official tours. During the festive season I had to inaugurate several Durga Pujas and take part in the distribution of clothing to the poor and the needy. Durga Puja was followed by Kali Puja. Another round of inaugurations and this time, distribution of blankets since it was already winter. On Kali Puja night we had the usual gathering on the terrace of Basundhara.

Soon after Diwali I joined one of the delegations to the UN. My loyal secretary, Vishwanathan, saw me off at the Delhi airport. At Heathrow I was joined by some others of my group— Digvijay Singh of the Samata Party who was then minister of state for external affairs, Yerran Naidu of the Telegu Desam, and others. This time I spoke at the General Assembly. When India was called on to take the podium, I walked up to the stage. Being a tiny person I wondered if I would disappear behind the podium. But I did not. There was a stool on which I stood and delivered my address. I was told later that the stool was always kept there since many south Asian leaders are of short stature. On weekends I would take the Delta Shuttle from New York on Friday evenings to Boston and come back on Monday mornings. Sometimes Sugata joined me in New York. Our favourite restaurant was 'Vong'. I did not go to Washington this time but our ambassador, Lalit Mansingh, came to New York. We had lunch together and discussed Indian foreign policy and world politics. My younger son Sumantra came from London and spent a few days with me in New York. Altogether it was a very fulfilling time that I had at the UN session in New York in November 2002.

After the end of the winter session I came back to Kolkata for our usual Christmas family reunion. Sugata and Sumantra arrived. On the eve of Netaji's birthday in January 2003, President Abdul Kalam visited Netaji Bhawan. He had promised me that on his first visit to Kolkata as President he would come to Netaji Bhawan to pay his homage to Netaji and he kept his promise. Along with all the members of the Netaji Research Bureau I welcomed him. Sugata showed him round the museum. When the President was taken to Netaji's sitting room, he sat down on a chair opposite that of Netaji's and said, 'I will now close my eyes and visualize Netaji before me!' The birthday celebration of Netaji Subhas Bose passed off with the usual glamour. The Netaji Oration was given by Arjun Appadurai. Apart from being an academic, he happened to be the son of S.A. Ayer, the minister of publicity in Netaji's provisional government of Free India established in Singapore in 1943. Ayesha was with us in Kolkata after she and Sugata had made a visit to Japan and we had a joyful time in January 2003. On 2 February 2003, Sisir's eighty-second birth anniversary, the road to the east of Netaji Bhawan formerly known as Allenby Road was renamed Dr Sisir Kumar Bose Sarani. This was the road through which Sisir drove his uncle Subhas on the historic night of his escape. My eldest grandson Tipu read excerpts from Sisir's book *The Great Escape* in which he describes the drive. Many in the audience said it was very touching to hear the grandson read from his grandfather's book.

At Home in the World

From mid-February 2003, my life took a rather peculiar and unexpectedly sad turn. I was, indeed, kept very busy. I had to travel a lot within India. I also went abroad several times in connection with my parliamentary work. In between I moved around my constituency keeping up public appointments. Parliament sessions also kept me busy. I spoke in many important debates. But in my heart of hearts there was suddenly a void. The previous year I had recovered at least partly from the grief caused by Sisir's passing away. Physically I felt much better after the two knee replacement operations. But from mid-February 2003 a new melancholy enveloped my life. I again lost the will to live. I felt all my work was done and it was time to quit: 'Sunset and the evening star and one clear call for me...' I waited for the call. This was a mood I could not share with anyone. My two sons knew about the despondency I was going through and the reason for it and they did their best to be supportive. I carried on my public duties without faltering because I remembered Sisir used to say private grief should never come in the way of public duty.

Throughout February and March I was commuting between Kolkata and Delhi. The budget session was on. Important visitors from abroad kept on arriving in Delhi. The prime minister of Poland visited. There was a lunch meeting with the Bangladesh foreign minister. The President of Germany arrived and the Federation of Indian Chambers of Commerce and Industry

(FICCI) and Confederation of Indian Industry (CII) arranged a luncheon meeting for him. There was also the usual Rashtrapati Bhavan dinner in his honour. Ambassador Richter was a very good friend and I seemed to be attending all the ceremonies including the press conference addressed by the German President.

In our committee we were discussing the budget allotment for external affairs. But since February the Ayodhya dispute had again raised its ugly head. On 27 February 2003, I spoke on Ayodhya during the debate in Parliament. I spoke my mind forcefully and of all the speeches I made in Parliament it is the one I would like to reproduce at some length in this book from the record of the Parliamentary proceedings:

SHRIMATI KRISHNA BOSE (JADAVPUR): 'Mr Speaker, Sir, I rise to take part in this debate with anguish in my heart. I have been listening to the allegations and counter-allegations that went on for a long time. I have listened to the different historical interpretations from different sides, and also the legal squabbles that went on. It hurts when you have to sit through and listen to all this because instead of concentrating on the real problems of our country, we are discussing this. What are the problems? The problems are poverty, illiteracy and disease. We are frittering away our time on, I do not know, some futile debate. What is the need of the hour now? The need of the hour is to have in our national life, peace, unity, and good sense . . . However, before I go any further, I would like to reiterate my party's stand on this. As part of the NDA, we are bound by the Common Minimum Agenda. Any deviation from that is not acceptable to us. I also reiterate that we renew our commitment to abide by the final verdict of the Court, whatever that verdict be and I can see that all of you are saying that. So, what is the quarrel about? All of you are saying that.

Having said that, I just want to raise one or two points. Is this all about a few acres of land and some bricks and mortar or are some real issues involved in it? There are some real issues involved in it. Nobody mentioned it but one real issue is democracy. In democracy, majority is not defined by religion. Religious majoritarianism is a dangerous thing for any country. Majorities have to be earned and have to be won by good programmes, good governance and good projects. As a partner of the NDA, I would like to see the NDA earn a majority that way and not in any other way.

Sir, apart from that, I am a fiercely secular person in public life. But I am also a Hindu—a devout Hindu, I claim, more than many other people who are now striding on the stage as Hindus. I have learnt my Hinduism from Swami Vivekananda and from Shri Aurobindo. I would like to remind the House of what they taught us. I am a Hindu and I want you to listen to that. I would quote just two lines from Swami Vivekananda and I would like my colleagues to listen to that carefully. As you know, he said that all religions are true. He spoke about universal religion. He said: "I shall go to the Mosque of the Mohammedan." I repeat—

"I shall go to the Mosque of the Mohammedan; I shall enter the Christian's church and kneel before the crucifix; I shall enter the Buddhist temple where I shall take refuge in Buddha and his law; and I shall go into the forest and sit down in meditation with the Hindu who is trying to see the light which enlightens the heart of everyone."

Sir, this is Hinduism. Hinduism is a very great philosophy. There is no place for hatred there. After reading the Upanishadas, the great German philosopher, Schopenhauer said that the Upanishadas would be the solace of his life and it would also be the solace of his death. What a great thing to have been said after reading the Upanishadas! I would, therefore, like all of you to rise to the occasion and condemn any spread of hatred in the name of religion and Hinduism.

Sir, another point that I would like to make is that India has a composite culture. We have seen the rise and fall of many empires, namely the Hindu empires, the Mughal empire and the British empire. What did Shri Aurobindo—whom we all revere—say about this composite culture? I invite all of you to listen to his historical assessment of the Mughal empire. He said and I quote:

"The Mughal empire was a magnificent construction. An immense amount of political genius and talent was employed in its creation and maintenance. It was as splendid, powerful and beneficent and it may be added that in spite of the fanatical zeal of Aurangzeb, it was infinitely more liberal and tolerant in religion than any medieval or contemporary European kingdom or empire and India under the Mughal rule stood high in military and political strength, economic opulence and in the brilliance of its art and culture."

This quotation is from the "Spirit and Form of Indian Polity" by Shri Aurobindo. This is what he had said. He also wrote another book in defence of Indian art where he said how much he appreciated the beauty of the mosques and tombs of India. I am not very sure that he would have been happy with what happened to a particular mosque in our country.

Sir, I am very much concerned that this is a blot on the good name of Hinduism and on the good name of India. We should try somehow to stop this. Let us go back to our real task of fighting poverty, illiteracy and disease. Let us build hundreds of schools and hospitals. I may tell my colleagues on this side that these are the real temples for Shri Rama. He will reside in these temples. He will bless us all. If an edifice is built, the foundation of which will be on bloodshed, on violence and on hatred, then Shri Rama will refuse to live in that temple. This is my view.

Sir, somebody just mentioned about India's struggle for Independence and reminded us to think about the Satyagraha under Mahatma Gandhi, to think about the Indian National Army under Netaji Subhas Bose. The Hindus, the Muslims, the Sikhs and the Christians, all rose to an ideal to liberate India from foreign rule and they all were fighting together shoulder to shoulder. Their sacrifice should not go in vain. We have inherited that independence from them. We must remember that all of us—the Hindus, the Muslims, the Sikhs and the Christians—would have to live in India. There is no point in quarrelling on such a poisonous sort of a conflict all the time. I would like to call upon all of you in the name of Mahatma Gandhi and in the name of Netaji Subhas Bose to rise above this petty thing and think of India. India has a great potential. We would be one of the great economic powers soon. Let us rise above this and think of a greater and bigger vision for India. Mr Speaker, Sir, I have done.'

I had strong personal views on the temple issue. I was emotional and passionate. After I finished, several members from the opposition congratulated me. I remember Somnath Chatterjee, who spoke before me, had been taunting me in the course of his speech, 'There is Krishnadi, an ally, what does she have to say, etc.' After my speech he told me, 'You spoke very well.' I thought today I must have completely alienated our big partner in the coalition. I was not even sure how some in my own party would take my speech. Fortunately, none from my own party was present in the House when I gave this speech.

But a surprise awaited me. I went to attend a Rashtrapati Bhavan dinner in honour of President Nujoma of Namibia. I was already late as I was speaking in Parliament. I arrived somewhat breathless. I found Prime Minister Vajpayee walking towards me, his hand outstretched and a big smile on his face. I was somewhat taken aback. I usually said, 'namashkar' to him from a distance. Since he offered his hand I took it. He said, 'I listened to your speech, I heard what you said.' I had noticed he was not present in the chamber when I spoke. He must have heard my speech on the TV monitor in his office. His smile and handshake told me that he at least, approved of my views.

I was very busy in my constituency as well, rushing from one corner to another of its gigantic sprawl. Usually, Dol or Holi in March would be a family affair on the terrace of Basundhara. This year I was on the streets of Santoshpur where women and children danced to Tagore songs and sprayed colour on one another. Sugata had come from Boston to see me during his spring break and he joined me on the streets of Jadavpur. I made a short trip to Mumbai to participate in a conference on foreign and defence policy where I met the chief minister, Sushil Shinde, my former colleague on the CEA.

The Iraq crisis which had erupted kept us all occupied. There was a demand from the opposition for an all-party resolution to protest against US aggression in Iraq. I had been following the Iraq crisis closely. I tried to keep the committee up to date on the issue through discussions and interactive meetings. In November 2002 I was present at the Security Council when the infamous resolution UNSC 1441 was passed. I saw fifteen hands go up— five permanent and ten non-permanent members—voting for the resolution. Till the last moment there were some doubts as to what Syria, then a non-permanent member, would do. But Syria also went along with the others.

At the committee meeting to discuss the budget I asked foreign secretary Kanwal Sibal to brief the committee on the latest situation in Iraq, which he did. Some members told me later that our anxiety about Iraq and the foreign secretary's much-too-detailed explanation distracted our attention from the external affairs budget. As a consequence the MEA officials escaped some of the usual grilling on that subject. There were a number of all-party meetings in the Speaker's chamber about the draft of the all-party resolution on Iraq to be placed in Parliament. Usually the leader of the party or the chief whip participated in these deliberations. But since this was a foreign policy matter I took part in these particular meetings. There were lengthy debates on what word to use to 'condemn' or to 'deplore' the US aggression against Iraq. Eventually, we settled on the Hindi word 'ninda' to express our disapproval. The communists wanted 'ghor ninda' to heartily disapprove, but 'ninda' was deemed to be enough. It fell on me to take part in the debate on the resolution which was passed unanimously.

In the meantime various diplomatic overtures were on regarding the Iraq crisis. I was in contact with the German ambassador, Mr Richter. The political counsellor of the German embassy came to my office and had a long discussion on Iraq. The first secretary and two other officers from the US embassy came to my office to put across their point of view. Mr Blackwill, the US ambassador, called a few of us Members of Parliament to tea to explain the US views on Iraq. He also wanted to come to my committee to talk about Iraq as he did at the time of Afghanistan crisis but I had different ideas on this occasion. I believed that the US policy towards Iraq was a catastrophe and was deeply worried by American requests to our government for support, especially in the form of Indian troops. I invited former foreign secretaries, former Indian ambassadors to Iraq and the Middle East, as well as former army officers to give their expert inputs on Iraq. J.N. Dixit, who later became national security advisor to Manmohan Singh, deposed before my committee. Another expert on the Middle East whom I invited was Hamid Ansari, who later became Vice-President. Mr Ansari acknowledged that my initiative on Iraq as chairperson of CEA had played a major role in preventing our government from committing any mistake on that front.

The German government invited me and a few other MPs to visit Berlin for a post-Iraq discussion and also to share ideas on how to combat terrorism. So we arrived in Wiesbaden in early May of 2003. I was delighted to be in Wiesbaden because Sisir and I had fallen in love with this beautiful town when we had come here more than thirty years ago. That was the year Sisir and I had travelled to Europe in search of history. We looked for old acquaintances of Netaji, old photographs and documents related to his life. Our collection enriched the archives of the Netaji Research Bureau and I ended up writing my first book *Itihaser Sandhane,* which literally means 'In search of history'. Wiesbaden was as beautiful as ever. Only the old friends were missing. Before we settled down to serious work we were asked to perform a pleasant task. We were taken for a wine-tasting trip to a cellar stacked with a variety of wines. We had Kapil Sibal, Suresh Prabhu, General Tripathy, and a few others in our group. I tasted two white wines and two red wines and then gave up. My companions were braver and went on to taste a dozen or so different varieties. We also met high-ranking administrative officials who dealt with terrorist crime. The members of the state assembly from the Wiesbaden area gave us lunch and took us around their assembly house . We also went to a spa since Wiesbaden is well known for its spas. On one of my drives through the town I spotted Hotel Klee where Sisir and I had stayed during our first visit to Wiesbaden in 1971.

From Wiesbaden we moved to Berlin. Apart from German officials, we were received by Ambassador Rangachari. I was very busy and could not go to Augsburg to meet Anita and Martin. So Anita and Martin came to Berlin for a couple of days. We had day-long conferences with senior security officials where we exchanged notes on combating terrorism. What struck me was the fact that the senior police officers and the officials of the crime department looked very gentle—I had expected them to look severe and forbidding. We had meetings with members of the Bundestag and a dinner at the German Parliament annexe was arranged by the Friends of India group of the German Parliament. I knew many of them as I had met them in India when they visited or had met them in Berlin in the course of my previous visits. It was good to see old familiar faces again.

I snatched some time from my busy schedule and sat in a café chatting with Anita and Martin. Ambassador Rangachari and his wife Kokila were holding a reception for Zubin Mehta who had been given a Padma Bhushan, or some such award, which he could not to go to India to accept. So he was presented the award at this reception by our ambassador. I had known Rangachari and Kokila in Delhi. I used to meet Kokila at all the FICCI meetings because she was involved in their work. The Rangacharis specially invited Anita, Martin and myself to the reception. Dinner was served on the lawns of the ambassador's residence and it was a particularly chilly evening. I was at the high table with Zubin Mehta. I had the chance to talk to him a lot and liked him very much.

Back home I hardly had time to repack my suitcase. I was slated to go to Washington and New York. The CII had asked me to lead a delegation of MPs and captains of industry to the US. Among others in the group were Satyavrat Chaturvedi from the Congress, Bikram Kesari Deo from the BJP, Salim Shervani from the Samajvadi Party, Rammohan Rao of the Telegu Desham Party, and General Shankar Roy Chowdhury, an independent member of the Rajya Sabha. Anand Mahindra, the president of CII, and Tarun Das, its director-general, were also members of the delegation. Sugata arrived from Boston to meet me in New York the day I arrived. We had dinner together at Vong, our favourite restaurant on 3rd Ave and 53rd Street. We walked to the restaurant and walked back to the hotel. I felt very happy to be able to walk on New York streets again after a long time since I had not been able to do that for a considerable time because of my knee problem.

The next day in New York began with a breakfast meeting at the New York stock exchange. It was a sit-down breakfast and discussion. Then came the ringing of the bell. I was a bit apprehensive about this meeting. I was confident I could carry on diplomatic conversations quite well. I could discuss politics and world affairs with ease. But I was not so sure about stocks and bonds. So I heaved a sigh of relief when the meeting went off smoothly. In the evening I had telephone calls from Sugata and Sumantra. 'How did you manage the stock exchange meeting?' both of them asked anxiously. I said, 'Well I went about as if I had done nothing in my life other than visiting stock exchanges.' I had meetings with Vijay Nambiar, our permanent representative at the UN and his deputy, Gopinathan. In Washington we had a minute-to-minute programme. The main function that the embassy had arranged was a ceremony to celebrate the tenth anniversary of the Caucus on India. The Caucus had started with a few members but now it had a large number of friends of India in it. It was an impressive ceremony held at the Capitol and was well-attended by senators and house representatives. I presented the Bharat Mitra or Friend of India award to a number of Congressmen and made an extempore speech on Indo-US relations which, I was told, impressed everyone.

We had a good meeting with Congresswoman Nancy Pelosi, the minority leader of the Democratic party, who later became speaker of the House of Representatives. We compared notes on American and Indian democracy at the National Endowment of Democracy and had a luncheon meeting at the highly conservative Heritage Foundation. At the Brookings Institution Strobe Talbott joined us and told me he had just finished reading the manuscript of Sumantra's new book on Kashmir and had written a blurb for its jacket. We were staying at the Mayflower Renaissance hotel. Ambassador Teresita Shaeffer arranged a meeting of the Centre of Strategic and International Studies at the hotel. My presentation went off well, but General Roy Chowdhury got into an argument with two veteran Pakistani journalists on Kashmir. Teresita had to intervene to stop it. The meeting was presided over by CSIS President Hamre.

In Washington Lalit Mansingh took me to see two very good properties for the planned Indian Cultural Centre. At almost every meeting of our committee we had been criticizing the external affairs ministry as also the Indian embassy for the extraordinary delay in setting up a cultural centre in Washington. As a matter of fact, every time the embassy spotted a good property, it approached the MEA, but there was always an inordinate delay in getting any response from the MEA and the property would go off the market or the price would go up. One of the properties that Lalit Mansingh showed me was a beautiful Spanish-villa-style building with a lot of space inside and an extensive parking area outside. The other property was less expensive but equally good. I wrote a strong letter to the ministry to take an immediate decision to buy one of these. I personally preferred the Spanish villa.

The delegation I led had a good meeting with Christina Rocca, assistant secretary of state who I had met earlier in Delhi and had found to be knowledgeable and friendly. At every official meeting I had to explain India's attitude to Iraq which was that India wanted a multilateral approach to the Iraq crisis and we disapproved of the unilateral approach taken by the US. We also disapproved of the way US had bypassed the UN. 'Did you have to pass a resolution in the Indian Parliament condemning US policy?' I was asked. I answered that we were elected representatives of the people and we had to reflect the opinion of the people and we did exactly that.

We had a most interesting meeting with Senator Hilary Clinton in her senate office. I had met her briefly when she came to Kolkata for the funeral of Mother Teresa. Here at her office we had a proper discussion and I found her to be a very sharp and intelligent person. She also had poise and grace. In the course of her conversation on Indo-US relations I noticed that she mentioned her husband several times, 'When my husband went to India.' 'When my husband said . . .' and so on. She was very busy at that time because her autobiography was about to be released. She seemed very excited about that. On my return to

India one of the first things I was asked to do was to review her book for the Bengali literary magazine *Desh*. Our days in Washington were coming to an end. Ambassador Lalit Mansingh and his wife Indira gave a reception in my honour at their residence. Sugata came from Boston to attend the reception. I met many interesting persons there and made a formal speech.

The delegation dispersed and its members went in different directions. I stayed back and took the shuttle to Boston to spend a few days with Sugata. It was a quiet holiday after a hectic tour. Many close family friends came to see me. I had a meeting with the President of Harvard University, Larry Summers, a former treasury secretary, and also with Dean Bill Kirby. I made the regular visit to my doctor, Dr Elena Masarotti, whom I had come to like very much. She herself was wheelchair-bound but always full of energy. It was early June and we had lovely weather. There was one thing that Sugata and I missed very much. That was our annual reunion on Tipu's birthday. It was his tenth birthday on 2 June 2003, but there was no family gathering.

Before I left for India there was a formal black tie dinner for some occasion at Harvard University which I attended. The wife of the Indian dean for engineering came up and said, 'You look familiar.' It transpired that they had seen my photograph in some newspapers presenting the 'Friend of India Award' to US Congressmen. Boston's Museum of Fine Arts was always my favourite haunt since the days Sisir and I lived in Boston in the late fifties when I used to push Sugata in a stroller and go round the galleries. Sugata suggested that we go and see the Impressionist exhibition that was on at the museum. This time Sugata pushed me around in a wheechair through room after room, as I used to do with him in a stroller once upon a time. On my way back I stopped in London and spent a relaxed few days with Sumantra.

On my flight back to India I thought I really have no home to go back to either in Delhi or in Kolkata. There was a time when I used to come back from trips and Sisir would be waiting

for me. These days when I go to Boston Sugata is there. When I
go to London Sumantra is there. But in India I come back to an
empty house, which is painful. It was good that I was totally
submerged in work.

In Delhi I attended to work at my committee office. I finalized
a tour plan for the committee to Srinagar and Leh. Harsh Bhasin,
who had just been named our ambassador to Denmark, came to
call on me. Bhasin was actually being groomed to be sent to
Pakistan as our high commissioner since it was expected that we
might renew normal diplomatic relations soon. But relations were
not improving as fast as was expected. So Bhasin was being sent
to Denmark. But as soon as this was done, there was a thaw in
our relationship. Shivshankar Menon, who was in China, was
named India's high commissioner to Islamabad and Aziz Ahmed
Khan was named as Pakistan's envoy to Delhi. Harsh Bhasin
had just called on President Abdul Kalam before he came to me.
President Kalam sat at his computer and gave him a thorough
briefing on Denmark. Kalam used to call groups of MPs for
breakfast meetings and he was a very good host. He would himself
bring the plate to me, not caring about protocol. Afterwards, he
took classes for us with graphs and charts and lectured us on
how we could develop our part of the country.

It was the third week of June when I arrived in Srinagar with
members of my committee. I had spoken on Kashmir many times
in Parliament, raising questions about our policy that no other
MP had the courage to bring up. In 1996 I had asked questions
about the murder of Jalil Andrabi, a human rights lawyer,
allegedly by our security forces. In 1998 I had urged the
government to creatively explore the prospect of substantial
autonomy even while rejecting a particular autonomy resolution
passed under the auspices of the Farooq Abdullah government.
In subsequent debates I suggested taking a leaf out of the book
of the Northern Ireland peace process in addressing the Kashmir
imbroglio. But I had not so far been able to visit Kashmir since

my election as MP. In 2003 there was a temporary lull in violence in Kashmir after Vajpayee had once more initiated a peace process in April that year. We checked in at Grand Palace hotel. I was pleasantly surprised to see the hotel full. The previous year Sumantra had visited Srinagar about this time and had found only a handful of rooms occupied.

The committee had meetings with passport officers, post and telegraph department officers and police officers. On visiting the passport office I was delighted to meet the smart, efficient passport officer of Srinagar, John Shilshi. He came from the another insurgency-affected part of our country—the northeast. He was a Manipuri from Imphal. I mingled with the crowd who waited at the passport office for new passports or renewals. Every one said they were happy since John Shilshi had taken over. This was a pleasant experience for us because in most passport offices we heard a lot of complaints. The one other exception was the Chennai passport office which was extremely well organized. Waiting in the crowd at the Srinagar passport office I suddenly spotted the father of Agha Shahid Ali, the well-known Kashmiri poet, who lived in New York. On enquiry he told me he was on his way to the US when at Delhi airport his overcoat was stolen with the passport in the pocket. I asked John to see to it that he got a duplicate soon so that he could resume his journey.

We had a tea-meeting with the chief minister Mufti Mohammad Sayeed. His daughter Mehbooba joined us briefly. I had met Mehbooba earlier when she came to attend a seminar on Kashmir at Netaji Bhawan. Yasin Malik, chairman of the Jammu and Kashmir Liberation Front, was also there at that time. I introduced them to each other. We congratulated the chief minister on the improvement in law and order and the lull in violence. But soon after we came away there was an attempt on his life—a bomb had exploded at the very place where we had met him.

One morning I was having early breakfast in the coffee room

of the hotel. I got a message that Yasin Malik had come to meet me. He was waiting in the room of Dr Kaul of Batra Hospital. We sat in the balcony of Dr Batra's room and talked. I had known Yasin for quite a while since the time he, Jalil Andrabi and some others had come to take part in a seminar on Kashmir at Netaji Bhawan at the time of Netaji's birthday in January 1995. That was the year when the prime minister, Narasimha Rao also came to attend the traditional birthday assembly at Netaji Bhawan. The IB (Intelligence Branch) and the SPG (Special Protection Group) had a hard time with the prime minister, on the one hand, and Yasin Malik, who had just been released from prison, on the other. That morning in Srinagar, Yasin and I continued our conversation in my hotel room. The telephone rang. It was Sugata from the US. He also exchanged greetings with Yasin. It was decided that I would go to Yasin's home one evening after I had finished my official work of the day.

That evening Yasin came in his car to pick me up. I was quietly going out with him when the officer in charge of our security spotted us. 'Madam, you are going out with him? You are going alone?' He could not allow it, he firmly declared. Yasin was furious. He shouted, 'I take responsibility. Nobody can touch a single strand of her hair. She is my mother.' A heated argument followed. 'You cannot defend your own people. Could you protect the life of so and so...who was shot dead?' the security officer shouted back. 'If anything happens to Madam I will be held responsible. If Madam insists on going she will be accompanied by a Gypsy-full of security men. And her own bodyguard must be in the car she is travelling in. The two were almost coming to blows. John Shilshi and I tried to intervene. Yasin had a point. He said a quiet visit was preferable. The area where he lived was known as the 'Gaza Strip' of Srinagar. I would be the first Indian MP to visit the area since the outbreak of the insurgency in 1989. A car full of soldiers would only invite trouble. A compromise was worked out. I would sit in the front seat next to Yasin in his car and my personal security would be in the rear seat. If the Gypsy followed, it would keep its distance. So I arrived at Yasin's home and neighbourhood. The 'Gaza Strip' gave me a warm welcome. Instead of flowers, walnuts were showered on me as I entered the house. Yasin had not told me before that his sister Amina had got married in the morning. The showered walnuts were presented to me in a bag and Yasin, in the traditional Kashmiri way put a shawl round my shoulder. I had no gift for Amina except my blessings. Amina and all the womenfolk sat around me and made me feel part of the family. Amina was a sweet girl whom I had always liked very much and I was happy for her. But I felt sad for Yasin. This was the sister who took care of him whenever he was in prison or was hospitalized in Delhi. I had known Amina to knock on all official doors, trying to bring some relief to her ailing brother. We enjoyed a Kashmiri meal together. We felt sorry for my security guard who stood at attention in one corner of the room with his hand on the automatic weapon. He was invited to sit down on the floor and join in the dinner. He pleaded that since he was on duty he was not permitted to relax or sit down. Late in the night, Yasin escorted me to the Grand Palace from the 'Gaza Strip'. No untoward incident had happened.

We visited Pahalgam, a favourite place of mine. But I missed the quiet beauty of the place. For some reason it was full of tourists and noisy that day. The committee was given a formal dinner in a tent by the Lidder river. One afternoon we went for a shikara ride on Dal Lake. We wished to go to the Char Chinar. The shikara-wallahs were happy to see a large number of customers occupying a number of boats. Soon we were in the middle of the lake. Boats selling saffron and stone jewellery slid up next to our shikara and tried to sell these goodies. I chose a stone necklace. The price seemed unreasonably high, but I decided to contribute my mite to boosting Kashmir's economy and bought it. We were in a joyful mood. Our shikaras passed each other and we waved. Some took photographs of our shikara from the passing one. In my shikara I was singing a boatman's song by D.L. Roy, '*Chotto moder panshi tari, sange ke ke jabi ayay, bela boye jay*'—come to our tiny boat, whoever wishes to join, time is running out. Minati Sen, a Bengali MP from the CPI(M) joined me in my song. Suddenly there was some commotion in the boats that had gone ahead of us. A message came that a storm was about to hit us and the boats should row swiftly to the nearest bank and take shelter. Before we could act on the message, a severe storm broke upon the Dal. The shikaras swayed dangerously. Some of the shikaras had their slender colourful hoods blown off. There was panic all around but in the midst of the storm I felt a strange calm. I would not mind if the shikara capsized and I drowned in the Dal Lake. I would not be able to swim because of my weak knees and I would not be able to scramble on to the bank because I would need steps and railings. Now we could see the bank. The shikara preceding us reached the bank and people jumped out of the boat. I saw my secretary Viswanathan taking off his shoes and rolling up his trousers—ready to jump into the lake to rescue me. He looked with desperation at our boat trying to reach the shore. He did not have to jump. He helped me out of the boat and to climb up the steep bank. We were at the back of the Centaur Hotel. Well, some of us were. Where were the others? Back at the hotel we took a head count. All the MPs had reached safely. There were jokes about how we had missed making the headlines with news of so many MPs being drowned in the Dal Lake.

I used to wake up early in the morning during our stay at the Grand Palace hotel and go into the garden for a morning walk. Kashmir always brought back memories of previous visits with parents, later visits with my husband and young children. It also brought back memories of a rather unusual sadhu, Swami Premananda, whom I had known. His place of sadhana was Kashmir although he was a Bengali. He had left home and Bengal when he was a student of Presidency College. He left the hills of Kashmir and came back to the plains of Bengal after 1947 leaving behind a large number of Kashmiri friends and devotees.

Our next stop was Ladakh. I had e-mails from my two sons who asked me not to go to Leh. The altitude was more than 11,000 feet, the air rarefied. People might experience breathing difficulty. In Delhi, I think it was the former foreign secretary, M.K. Rasagotra, who told me that as a young officer on his first visit to Leh he came out of the plane and fell flat on the ground, unable to breathe. As chairperson of the CEA I gave strict instructions to all members that the first day would be a rest day. Nobody must stir out of the hotel room till they had given themselves enough time to get acclimatized. They obeyed the order till late afternoon. Then I noticed they came out on to the main street of Leh where there were shops on both sides and enjoyed themselves. The meetings in Leh were quite interesting. The Ladakhi people are simple and friendly. Some citizens of Leh asked me to put in a word with the prime minister for the Leh to Mansarovar road to be reopened. The old road already existed and there was no need to make a new one. But permission was necessary from the Chinese government. This would make the approach to Mansarovar very easy. At present it takes weeks to reach Mansarovar by the route that goes through Uttar Pradesh. Prime Minister Vajpayee was visiting China at that moment. We heard that an alternate route to Mansarovar was on the agenda but it later turned out that the official alternate route would be through Himachal Pradesh and not Ladakh.

We planned to go up to the highest point near Leh, travelling as we were told, by the highest motorable road in the world. Khardung La (pass) was at a height of 18,350 feet. Frantic e-mails reached our Ladakhi friend Siddiq's computer from Sugata and Sumantra, 'Ask Mamma not to go to that height.' I gave in to my sons' anxiety and said, 'All right, I will not go.' That morning after we had concluded an official meeting the convoy left for Khardung La with all the MPs. There was a car with first aid arrangements and a doctor in case medical assistance was needed. After everyone had left I got into the small car I was using and asked the driver to take me for a little drive on that route so that I could have an idea of the surrounding landscape. In my car I had two Ladakhi women—an elderly Buddhist lady and a young Christian girl. The convoy had left earlier, so we were totally alone on the road. But as we went up the mountain, the rugged landscape was breathtakingly beautiful. The grandeur naturally made one bow one's head to the Creator. I uttered the mantra, '*Jatraiba chitte samudeti bhakti tatraiba pashyati tabaiba murtim*'—wherever bhakti (devotion) is inspired in my heart, I see you there.

I asked the driver to go further uphill. The young Ladakhi girl was already feeling sick. But I was in a daze. I sang to myself, '*Amar matha nata kore dao he tomar charana dhular tole*'—let me bow my head and touch the dust of your feet. I realized we had reached a small group of huts—the last inhabited locality. We were at the altitude of 15,000 feet. We made a halt and gave water to the young Ladakhi girl who was sick. I talked to the driver. Since we had come up to an altitude of 15,000 altitude, why not go all the way up to Khardung La? The last stretch of the road was steep and somewhat rough and took a longer time to cover than the earlier part. But at last there I was at Khardung La. Our convoy of MPs was still there. They were most surprised to see me get down from the car. They were delighted but said to come alone was much more dangerous. It would have been safer to be with the convoy. I remembered the anxiety of my two sons and tried not to exert myself. I walked slowly, took a few photographs and returned to my car while others enjoyed the views of the snow-capped mountains.

We were back in our hotel before sunset. It would have been wise to take rest. But a dinner had been arranged in our honour on the terrace of the hotel. It was preceded by a Ladakhi dance performance. A group of men and women in traditional Ladakhi dress went round and round singing and dancing. The dance movement was quite slow. As I watched them, the leader of the troupe came up to me, held my hand and invited me to join the dance. So I got up and joined them. They gave me a scarf. There was a general cheer from the audience when they saw me dance. After some time, one by one the other MPs got up and joined me. Most of them were not very good at dancing so it looked as if a row of people were walking at slow pace following our movements. But it was fun. Everyone enjoyed the dance and the food. Our friend Siddiq sent an e-mail to Sugata and Sumantra to say that in spite of the Khardung La adventure and the dance, their Mamma was all right. There was no need to worry.

Siddiq and his wife took me to the source of the Sindhu river. We sat at the bank and I dipped my fingers in the water. So this was the river that flowed down to Pakistan. Our two nations are inexorably bound by nature. I remembered our Pakistani friend Iqbal Ahmed who told me in Kolkata—'If I sow a new plant in Peshawar today you will find it in Bengal in a couple of years.' I avoided trips to the monasteries because of the innumerable steps one had to climb, but the others went. Viswanathan bought a garland of beads for me from one of the old monasteries. You were supposed to count the beads and do your prayers.

From Ladakh we came down to Jammu. Coming from peaceful Ladakh, Jammu seemed tense to me. I told my Jammu friends that even Srinagar was more relaxed. They said all the terrorists were targeting the plains now. Some of them who lived outside the city told us that they did not sleep at night but kept vigil. They took rest in the day. Jammu was a short stop. I had official meetings and could not visit friends. Our good friend Ved Bhasin, editor of the *Kashmir Times*, came to meet me at the hotel. We discussed the situation in Jammu and Kashmir.

Usually from Jammu people go to Vaishno Devi temple but

we decided to go to the mountains. On our way up, as also on our way down, I noticed soldiers standing guard at regular intervals. I was told they were on duty. They could not leave their posts and food would be brought to them. Against the beautiful natural backdrop of the mountains, they looked incongruous. I felt sad for the poor soldiers who had been given an unenviable task. I could only hope and pray that the political leaders would work towards a just solution of the Kashmir problem.

That summer, July and August 2003, I was very busy in Delhi and Kolkata. The monsoon session was on in Parliament. Sugata and Sumantra were with me for part of the session. They took turns to be with me. They were always anxious about me and tried to ensure that I was not left alone for long stretches of time. Interactions with the diplomatic community went on. In Parliament, Vajpayee made a statement on his visits to Germany and China. In mid-August the opposition brought a no-confidence motion against the NDA government. Voting took place after a long-drawn-out debate and very mediocre speeches from both sides on 19 August 2003. The result was as expected. Sometimes Sugata joined me in the Central Hall for lunch. Other members, irrespective of party affiliation, would come and join us now and then. I remember a lunch that we shared with Sunil Dutt, the actor, a Rajya Sabha MP and a fine person.

The Central Hall, with its domed roof, its antique standing fans which revolved in slow motion and where the heroes of yesteryears looked down from their framed glory was a most fascinating place and it will remain etched in my memory forever. I had been present here on historic occasions as well as at lighter moments. Above all there was an atmosphere of friendship and fellow-feeling among Members of Parliament who belonged to diverse political persuasions. Nobody would believe that two Parliamentarians now enjoying a cup of coffee together had been shouting at each other five minutes earlier inside the chamber.

For awestruck newcomers to the Central Hall it was an opportunity to watch important political leaders in different moods.

Atal Behari Vajpayee had been the leader of the opposition in the eleventh Lok Sabha, my first term in Parliament. He did not usually sit in the Central Hall. But I often saw him at the coffee corner where he stood alone, munched a toast and sipped coffee. On my way to the chamber I folded my hands and said namashkar. He looked up absentmindedly and nodded. He obviously did not have a clue as to who I was. Later, of course, I came to know him well. Most ministers did not usually sit or chat with lesser mortals in the Central Hall. But there were exceptions. I remember Indrajit Gupta as home minister used to sit with us at lunchtime regularly. He would call out to me, 'Mrs Bose, come and join us. What will you have, upma, pongol?' It was a pleasure to have a conversation with him. He belonged to the bygone days when Parliament was a civilized place for debate on national issues. He was sad at the decline in the standards of debate as also the unruly and irresponsible behaviour of members on various occasions. Indrajitbabu's successor as home minister, L.K. Advani, could be often seen crossing the whole length of the Central Hall on the way to his Parliament office from the Lok Sabha. He was always courteous and greeted people. If I happened to be in his orbit he would stop by without fail. 'How are you, Krishnaji?' he would say, and enquire about my husband and children. A very interesting figure, then in opposition, was Lalu Prasad Yadav. Laluji was always surrounded by courtiers. He moved around in a mini procession. But he was always friendly and full of exuberance. If his eyes fell on me through the crowd of courtiers he was sure to shout, 'Didi, namaste.'

Another erstwhile leader of the opposition was none other than Sonia Gandhi. She also sat now and then in the Central Hall surrounded by courtiers. Women members of Congress sometimes clustered around her. There was always a visible competition among them to attract her attention or to show their concern for her. Some would call the bearer and tell him to remember that she liked the coffee strong. But these were rare occasions. She was seen more often walking briskly up or down the hall. In winter she wore a black short coat over her sari. In the height of summer it could be a white Kerala sari with a golden border. Her short ponytail shook in rhythm with her brisk gait. By some strange coincidence, on several occasions when we spoke to each other was not exactly in the Central Hall but in front of the ladies' washroom while we patiently awaited our turn. When our turn came she would always graciously give me precedence. Once when both the doors opened simultaneously—to my mild surprise—she chose the Indian-style toilet leaving the western one for my use. That was a sure sign, I thought, that she was truly Indian. The last time we met at that spot I told her that next time we really must meet somewhere else. There were brief, serious conversations occasionally. She knew I had an alternative to the official Women's Reservation Bill and had introduced it as a private member's bill. She had taken serious note of it and asked Kapil Sibal and other colleagues to go through it. But she told me she would prefer the thirty-three per cent Reservation Bill. If we failed absolutely to get that bill through, we might think about my alternative.

The joint sessions of Parliament addressed by the President were sombre, impressive occasions in the Central Hall. I saw three Presidents—Shankar Dayal Sharma, K.R. Narayanan and A.P.J. Abdul Kalam—in that role. The President came in a solemn procession followed by the vice president, the Speaker, the prime minister and others. There were the turbaned sentries with colourful flags. As chairperson of a Parliamentary committee I was supposed to sit at a special place earmarked for all chairs. We were considered semi-VIPs. But I always chose to sit at the back where I managed an aisle seat and watched the progress of the solemn procession. But the session at the Central Hall that I shall carry in my mind forever is the midnight session of 15 August 1997. It was the golden jubilee of India's independence. It was a very impressive and emotionally charged session. The hall was full to capacity. We huddled together on the benches and Sisir sat by my side. The 'Tryst with Destiny' speech by Jawaharlal Nehru was played. I wondered whether there were many in that hall who might have listened to the speech fifty years ago? I was a young girl at that time. I remember I heard it over the radio as I sat at our Nicholson Road home near Kashmere Gate. After Nehru the husky voice of Mahatma Gandhi cast a spell over the gathering. The announcement by Sangma that a speech by Netaji Subhas Chandra Bose will be played was greeted with a thunderous roar from the audience and a continuous thumping of desks. Then there was Netaji's voice speaking in Hindustani. During the five-minute speech people burst into spontaneous applause at the end of every sentence. I looked up at his portrait. There he was reading the proclamation of the Provisional Government of Azad Hind as his voice echoed through the hall on the fiftieth anniversary of India's freedom.

One afternoon in July 2003 I.K. Gujral, who as prime minister had supported me in including Netaji's speech at the midnight session, asked Sugata and me to come over for tea at his residence. We later invited him to deliver one of the Netaji Orations. Mrs Sudha Murthy, wife of Narayan Murthy of Infosys, came to my Delhi apartment one morning and had breakfast with Sugata and me. She was an unusual person who did a lot of good work for the down-trodden and poor. She too came later to Kolkata and visited Netaji Bhawan.

Shyam Benegal came to see me one day. He was busy shooting his Netaji film and had asked for the army's help for some of the war scenes. The army, he said, usually helps in such films. There have been films on Kashmir, films on Indo-Pak wars, and the Sino-Indian war. Shyam was shocked because he was told that for the purpose of these films the soldiers of the Indian army can don the uniform of the Pakistan army or the Chinese army, but they were banned from wearing the uniform of Indian National Army which under the leadership of Subhas Chandra Bose fought for India's freedom. I tried to reach George Fernandes, the defence minister, but he was out of India. I raised the issue in Parliament during zero hour. While I was speaking on the issue, the Congress chief whip Priya Ranjan Das Munshi got up in support and said, 'We associate ourselves with her point of view.' The Speaker asked these sentiments to be communicated to the defence minister. I later got an unsatisfactory official reply from the defence minister on my zero hour submission. George Fernandes later spoke to me personally and said this was the policy which Mountbatten started and Nehru continued, but he seemed unwilling or unable to change the policy. I finally understood the meaning of the term 'post-colonial' that is often used to describe our state.

My committee devoted time to discussing Indo-Pak relations as another peace process was in its incipient stages. I also convened an interesting meeting on the activities of the ICCR, the Indian Council of Cultural Relations. ICCR had immense possibilities to take cultural diplomacy forward. But I felt it worked more as a bureaucratic wing of the MEA. So I arranged a meeting where I invited painters, musicians, dancers to come and share their views on the activities of the ICCR. The members of the committee always enjoyed these unconventional meetings that I arranged.

In Kolkata I was busy with usual constituency work. The mayor of Kolkata had arranged a reception for Sourav Ganguly, our famous cricket player, who lived in my constituency. He invited me to the occasion and asked me to present gifts to Sourav and his wife Dona. The reception was held at the Town Hall. I remember putting a gold chain around Dona's neck. On the eve of Independence Day, 2003, I hoisted the flag at a big gathering in Behala. On the morning of Independence Day I went round Kabitirtha and Behala and hoisted flags at different schools and various functions. In the afternoon I was at the traditional tea-gathering at the Raj Bhawan.

I was never very closely involved with internal party activities of the Trinamool Congress. I preferred it that way. As a Member of Parliament I disbursed the funds that the central government gave us for local area development without consideration of political affiliation. Thus CPI(M) petitioners always got whatever they wanted from me, particularly for educational institutions even though since theirs was a regimented party and there was no hope of reciprocation of my liberal views. So far as my party's views on broader issues like economic reform or foreign affairs were concerned, I was never very sure where Mamata stood. I do not think anyone else had any inkling about these either or if she at all had any informed views of her own. Whenever I spoke on issues like saffronization of education, the Ayodhya controversy, Indo-Pak relations, or the Kashmir dispute, I articulated my personal views. Fortunately, Mamata never objected to any of that. Unfortunately, on the all important question of Gujarat I was unable to get my way with Mamata and her party.

In the early days of Trinamool I had asked Mamata to form a working committee. She accepted the suggestion immediately and constituted a committee with twelve persons. But whenever a meeting of the working committee was convened, it would be described as an 'extended' committee meeting. There could be a hundred people present. It was impossible to have any serious discussion on policy matters. There would always be sycophants who would flatter her in an unashamed manner. Here was a leader who led a simple life, was personally not corrupt, and had a certain mass appeal. Even the intelligentsia, who wished to be emancipated from the shackles of years of communist rule, reposed their faith in her for a while. She was in no need of sycophants and flatterers. It was sad to see the fast erosion of confidence in her abilities in the minds of the people.

In August 2003 Mamata had called a conference of the Trinamool Congress in Asansol which was about a four-hour drive from Kolkata. I had avoided going to other such conferences, but I agreed to go this time. I was told I would have to move the resolution on foreign policy. So I hired a Toyota Qualis since some of my workers wished to go with me and started for Asansol. Huge lorries overtook us or crossed us every now and then. I was in the front seat beside our young Muslim driver. At the back were Anirban, Ratan, Sambhu, Gomma and others. I had dozed off. And in that half-awake state I thought that if there were to be some mishap now, nobody would know what happened to us. The story unfolded in my dream. The newspapers would get the news first. So Suman in his newspaper office will be one of the first to receive the news. Then he would go to his boss Aveek and ask for permission to leave for Asansol immediately. In my dream Aveek was shocked and asked Suman to rush to the spot. In the middle of this dream I opened my eyes. And there was a gigantic truck just about to collide with our car. I was strangely calm. My only reaction was oh, my God, there would be a tremendous noise now, as if it was only the noise that mattered. There were shrieks of panic from behind. Our driver tried to swerve the car to the left and slammed on the brake. The Qualis came to a halt and stood face to face with the truck. It was literally a hair's breadth escape.

The conference was the usual chaotic conglomeration of people. I did not think much serious work could be done. The main conference was held in a cinema hall. I scrambled on to the stage and read my piece on foreign affairs. It was in English and I was not sure how many appreciated it. Next day some of us went to visit the Kalyaneswari temple nearby. Kalyaneswari is a temple for Goddess Kali and a well-known place of pilgrimage. In my childhood I used to visit the temple from my father's country house in Mihijam and I noticed that now the place had lost some of its quiet beauty. There was a huge crowd of devotees. Gomma, my devoted housekeeper, insisted that we make a mannat there. You have to tell Goddess Kalyaneswari your wish and tie a small pebble on a branch of the tree in the courtyard.

And when Kalyaneswari fulfilled your wish—which she was sure to do—you would have to come back, offer a puja, and untie the pebble. Of course, the wish has to be kept secret. I am still waiting for my wish to be fulfilled. Next day there was a meeting to be addressed by leaders of the party. I decided to skip it and took the journey back home. If ever you drive that way, there is a 'must' that you had to perform. You had to stop your car at a place called Shaktigarh and buy a famous sweet of the locality called 'langcha'. We dutifully brought an earthen-pot full of langchas and returned to Kolkata. Somehow it was Kalyaneswari and the langchas that I carry in my mind rather than the political inanities uttered by the leaders.

I continued to shuttle between Delhi and Kolkata. Christina Rocca had arrived in Delhi. There was a FICCI lunch and a CII dinner for her. She had come with a team and one member of her team, David Good, who was in charge of India, Nepal, Bhutan and Sri Lanka, came to Kolkata and visited Netaji Bhawan. In early September we always had the Sarat Bose Memorial Lecture. I had asked Kapil Sibal to give the lecture that year and he gave a good speech on minority rights.

In September I was back at Harvard. The South Asia Initiative, that Sugata and some of his colleagues had started, was hosting its inaugural conference on *South Asia: Bridging the Great Divides* for three days from 17 September to 19 September. I spoke along with Syeda Abida Hussain of Pakistan and Abul Hasan Chowdhury of Bangladesh at one of the sessions chaired by Nur Yalman. There was a big dinner at the Kennedy Room of Charles Hotel where Amartya Sen gave the keynote address. Harvard's president, Larry Summers, spoke on the occasion. The lunch meeting where Amitav Ghosh read from his new novel was presided over by Bill Kirby. Sugata's friend and colleague Homi Bhabha gave a most eloquent introduction at the literary lunch. On the last day of the conference there was a dinner at Sugata and Ayesha's home. They had only recently moved to their new

Orchard Street residence. One day I quietly sat in the last row
and listened to one of Sugata's audio-visual lectures on the
Mughal Empire at Harvard. In the evenings we relaxed and
watched films on DVD at home. At Ayesha's insistence I watched
Ram Gopal Varma's *Company*. I dislike violence in films and
resisted seeing it for quite some time. But I must confess I enjoyed
this gangster movie.

On my way back I stopped at London for a few days and
spent some time with Sumantra. I met Ronen Sen, who was still
our high commissioner, and also spoke to his deputy, Satyabrata
Pal. President Bush visited London that week. There were protest
meetings and processions against him at Trafalgar Square. We
had sunny weather in London and I enjoyed the rear garden of
Sumantra's house. I left London on 30 September. It was the
third death anniversary of my husband Sisir. I felt rather sad on
the flight. Three years had passed but I still had no idea when I
would meet him 'up there' as my five-year-old grandson had
predicted.

On my arrival at Kolkata, it was Durga Puja time. There was
the usual round of inauguration of Pujas and distribution of
new clothes to the needy. The CEA met in Kolkata and we visited
the ICCR building which was coming up on Ho Chi Minh Sarani.
In the evening there was a dinner and a sarod recital by Bahadur
Khan's son. I checked in at the Taj with the other MPs because
early morning on the next day we left for Chennai on our way
to the Andaman Islands. We arrived at Port Blair and drove to
the Hotel Bay island. I stood on the balcony of my hotel suite
and there before me lay the vast greenish blue stretch of the sea.
Nearer the shore were rows of coconut trees. I remembered my
earlier visit to Port Blair long ago. Sisir and I had arrived with an
exhibition on Netaji Subhas Chandra Bose accompanied by our
team from the Netaji Research Bureau consisting of Atul Sen
and Naga Sundaram. The government of India had sent a
delegation of MPs to be present for the inauguration of the

exhibition. Streams of visitors poured in to see the exhibition. Netaji Subhas Chandra Bose had visited the Andamans on 30 December 1943. The Andaman and Nicobar islands were the first Indian territories to be declared independent. Netaji had named the two islands 'Shahid' and 'Swaraj'. It was a sentimental journey for me and Sisir. I had not visited the Andamans again but Sisir went with President Venkataraman on 23 January 1988 so he was not present that year's for Netaji birthday ceremony at Netaji Bhawan and I had to conduct the proceedings. The committee had a meeting with the Governor N.N. Jha who told me he knew Sisir as he had once presented him a copy of his book *The Great Escape*. Francis Xavier of the Andaman administration said, 'I was in charge of Dr Sisir Bose when he came with President Venkataraman. I took him around the Cellular Jail and other places associated with his uncle.'

In between official meetings we also did one round of the Cellular Jail. It reminded one of the colossal sacrifices that the youth of India made in the fight against British imperialism. Hundreds of young men in those days, mostly from Bengal and Punjab, had died on the gallows there. People thronged to see the gallows as if they had come on a pilgrimage. Next day we got into motor boats and went to Ross Island. It was once upon a time the seat of the British commissioner and later the seat of the Azad Hind government in exile led by Netaji.

With the trip to the Andamans my travels for the year more or less came to an end, excepting the Kolkata-Delhi commute. On Kali Puja day Prime Minister Vajpayee was giving a dinner for the visiting Canadian prime minister. But my staff in Kolkata demanded that I come back to Kolkata and celebrate the festival of lights there. So I chose to give the prime minister of Canada a miss and came to Kolkata to be with them. I also visited some of the Kali Puja pandals. The usual distribution of blankets for the poor was also done. Kali Puja was followed by Eid on 26 November. As was my practice every year, I went up to the

Sola Anna Masjid in my constituency and stood at the door. As people came out of the mosque after offering namaz, we wished each other Eid Mubarak. I had given the Sola Anna Masjid funds for the development of their cemetery. I had also done more than any other public representative since independence to help the madrasas and schools of the relatively poor Muslim segments of my constituency.

In Delhi Sanskriti, the art gallery, asked me to inaugurate a wonderful exhibition of contemporary Bengali paintings. In my speech I recalled my close association with the Bengali artists of yester year, particularly Jamini Roy, Gopal Ghose, the sculptor Pradosh Dasgupta, and Atul Bose, the master of portraiture, all of whom had been close friends of my father. The Empowerment of Women Committee met in Delhi. My own committee also held meetings on a range of subjects including Indo-Pak relations. One day I might be having dinner at the Rashtrapati Bhavan with the President of Switzerland hosted by Abdul Kalam or entertaining women MPs from Laos. The next day I would be inaugurating an ambulance or opening a book fair in Baruipur or visiting Atghara, a small village in the same area. Villagers were always very happy to have me with them and I enjoyed their company.

At the end of the winter session in December 2003, there was a big dinner given by the prime minister at the convention hall in the Ashoka Hotel. The parliamentary affairs minister, Sushma Swaraj, was in charge. The favourite slogan of those days was—feel good. The BJP believed that the people of India were feeling good and that the 'feel good' factor would see them through the next elections. Theoretically, they might have been correct. The macro-economic indicators looked good. Indo-US relations had improved considerably over the years. India and Pakistan were ready to talk to each other. There was a visible warming of relations between the two neighbours. The BJP had won the Rajasthan and Madhya Pradesh assembly elections and felt mighty pleased with themselves. There were loud whispers in the air that Parliamentary elections were round the corner. The one black spot during the tenure of the NDA regime of a little over four years was Gujarat, 2002. Yet even there, in spite of the horrendous calamity and the absolute callousness of the state government, the same wicked lot had won the election and come back to power. Inscrutable are the ways of the Indian electorate. This Parliament's life was till October 2004, but the BJP had made up its mind to bring the elections forward. They had not taken into account the long shadow the black spot of Gujarat would cast on the next elections. In seeking to win Gujarat by means most foul, they had gambled away India. To me this hara-kiri syndrome, the suicidal tendency, was quite familiar. I had seen the same tendency in the Congress in earlier times. With the BJP keen on early elections, we knew that this was the last full session of the thirteenth Lok Sabha that we were attending.

I always admired the majestic buildings of the South Block, North Block and the circular and stately Parliament House that surrounded the open chowk. I have a hazy memory of a tonga ride in the early forties with my father and others of the family in that area. As a child I looked awe-struck at those huge buildings. At the inaugural moment of free India in August 1947, I was one among the milling crowd in the flying dust of Lutyens' Delhi. Now as I drove in my small car and looked at the familiar sight, I bade goodbye to the majestic landscape. On 26 December 2003, I turned seventy-three. It was a quiet birthday in Kolkata. My two sons, Sugata and Sumantra, were with me. I thought, maybe, it was time for another journey, uphill all the way. At the end of that journey 'shall I find comfort, travel sore and weak?' The answer we all knew—'Of labour you shall find the sum.' And the promise that there would be—'Yea, beds for all who come.'

Epilogue 2007

It was fall 2007. I was in New York. As I walked down Fifth Avenue, I found large and attractive banners with catchy slogans at every street corner proclaiming the wonders of 'Incredible India'. I sat down on the steps of the New York Public Library. The September sky was beautiful and clear. There was just a touch of chill in the late afternoon breeze. Sixty years had passed since the day I walked the dusty roads of Delhi on the day India attained freedom. The newly independent country had just begun its long journey after breaking the shackles of foreign bondage. A decade later I came to the US. India was still an object of curiosity. I entered the United Nations building for the first time in 1959 to be greeted with flash bulbs—a woman in a sari! The grand, expansive steps of the New York Public Library were now filled with women in beautiful saris and salwar-kameezes. It seemed the most natural thing in the world. Inside, preparations were on for a gala evening to celebrate the sixtieth year of India's independence. A few days later the strains of the 'Desh' raga wafted gently across the courtyard of Harvard's Fogg Art Museum as the University observed the diamond jubilee of south Asian independence. Has India arrived? Has India found its place of pride and honour in a globalized world?

During our six-decade long journey we have sometimes lost our way. Many promises made during the struggle for independence have remained unfulfilled. Our leaders had promised us eradication of poverty and education for all. Poverty still stalks our land, despite an uneven spread of prosperity, and universal education and health care remain unattained dreams. Yet on the whole we have not allowed ourselves to be deflected from the path of political democracy. Our democracy is not perfect. Despite the flaws of dynasticism, criminalization and regional aberrations in the practice of democracy, our political processes have ensured a substantial measure of liberty and led to the empowerment of long subordinated sections of our society. It is no mean feat that we clung to democracy when most of our neighbours slipped into different forms of dictatorship. Soon after independence India opted for universal suffrage. No one was quite sure how it would work out. But the masses of India by and large showed a kind of canny common sense which pulled us through difficult times. I feel a sense of fulfillment in having played a small role in the gigantic drama of Indian democracy. I would have felt happier if our efforts to ensure gender equity in political representation had been successful and if we understood in a clearer fashion the difference between democracy and majoritarianism.

Soon after independence India also opted for an independent foreign policy. During the four decades of the cold war India resolutely pursued a policy of non-alignment. My years as a Parliamentarian coincided with the challenge that we faced in the post-cold war era of re-orienting ourselves in a world that was at once more multi-polar and globalized economically and culturally, and yet unipolar in military-strategic terms. During the years that I served as chairperson of the Parliamentary standing committee of external affairs I can say categorically that India's people's representatives successfully negotiated that challenge. Even in an age of the unilateral exercise of military might, India still followed its own independent policy as was evident at the time of Iraq war. India has legitimate ambitions to play a significant role on the global stage. In order to achieve those aims, a constructive engagement with the US is necessary, but not at the cost of close ties with our neighbours in Asia and the Middle East and other countries of the global South. How well we can fine-tune and balance our regional and inter-regional imperatives with our global role will determine the scale of our foreign policy successes in the future. I would have liked to see the Parliamentary standing committee on external affairs play a more active role in deliberations on the proposed Indo-US nuclear deal. There is need for Parliamentary oversight of the conduct of our foreign policy. While a lot of time gets wasted in disruptions of Parliamentary debates and grandstanding by parliamentarians for the TV cameras, my own experience suggests that a lot of constructive work can be done in the Parliamentary standing committees which need to be strengthened further.

For thirty of the sixty years of independence I have lived in a state ruled by the communists. They proclaimed themselves to be friends of the poor. They had the opportunity to rule with near-absolute power since there was no viable opposition for much of this period. Despite some initial successes in the area of land reforms and agricultural performance, the state was rapidly turned into an industrial wasteland. Ironically, it was precisely in areas where one might have expected self-avowed communists to deliver something of real substance that they failed most miserably. The last three decades have been a catastrophe in the spheres of primary education and health care. Literacy rates and indicators on school enrollment and attendance showed West Bengal falling behind the already dismal Indian averages during this period. Being a college professor and principal, I watched in despair the collapse of our system of higher education as well. With party loyalty the key factor in educational appointments at every level and excellence derided as elitism, our communist masters presided over the triumph of mediocrity. For some twenty years English was banished from the school curriculum before the government recognized its mistake and did a U-turn. Not that Bengali or Hindi, the link language, was taught especially well. Students who remained in West Bengal found it increasingly hard to compete nationally and internationally. Some opted for other states of India or, if possible, went abroad. The flight of capital from West Bengal in the last two decades of the twentieth century has been the cause of much lament. Far more disastrous for the long term was the exodus of our most talented youth.

In the late seventies and early eighties, the ruling Left Front could take credit for its moderately progressive land reforms and local panchayats and during the eighties it could boast about an acceleration in the rate of agricultural growth. In the nineties, however, the CPI(M)-led Left Front in West Bengal had little to recommend itself. I entered Parliamentary politics as a candidate of the Indian National Congress, the principal opposition party in the state. But it soon became clear that the Congress, hobbled by its central high command, was unable to take a genuine oppositional stance in West Bengal. I joined the Trinamool Congress at its founding moment and between 1998 and 2001 we raised high hopes of providing a real alternative after more than two decades of communist rule. As a Congress MP in the eleventh Lok Sabha, I had limited freedom of manoeuvre to articulate West Bengal's regional aspirations. As a Trinamool Congress MP in the twelfth and thirteenth Lok Sabhas I felt I could represent my region's interests without sacrificing my national and international outlook. In the Parliamentary election of 2004 for the fourteenth Lok Sabha, however, the Trinamool Congress suffered terrible reverses. Of the nine Trinamool MPs in the Lok Sabha, eight of us were defeated. Mamata was the only one to win in her safe south Kolkata constituency. But even her margin of victory was slashed from 217,000 to 97,000 votes. There were various reasons for this setback. One, people did not take well to Mamata's flip-flops, inexplicably leaving the NDA and going with the Congress in 2001 and then returning to the NDA at the wrong moment. Mamata's tremendous popular appeal in 1998 and 1999 had all but dissipated by 2004. Second, there was a decline in the NDA's fortune as well. Even though the macro-economic indicators looked good, large segments of the populace had not yet partaken of the much-trumpeted economic boom. People rejected the self-congratulatory 'India Shining' slogan propagated by the NDA. In a way it was ironic that when the BJP sought votes not so much on their plank of Hindutva, but on economic development, they lost. Gujarat was an indelible blot on the BJP. The party won Gujarat, but in the process lost India. Mamata's decision not to break decisively with the BJP on the question of Gujarat was resented by Muslim voters, who formed a quarter of the electorate in West Bengal. My experience, however, was that the Bengali Muslims who were Trinamool supporters did not wholly abandon the party. But the non-Bengali Urdu-speaking Muslims definitely switched loyalties. Last, but certainly not the least, was the massive rigging of the electoral process by the CPI(M) and the fierce intimidation let loose on rural voters. Rigging was, of course, present in previous elections. But in 2004 it reached devastating and unprecedented proportions. The weak organization of the Trinamool Congress was no match for the ruthless communist machine. In a constituency with nearly 1,300 polling booths, the capture of about a hundred was more than sufficient to ensure a communist victory. Village women protested that they were intimidated the evening before. Communist cadres had shown them widows' weeds as a warning to their menfolk not to venture near the polling stations the next day. Those who still dared to go were ordered home, being told that their votes had already been cast. In my own constituency I paid the price for not paying sufficient attention to one crucial fact. Buddhadeb Bhattacharya, who was a member of the state assembly from one of the seven segments of my Parliamentary constituency, was now the redoubtable chief minister of West Bengal, which he was not during my first three elections.

By the time of the 2006 state assembly elections the long-time number two in the Left Front's government hierarchy which had presided over the state's industrial decline, had managed to re-invent himself as the poster boy of capitalist industrialization of the state. To the communists' electoral machine was now added the glittering image of 'Brand Buddha' as the Left Front stormed back to power for the seventh time in a row. But in less than a year the tide turned. The year 2007 finds the government of my state of West Bengal in a peculiar situation. In their attempt to undo some of their own past mistakes they have landed themselves in great trouble. After thirty years of hibernation the communist government woke up suddenly and seemed to be in a tearing hurry to woo big industrialists, domestic and foreign, to the state. Their slogan once upon a time was 'grab the land' from landlords and rich farmers to give to the rural poor. Suddenly the perception gained ground that they had changed the principle and were now saying 'grab the land' from the peasants and give it to the capitalists for industrialization. Two rural localities, Singur in the Hooghly district, and Nandigram in the Midnapur district, came to symbolize the perfidy of the CPI(M). In the first, the government had acquired land for a car factory to be set up by the Tatas. In the second, peasants feared plans to take away agricultural land for a chemical hub to be set up by the Salim group of Indonesia.

The attempt to acquire land met with strong resistance from the peasants. No one doubts that employment-generating new industries are desperately needed in West Bengal. But instead of creating a more conducive environment for investment with improved infrastructure and encouraging market competition, the government has chosen to grant special favours to certain big capitalists. By contrast, there has been inadequate attention to plans of rehabilitation and adequate compensation for displaced people, no attempts at serious consultation and discussion with the opposition or to explain the necessity of land acquisition and any ultimate benefit to the peasants. The rural protests were put down by police firing. And to the horror of everyone, armed party cadres were used alongside the state police in a campaign of brutal reprisals. Outsiders were aghast to see the kind of state and party terror unleashed on poor villagers—men, women and children—some of them their own erstwhile supporters. This was nothing new. I had seen exactly the same kind of terror let loose in Keshpur and Garbeta in 2003 and intimidation during election time across broad swathes of rural Bengal is an old story. But by 2007 there had been such a proliferation of the electronic media that much larger numbers of people across the whole country saw with their own eyes what had happened. There were spontaneous protests from civil society, and for the first time in thirty years, an overwhelming majority of left-oriented intellectuals came out in open criticism of the shenanigans of the Left Front government. Disenchantment with the communist government is at its peak, their arrogance of power having proved to be their ultimate undoing. But it remains to be seen if a credible alternative with a positive programme can emerge and win the confidence of an electorate thoroughly disillusioned with communist rule.

For me and for those of my generation it was great to have lived through fascinating times. I was born in a subject nation. When I was a child my maternal grandmother used to tell me not fairytales but the true stories of young revolutionaries who frequented her Dhaka home. The children would be woken from sleep by sounds of police boots surrounding the house, a sure sign the house would be subject to a search. I witnessed the advent of independence and the struggle of a newly independent nation to address its own problems and play a role on the world stage. After four decades as a teacher and a writer, I was happy to get a chance to serve my country during my three terms in Parliament. Until I was thrown into the political arena I did not know how I would cope with the new environment. I discovered that I felt completely at home with the simple peasants of Mograhat or

Bishnupur or Baruipur and with a slight effort and a change of gears I could also converse with high dignitaries of foreign lands with whom I had to deal as part of my Parliamentary work. I had been warned by friends and well-wishers that the political world was full of intrigue and not at all a nice place for an outsider like me. But which walk of life is free of politics? Does not the academic world have its share of petty politics? By taking active part in India's democratic processes, I learnt more about India and its peoples than I could have in any other way. And in doing so I learnt a great deal about my own self. Being essentially an introvert, I had looked for a quiet, secluded life. My favourite lines from Tagore were *Dhan noy, man noy, etotuku basa, korechhinu asha*—not wealth, not fame, but a dear little home was all that I hoped for. But that was not to be. My professional life as an educationist, my involvement with public organizations, and, above all, my life as a Parliamentarian put me in constant touch with people. After my first election victory I received many congratulatory messages among which the one I liked best came inscribed on a simple postcard. It read: 'Since the Almighty has taken you by the hand and placed you in the midst of the people of your country, maybe some service is expected of you.' The spirit of public service—service of the country and the service of humanity—was the best legacy of our freedom struggle. I hope, sixty years after freedom, that this spirit will continue to inspire a new generation.

Postscript 2015

It was 21 July 2009, a rainy morning. I sat down and wrote the preface to my book *Parliament-er Andarmahale* (Inside Parliament), the Bengali version of *An Outsider in Politics*. As I wrote, memories of many 'Ekushe July' rallies came back to me.

Since the mid-1990s, when she was still in the Congress, Mamata Banerjee has observed 21 July as *Shaheed Divas* or 'Martyrs' Day' with a big rally in the centre of Kolkata. The event commemorates thirteen young men killed in police firing in central Kolkata during a demonstration against the Left Front government she led on 21 July 1993. For over a decade starting in 1996, I was present on the dais at every Shaheed Divas rally. From the dais erected in front of Victoria House in Dharmatala, at the heart of central Kolkata, one had a panoramic view of a sea of humanity. Lakhs of people flooded into the area every year. From one side of the main dais, the speakers addressed the gathering from a small, elevated platform. First, senior party leaders addressed the crowd, then it was the turn of Lok Sabha MPs like myself. I spoke every year. Mamata always spoke last. The climax would be the sloganeering she would lead from the dais: '*Amra kara?*' (Who are we?) she would shout in her high-pitched voice. 'Trinamool!' lakhs would respond in unison. '*Ashchhe kara?*' (Who is coming?) she would ask. 'Trinamool!' the crowd would roar back. '*Ei Banglay?*' (In this Bengal?) 'Trinamool! Trinamool!'

But somehow the huge turnouts and the enthusiasm did not translate into electoral victory. After more than two decades of Left Front rule, a desire for change was palpable among a large section of the people. But *paribartan* (change) proved elusive in election after election. In the mid-term Parliamentary election in autumn 1999 our party won eight of the forty-two Lok Sabha seats from West Bengal (up from seven in the mid-term Lok Sabha poll in spring 1998, when the Trinamool Congress was newborn), and we became nine after a by-election win in 2000. This was the situation until mid-2004. But our result in the much-anticipated assembly election in West Bengal in May 2001—the first state election after Trinamool's emergence—was disappointing. We were able to win only sixty of the 294 seats in the assembly. This further came down to only thirty MLAs in 2006.

I finished writing the preface and switched on the television. The rally had reached its final stages, the sloganeering had begun. But this time, the prospect of a change of government in West Bengal in the assembly election due in 2011 had emerged as a real possibility. Two years earlier, in May 2009, Trinamool had won as many as nineteen of West Bengal's forty-two Lok Sabha constituencies. Its alliance partner, the Congress, had bagged another six.

The path to Trinamool's alliance with the Congress, thereby preventing any split in the opposition vote, was paved by the CPI(M)'s then general secretary, Prakash Karat. Karat withdrew his party's support to the Congress-led UPA-I coalition government in July 2008 in protest against the civil nuclear cooperation agreement with the United States. Sonia Gandhi was not pleased at all and gave the go-ahead to a new alliance with the Trinamool Congress in West Bengal. Mamata drove a hard bargain in the seat-sharing talks for the 2009 Lok Sabha election (and later for the 2011 assembly election). Despite protests by its state unit, the Congress was compelled to accept Mamata's terms on seat-sharing in both these elections.

Mamata became the Union minister for railways in May 2009, regaining the portfolio she had held in Vajpayee's NDA government. She was quite pleased, as she always had a preference for the railways portfolio. Trinamool also got six minister of state (MoS) slots in the UPA-II coalition government. As MoS positions are usually without much clout, some felt that Mamata could have asked for three full cabinet positions, to which Trinamool was entitled as the second-largest constituent of the UPA-II. But eventually Mamata decided to accommodate a greater number of her colleagues in the ministry through the MoS route.

From 2009 to 2011, the Trinamool Congress experienced a meteoric rise in West Bengal as, after three decades in power, the CPM's edifice of hegemonic rule rapidly unravelled. This was a remarkable turnaround from the post-2004 situation, when Mamata was the sole Trinamool MP in the Lok Sabha, elected with a much-diminished margin compared to 1998 or 1999 from Kolkata South. All the other sitting MPs lost their seats in 2004, including me after three consecutive victories from Jadavpur. Mamata used to tell me during those years that she didn't feel like going to Delhi to attend the Lok Sabha all alone, and that the small army of CPM MPs would jeer whenever she made an appearance.

Several of my former parliamentary colleagues left for other parties. Sudip Bandyopadhyay, the MP from north Kolkata whose relationship with Mamata soured from 2002, had already rejoined the Congress. Dr Nitish Sengupta, who was the MP from Contai in Midnapore district, also became close to the Congress after 2004. Bikram Sarkar, another of my fellow MPs, went to Sharad Pawar's NCP (and later to the BJP). The eminent skin specialist Dr Ranjit Panja, elected twice on a Trinamool ticket from the Barasat Lok Sabha constituency in North 24 Parganas, fought the 2004 election in poor health and narrowly lost. He passed away soon afterwards. Another fellow MP, Akbar Ali

Khondkar, narrowly lost his Serampore seat in Hooghly district in 2004 and soon afterwards also passed away at a young age.

Amid the deaths and desertions, I chose to remain beside Mamata in the defeated, demoralized party.

I initially thought that I might look forward to a less hectic life. But that was not to be. At the end of 2004, Gopal Gandhi was appointed as West Bengal's Governor. Soon after his arrival in Kolkata, I received a handwritten letter from him: 'Krishnadi, I see you are as busy as ever.' Indeed. Apart from my writing and various speaking engagements, my involvement with several institutions kept me on my toes. One was the Institute of Child Health, the children's hospital in Kolkata's Park Circus area which my paediatrician husband Sisir Kumar Bose was associated with since its inception in 1956 and later served as director for over two decades. I became president of this teaching hospital's trust after his death in 2000. I also served as president of Vivek Chetana, an NGO inspired by Swami Vivekananda's life and teachings, which works for the welfare and uplift of women and children from poor families in south Kolkata. Then, of course, there was the Netaji Research Bureau, the museum, archive and research and conference centre dedicated to preserving Netaji Subhas Chandra Bose's life and work, which Sisir established at the Boses' ancestral house (Netaji Bhawan) on Kolkata's Elgin Road in 1957 and built up over the next four decades. I had become the bureau's chairperson after his death on 30 September 2000.

I also continued to be actively engaged with politics. In June 2005, the elections to the Kolkata Municipal Corporation (KMC) came around. Five years earlier, the then two-year-old Trinamool had scored a major triumph by winning the corporation polls. This time there was a serious complication. The outgoing mayor, Subrata Mukherjee, a veteran politician whom Mamata had been close to since her days as a young Congress activist, had fallen out with her and contested the elections separately at the head of a rebel group. Subrata had not joined Trinamool at its inception at the end of 1997, the obstacle being his senior role in the Congress's trade union wing, the INTUC. But he was sympathetic to us and was a regular visitor to our MP flats in Delhi from 1998 onwards. Two years later, he became the mayor of Kolkata as a Trinamool leader. Mamata used to tell me before he formally joined, 'Krishnadi, Subratada is with us in his heart.' She always had a soft corner for Subrata. Their on–off political relationship mended in 2008, when Subrata patched up with Mamata. Today he is a key cabinet minister, holding the charge of panchayat affairs and rural development in her government in West Bengal.

But in 2005 the Mamata–Subrata conflict cost us the KMC. The Trinamool Congress did reasonably well in the circumstances, winning one-third of the 141 wards, but the Left Front staked out a narrow majority thanks to the internecine feud, and a CPM mayor took office for the next five years. I campaigned extensively for Trinamool candidates in areas under my Jadavpur parliamentary constituency. A number of my loyal political workers—Ratna Sur, Ashoka Mondal, Tarak Singh, Gopal Roy, Anita Kar Majumdar and others—were running for election or re-election in wards across the sprawling areas of Behala and Jadavpur. Most of them were elected or re-elected as councillors. A senior Trinamool leader, Sobhandeb Chattopadhyay, was put up against Subrata in a south Kolkata ward. Sobhandeb was also an old colleague. When I first ran for Parliament at Mamata's suggestion and won from Jadavpur as a Congress candidate in 1996, he was the only Congress MLA among the MLAs from the seven assembly segments comprising the parliamentary constituency—the other six had Left Front MLAs, all bar one from the CPM. Sobhandeb had narrowly won the Baruipur assembly seat in 1991 and was re-elected from there in 1996, in the assembly election held simultaneously with the Lok Sabha poll. I campaigned for Sobhandeb in 2005.

I also remember speaking at a couple of bigger public meetings with Mamata.

Around this time, several seats in the Rajya Sabha from West Bengal came up for election. With its sixty MLAs, the Trinamool Congress could win one of those seats. Mamata told me that she was considering Derek O'Brien. Derek, a member of Kolkata's Anglo-Indian community and a quizmaster by profession, was then a recent entrant to the party. In January 2005, he had helped organize the first public exhibition of Mamata's paintings and sketches. I attended the inaugural ceremony with my sons, Sugata and Sumantra. Mamata gifted me one of her paintings.

My name was also doing the rounds for the Rajya Sabha nomination. The gossip increased when at a rally in Dharmatala, Mamata said to me '*Katha achhe*' (we need to talk) as I was getting down from the dais. Mamata also had a chat with Sugata at her Kalighat home. However, I felt that in the end it would be someone other than Derek or myself. I was proved right when a few days later Mamata let Sugata know that she had chosen a 'non-political' person. That person was Swapan Sadhan Bose alias Tutu Bose, a businessman who also owned a Bengali daily newspaper. Derek did eventually make it to the Rajya Sabha— six years later in 2011.

Mamata told Sugata that Trinamool would soon get another Rajya Sabha seat, in another round of elections due in March 2006. 'I will send Krishnadi then,' she told him. When that election came around, she chose her close aide Mukul Roy to fill the seat. My name did come up in discussions at her Kalighat home, where Sugata, Mukul and Subrata Bakshi, a senior party leader, were present. Mamata explained that Mukul did party work on a 24/7 basis. She also said that Mukul feared the CPM and he felt that being an MP would afford him some protection from being murdered. Once Mukul's name was finalized, Mamata looked at him and said, in Bengali of course, 'Well,

I am sending you, but who knows what incarnation you will assume in the future.'

This discussion took place around mid-March of 2006— the so-called 'ides of March' in the ancient Roman calendar, the day Julius Caesar was betrayed and assassinated by his courtiers. In Shakespeare's play, *Julius Caesar*, the soothsayer warns, 'Beware of the ides of March!' By a coincidence, I am writing this postscript, sitting in New Delhi, during another 'ides of March'. In mid-March 2015, the newspapers and television channels are agog with news of the political fall of Mukul Roy, Mamata's undisputed and increasingly all-powerful deputy for nearly a decade. Mamata has removed Mukul from his national general secretary post in the party, and he has been relegated from the front row of the Rajya Sabha to a seat in the very last row. Mukul, for his part, is taking potshots at the party and its leader in the manner of an expert sniper. He has even told the media that it is he who founded the Trinamool Congress—on the grounds that he submitted the papers applying for recognition to the Election Commission in Delhi on 17 December 1997. According to his account, Mamata then joined the new party on 23 or 24 December. I remember that time well—I formally left the Congress and joined Trinamool on 28 December 1997.

The whole country knows that the Trinamool Congress is Mamata's child. Much like a single mother, she has reared that child from infancy onwards. When the media talks about Mukul's fall as the 'end of an era' in Trinamool, I am reminded of an era in Trinamool before Mukul's rise to prominence post 2006. I remember Mukul as a quiet and reticent party worker. Until 2004, the Trinamool parliamentarians—and sometimes, leaders visiting from Kolkata—would often meet in Mamata's flat on the third floor of the housing complex for MPs on Delhi's Baba Kharak Singh Marg, close to the Lohia Hospital (my flat was in the same building, on a lower floor). The flat's small front office was manned by Ratan Mukherjee, Mamata's long-standing man

Friday in Delhi. Sometimes there was a second man there whom we barely noticed—that was Mukul. Even after 2004, when meetings were held in the new Trinamool Bhavan in Kolkata, we barely noticed Mukul's presence still. Sometimes, when a particular document or file was needed, Mamata would call out, '*Ei, Mukul kothay?*' (where's Mukul?). A quiet man would unobtrusively appear, place whatever was required on the table, and silently exit the room.

I feel, though, that the Mamata–Mukul rift may heal with time. Mamata is an emotional person. When she gets angered she can be hard on people, including formerly close and trusted colleagues. I have already mentioned how she and Subrata Mukherjee made up a few years after an acrimonious split. The same happened with Sudip Bandyopadhyay, who was rehabilitated in Trinamool in 2009 after a bitter estrangement that lasted several years. Then there is Saugata Roy, another West Bengal political veteran who stood from Kolkata South against Mamata in the 1998 Lok Sabha elections and was for a time a severe critic of hers, only to be accepted into Trinamool a few years later. That Mamata eventually made a rapprochement with all these career politicians speaks of her underlying generosity of spirit as well as her political sense.

The Trinamool Congress's resurgence began, as is well known, with the Singur and Nandigram land agitations. When Mamata went on a hunger strike in solidarity with the Singur peasants in December 2006, I could not go to see her personally at the site of the fast in Dharmatala. I had just had an eye operation and was convalescing at home; going to the dusty area where she was conducting the protest was forbidden by my doctor. Sugata and Sumantra went to see her there. She was happy to see them, and was sorry that she wouldn't be able to visit me on my birthday (26 December) because of the ongoing crisis. For many years now, Mamata has turned up at our home at 90 Sarat Bose Road on the evening of my birthday. That year was a rare exception.

In August 2008, as the Singur movement entered its climactic phase, I remember a brief conversation with Mamata during a visit to her Kalighat home. Sumantra, my younger son, was with me. I had wondered whether some kind of compromise could be reached to solve the crisis. By that time it was clear that in the event of a Tata pullout it would be very difficult to return the acquired lands to the peasants to start farming again, while those locals who had hoped for jobs from the Nano plant and its ancillary facilities too would be left high and dry. Mamata was, however, in a combative mood and was scathing about the Tatas. She said, 'They want to do business everywhere, in Russia, in China, they dabble in everything, from salt to tea to cars. They think they can kick out the poor farmers here. I won't allow it.' She was preparing for the final phase of the agitation— '*Dhamaka hobe*' (there will be fireworks), she said. A month later, in September, Governor Gopal Gandhi made a failed last-ditch attempt to facilitate a compromise by bringing Mamata and Buddhadeb Bhattacharya, the CPM chief minister, together in a face-to-face meeting. I learned about this while on a cruise on the Nile in Egypt.

Indeed, at that time, packets of tea and salt produced by firms of the Tata group of companies would regularly be thrown on the streets of Kolkata by the protesters. I noticed that while middle-class opinion was divided on the issue, the working classes—the majority in society—were largely in favour of Mamata's anti-capitalist campaign. In early October 2008, Ratan Tata fled from what he called the 'Bad M' of West Bengal and relocated his factory to Gujarat, governed by the 'Good M'.

By that time, the CPM government was in serious trouble. The killings in Nandigram in March 2007 were followed in November that year by a botched attempt by the CPM to forcibly recapture the area, which had virtually become a 'no-go zone' for the police and CPM supporters since March. Thanks to the profusion of television channels broadcasting in Bengali, the tragic dramas of Singur and Nandigram were beamed into homes across the state. In both cases, but especially in Nandigram, the collusion of the police with armed gangs of CPM cadres was thoroughly exposed. In May 2008, the beginning of the end of CPM rule in West Bengal was signalled by the results of the panchayat elections. In these elections, the CPM suffered serious reverses and Trinamool made impressive gains. A major political shift was underway in rural West Bengal. Meanwhile in Kolkata, artists, intellectuals and assorted 'celebrities' hit the streets to campaign against the government—significantly, these included many who had long been known as fellow travellers of the CPM.

After that, there was no stopping the fall of the CPM and the rise of the Trinamool Congress. After its impressive showing in the 2009 Lok Sabha election, Trinamool won a two-thirds majority in elections to the Kolkata Municipal Corporation in May 2010. Then, in May 2011, thirty-four years of CPM-led Left Front rule finally came to an end in West Bengal as Trinamool won a smashing victory in the assembly election. With victory came a mass of expectations from the electorate that had voted for change.

The day of counting of votes in May 2011, I had just arrived in London and watched the results come in on television. When Mamata took oath as chief minister a few days later, I had just arrived in Boston and watched her swearing-in on television there. I saw her walking among masses of people from the ceremony at the Raj Bhavan to the Writers' Buildings, the headquarters of the state government. I felt a sense of fulfilment that the long, hard years of struggle had finally come to fruition.

The editor of the Bengali daily *Anandabazar Patrika* had asked me for an article on Mamata as I had seen and known her over three decades, to be published on the morning of the oath-taking of the new government. I read the article on the Internet. I had finished it with a small anecdote: Shortly before the May 2011 election I had gone to the Central Hall of Parliament in

New Delhi. There the security personnel and the waiters who serve tea, coffee and snacks gathered around me and asked about events in West Bengal. They wanted to know about 'Didi's' prospects. I assured them that Didi was going to win. They were all highly pleased to hear this. Then one elderly waiter told me to tell her, *'Gussa mat karna'* (not to get angry easily). It was well-meaning advice from a man of goodwill.

A full assessment of Mamata's transition from fiery opposition leader to chief minister is premature as yet. During her first year in office, Mamata ensured that peace returned to Jangalmahal, the area in south-west West Bengal with a large population of Adivasis (Santhals) that saw an intense Maoist insurgency from 2008 to 2011. The poverty-stricken people there—mostly Santhals and Mahatos—just wanted their basic needs to be met, and some respect. After decades of neglect and years of oppression, they got a government sensitive to their grievances. Many tribal men and women who had taken up arms surrendered and were honourably rehabilitated. Mamata also made sure to reach out quickly to the agitators for Gorkhaland in the Darjeeling hills. An agreement for enhanced autonomy for that bit of West Bengal was signed within months of her taking office.

Mamata's hands-on approach and personal touch are a contrast to the remoteness and aloofness of her two communist predecessors: Jyoti Basu and Buddhadeb Bhattacharya. These men commuted between Writers' Buildings and the CPM headquarters on Alimuddin Street in central Kolkata. Mamata spends the greater part of every month on the road, travelling the districts. Her personal energy has brought back a degree of life to the long-moribund administrative machinery. For example, when she decided that the roads of Kolkata and other towns should be decorated with trident-style lamps, and that dividers should be installed on Kolkata's main roads, the work got done rapidly. In the rural areas which make up the bulk of the state, the basic welfare, developmental and infrastructural programmes are generally being implemented, an improvement on the stasis of the later years of the Left Front rule.

Most new governments enjoy a 'honeymoon' period with the media. In West Bengal, the change of guard materialized after a very long time—thirty-four years. So it was somewhat unexpected when an influential part of the media in the state turned hostile to Mamata's government from about the six-month mark. It caught on and a torrent of bitter criticism of the government and the chief minister is aired every day on some television channels and in some newspapers. Criticism of those in office is a normal and necessary part of democracy, but sometimes I'm taken aback by the petty spite and negativity of some of the critics. It is also clear that the confrontation with some parts of the media is damaging for Mamata and her government.

I am personally concerned about two issues. One is the state of higher education in West Bengal. The other is the dignity and security of women.

I was strolling in west London's Portobello street market with Sugata and Sumantra one Saturday afternoon when Mamata called on my mobile phone. She wanted Sugata to organize and lead a 'mentor group' to restore Kolkata's Presidency University to intellectual standing. That was in June 2011. One of the most ruinous legacies of three and a half decades of CPM supremacy was the destruction of the state's higher education system through party penetration and control at all levels. As a professor and academic administrator at a Kolkata women's college before my entry into politics, I was a hapless eyewitness to this in the 1980s and 1990s. Presidency—an institution with a distinguished past—was a prime victim. The new government held out the promise of remedying this state of affairs.

In fact, with the exception of Presidency, the party politicization of the higher education system has continued—in teacher appointments, student admissions and other matters.

Student union elections in the colleges and universities have remained dominated by the interests and rivalries of political parties. The losers are the young generation, for whom quality learning in a decent environment continues to be a mirage. The long-term trend of young people leaving West Bengal after finishing school to take up higher studies in cities elsewhere in India (and in some cases, abroad) continues. The depoliticization of higher education is the joint responsibility of all political parties, not just the party in government. The students also have their share of responsibility—to not be used as willing tools of political parties on campuses.

The issue of women's dignity and security is a national one, not specific to West Bengal. But West Bengal's reputation on this front could—and should—be much better than it is. Again, it is not fair to simply put the blame on the ruling party and the government. But a much more sensitive approach to the issue by those in office is certainly called for.

In 2014, I made a return to the rough and tumble of electoral politics—in a way. Mamata asked Sugata to contest for the Lok Sabha from my old constituency, Jadavpur. The borders of the constituency had changed substantially due to the 'delimitation' process of the Election Commission, which came into effect from the 2009 Lok Sabha election. The vast urban and suburban sprawl of Behala had gone into the Kolkata South constituency; and rural assembly segments like Mograhat and Bishnupur were now part of other, rural South 24 Parganas parliamentary constituencies. But sizeable parts of my old constituency remained part of the redrawn one.

When I went to these areas—whether in urban Jadavpur or suburban and rural Baruipur—during the campaign, I was touched to find that the people had not forgotten me. I was welcomed back into their midst with great warmth and enthusiasm. People often pointed out schools that had been upgraded or deep-water tubewells that had been built with money from my MP LAD (Local Area Development) fund. In the intervening years, a new generation had come of age. During one campaign outing, a bunch of young men told me, 'Didi, when you used to lead *michhil*s [marches] here, we kids used to run along in excitement beside the procession.'

All my Lok Sabha campaigns as a Trinamool candidate were hard struggles. We had to fight the CPM's election machine, and deal with a largely hostile administration and police. The Election Commission tried to ensure free and fair polls but was not so effective then. The first West Bengal election in three decades since the Left Front came to power in 1977 in which the Election Commission managed to ensure more or less free and fair polls was the 2006 assembly election. In all the four Lok Sabha elections I contested, my party workers faced systematic intimidation and violence from the then ruling party. My mainstay was the goodwill of common people, my constituents.

Now, since the tables had turned, it was easier—the stress and strain was much less. Trinamool workers were everywhere and Trinamool publicity dominated the streets, lanes and walls—sometimes rather excessively so.

When the results came in on 16 May, Trinamool had both held off the 'Modi wave' and decimated the CPM, winning thirty-four of the state's forty-two parliamentary constituencies.

My father-in-law Sarat Chandra Bose used to say, 'Life is larger than politics.' And so it is. I gained great fulfilment from my life in politics. But the respite from the daily grind of politics in recent years enabled me to give time to other fulfilling pursuits, particularly my own writing and the busy work of Netaji Bhawan that is Sisir's legacy. And the older I get, the more I seem to travel, usually accompanied by Sugata or Sumantra or both. It is in recent years that I have seen several of the wonders of the world: the Great Wall of China, the pyramids and temples of ancient Egypt, the fabulous Angkor ruins of Cambodia. Once, I went as part of a non-official delegation from West Bengal to Pakistan.

In Peshawar I was mobbed by the media and members of the local elite and public. The reason was that Netaji had travelled to Kabul and beyond through Peshawar in 1941. I was struck by how important this was to people there so many decades after the Partition. I also travelled to conferences in Singapore, the main base of Netaji's movement in South East Asia during the Second World War, and Taipei, a place associated with his memory.

Then there have been the purely recreational trips: a Bay of Bengal cruise from Kolkata's Kidderpore docks, an Indian Ocean cruise from Chennai to Colombo where we were warmly hosted by the then Indian ambassador Nirupama Rao, whom I first met when I was chairperson of the parliamentary standing committee on external affairs and she was the spokesperson of the ministry of external affairs. And of course, the vacations twice a year with Sumantra in London and Sugata in Boston, and once every couple of years with Netaji's daughter Anita and her family in Bavaria, just outside the pretty city of Augsburg. It was while in London in June 2012 that I learned that Mamata had proposed my name for vice president of India.

When I ponder the lessons I have gleaned from life, two stand out. From my life in politics, I have learned the importance of rising above narrow party affiliations and interests and thinking in broader terms, of the people and the nation. That not only serves the public and national interest but is also ultimately beneficial to the prospects of political parties and their leaders. From my life outside and beyond politics, I have learned that human existence is bound to be a mix of joy and sorrow, of happiness and pain. Our *shastra*s teach us that we must remain balanced in joy and stoic in sorrow. Life, in the words of my favourite English poet Robert Browning, is the search of the finite soul for the infinite.

Index